Occupied Voices

Occupied Voices

STORIES OF EVERYDAY LIFE
FROM THE SECOND INTIFADA

Wendy Pearlman

Photos by LAURA JUNKA

State Library OF Ohio

SEO Library Center
40780 SR 821 * Caldwell, OH 43724

THUNDER'S MOUTH PRESS / NATION BOOKS
NEW YORK

OCCUPIED VOICES: *Stories of Everyday Life from the Second Intifada*

Copyright © 2003 Wendy Pearlman

Photos © Laura Junka 2003

Published by
Thunder's Mouth Press/Nation Books
161 William St., 16th Floor
New York, NY 10038

Nation Books is a copublishing venture of the Nation Institute and Avalon Publishing
Group Incorporated.

Library of Congress Cataloging-in-Publication Data

Wendy Pearlman.
    Occupied voices : stories of everyday life from the second Intifada / by Wendy
      Pearlman.
      p. cm.
    ISBN 1-56025-530-7
    1. Al-Aqsa Intifada, 2000–Personal narratives, Palestinian Arab. 2. Palestinian
Arabs–West Bank–Interviews. 3. Palestinian Arabs–Gaza Strip–Interviews. I. Title.

DS119.765.P43 2003
956.95'3044'09239274–dc21

                                                                    2003042623

9 8 7 6 5 4 3 2

Book design by Simon M. Sullivan
Printed in the United States of America
Distributed by Publishers Group West

For our grandmothers,
who taught us to follow our passions and convictions.

Acknowledgments

This book is the product of the commitment and encouragement of so many friends, we are not able in this space to thank them all.

First and foremost, we are indebted to the countless Palestinians in the West Bank and Gaza Strip who welcomed us into their homes and hearts. They trusted us, fed us, and cared for us. They took us by the hand when we were lost, and we were lost often. Their strength and courage inspired us, and their boundless kindness amazed us time and time again.

We also express our gratitude to friends whose support, both personal and professional, was instrumental in transforming this book from an idea into a reality. Among them, we thank Lori Allen, Fida Abu Humeid, Ala Francis, Issam Younnis, Ghada Snounu, Mohammed Abdullah and family, Hedaya Shamoun, Samya Wazwaz, Rolla El-Aydi, Bradley Brigham, Ghaith Omari, Gretchen Merryman, Sofia Ahmed, Mike Loetze, Almas Sayed, Alyce Abdulla, and Mirna Adjami, as well as Justice for Palestine at Harvard Law School, and the staffs of both the Palestinian Independent Commission for Citizens' Rights and Al-Mezan Center for Human Rights.

We are also indebted to those who volunteered to help translate and transcribe some of our tape recordings of interviews from Arabic to English: Jenny Peterson, Leah Harris, Shira Robinson, Sherene El-Ezaby, Dallal Aboul Seoud, and Ayman Amer. Giving of their time and talent without recompense, their contributions represented true solidarity with the goal of making Palestinian voices heard.

And, of course, we thank our families, who have stood behind us in doing what we believe that justice demands.

Wendy Pearlman
Cambridge, Massachusetts

Laura Junka
London, England

TABLE OF CONTENTS

Introduction ... *xi*

PART ONE *Generations of Intifada*

1. SAMIA, *community volunteer* ... *3*
2. SABER, *professor* ... *15*
3. SULTAN, NARIMEN, AND JAMILA,
   three friends in a village near Bethlehem ... *25*
4. OSAMA, *financial adviser* ... *37*
5. SUZANNE, *TV reporter* ... *47*
6. SANA' AND SAMI, *schoolchildren* ... *59*

PART TWO *Loss and Longing*

7. MUNA AND SOHA, *mother and sister of a child martyr* ... *73*
8. MOHAMMED, *surgeon* ... *91*
9. MOHAMMED, *injured in the second* Intifada ... *101*
10. ISSAM, *injured in the first* Intifada ... *111*
11. AHMED, AMAL, MANOA, AND IBRAHIM,
    members of a family in Beit Jala ... *119*
12. MAHMOUD, *owner of a demolished home* ... *135*

PART THREE *Faces of Everyday Resistance*

13. AZZA, *filmmaker* ... *145*
14. SAAD, *agricultural engineer* ... *155*

15. IMAN, *college student* . . . *167*

16. SAMI AND SHAABAN, *shop owners* . . . *179*

17. AHMED, *psychologist* . . . *191*

18. KHALED AND MARINA, *theater directors* . . . *203*

Postscript . . . *217*

Occupied Voices

INTRODUCTION

ON SEPTEMBER 28, 2000, Ariel Sharon, guarded by an entourage of Israeli soldiers, visited Jerusalem's Temple Mount/ *Al-Haram Al-Sharif* in an assertion of Israeli sovereignty over the structure sacred to both Muslims and Jews. The next afternoon, Friday prayers at the Al-Aqsa Mosque ended in violence leaving 70 Israeli police injured by Palestinian rock throwing and four Palestinians killed and over 200 wounded by Israeli gunfire. As days passed and clashes spread from Jerusalem throughout the West Bank and Gaza Strip, Israelis accused Yasser Arafat of engineering a revolt in order to win through armed resistance that which he had failed to achieve at the negotiating table. Palestinians, in turn, asserted that they were expressing their legitimate exasperation with seven years of talks that saw the transfer of administrative duties to the Palestinian Authority but left Israel with real control over their lives. The peace process, it appeared, was over. A new *Intifada,* heir to the Palestinians' first mass uprising from 1987 to 1993, had begun.

One would not guess that the renewed fighting in the Middle East conflict would mean anything particular to me, a Jewish girl from Nebraska. Attending religious school on Sunday mornings as a child, my introduction to Israel had been conventional. I remember that our lessons on Jewish traditions and history seemed to comprise one merciless tale of oppression and forbearance. We celebrated holidays that recalled time after time in which others attempted to destroy us, but we survived. We studied the Holocaust, its collective trauma shaping our own senses of self and duty in the world.

In this context, the State of Israel was presented to me as a triumph over pain and weakness. It represented fulfillment of Jews' struggle to create their own country where they could protect themselves at last. I was taught that Israelis were my brethren and that I should be active in supporting them to surmount ongoing threats. But I could not honestly say that I felt much personal connection to Israelis or the homeland that was supposed to be mine. I was from the American Midwest, and did not want anymore homeland than that. That Judaism had profoundly shaped my identity, values, and worldview, I had no doubt. But I could not see what Israel—a foreign place in a desert on the other side of the ocean—had to do with me.

Meanwhile, my sense of international affairs evolved. At age fourteen, I joined my local chapter of Amnesty International. When the group leader stepped down during my second meeting, I volunteered to take the position. In leading the all-adult group for the next two years, I read and wrote letters about countless particular cases of human rights abuse. Early on, therefore, I developed a deep concern not only about oppression, but also about what oppression means for the real people who suffer its consequences: real people with names and families, real people with lives and dreams cut short. Attention to the lived experience of injustice formed itself as the bedrock of my political consciousness, long before I was old enough to imagine the directions in which it would take me.

It was years after finishing both Sunday school and my tenure as Group Coordinator for Lincoln, Nebraska Amnesty International Local Group #173 that I came into contact with Israel again. This time, however, I came through the back door. In college, the desire to combine travels to both Europe and Africa led me to spend a semester abroad in

Morocco. Having never had contact with Arab society before, I was fascinated by the challenges and rewards of living with a local family, participating in celebration of the month of Ramadan, and learning Arabic. In subsequent years, I returned to Morocco several times, continued with Arabic lessons wherever I found myself, and eventually started doctoral studies in the politics of the Middle East and North Africa. I knew that Morocco was the tip of the Arab world, however, and that I would have to move eastward if I were to develop a real understanding of the region's political dynamics. No issue had shaped the history of the region more than the conflict between Arabs and Israelis. If I really wanted to understand contemporary Middle East politics, I decided, I would have to visit the land that each claimed and both seemed destined to share.

At the start of the year 2000 I had my chance. I signed up for a free trip to Israel for young American Jews, participated in the ten-day tour of seminars and sightseeing, and extended my return ticket in order to stay an extra six months. When the rest of my tour group caught a flight back to the U.S., I went to East Jerusalem and caught a taxi to the West Bank. I moved in with a Palestinian woman, enrolled in political science courses at Birzeit University, and got an internship at a human-rights organization in Ramallah. My passage to Israel thus became my passage to Palestine as well.

I stayed in the Palestinian Territories from January to June 2000, in what now appears to have been the calm before the storm. Six and a half years beforehand, Yitzhak Rabin and Yasser Arafat shook hands on the White House lawn, signed the Declaration of Principles, and kicked off what became known as the Oslo peace process: a framework for a five-year interim period in which Israeli withdrawal from the territories occupied in 1967 was to end in permanent status negotiations on the toughest issues of the Arab-Israeli conflict. According to the original timeframe, Israel's military occupation was supposed to have ended the year before I arrived. The three million Palestinians in the West Bank and Gaza Strip were to be allowed to govern themselves at last, a monumental change after centuries of being the subjects of one foreign power or another.

I arrived in the West Bank to find that in contravention of these signed agreements, a full 61 percent remained under exclusive Israeli control. Only 18 percent of the West Bank had been transferred to the full sovereignty of the newly formed Palestinian National Authority, while another 21 percent fell under shared Israeli-Palestinian over-sight. Far from forming a contiguous base for the development of meaningful self-rule, Palestinian territory was intersected by Israeli territory such that it was splintered into no less than two hundred dis-crete fragments of land. The overwhelming majority of these pockets were less than two square kilometers in area. For Palestinians, this jigsaw map made a mockery of their trust that Oslo would lead to the creation of two independent nations living side by side as equals. Instead of the viable state that they believed would be the fruits of peace, Palestinians found themselves imprisoned in isolated islands of Palestinian-governed territory surrounded by a sea of Israeli control.

Israeli control, furthermore, was growing. From the signing of the Declaration of Principles until the time that I arrived in the West Bank, Israel had demolished 950 Palestinian homes and confiscated tens of thousands of acres of Palestinian land. Much of this land, the lifeblood of Palestinian farmers and their families, was used to build new Israeli settlements. Although settlement in occupied territory was patently illegal according to international law, the Israeli government offered its citizens tax breaks and other benefits in order to move from Israel proper to Palestinian territory. In consequence, the number of settle-ment housing units increased by 50 percent during the years of the peace process. The settler population in the West Bank and Gaza Strip, as well as East Jerusalem, nearly doubled to reach some 400,000. The network of Israeli-only settler bypass roads grew likewise, with Israel paving approximately 250 miles of such roads during the Oslo years alone. Maps of the Occupied Territories suggested that the strategic location of settlement and road construction, as much as its constantly increasing magnitude, practically preempted the achievement of genuine Palestinian sovereignty over land and resources.

While settlers crisscrossed the Palestinian Territories at their convenience, Palestinians themselves could not travel without facing Israeli checkpoints, searches, delays, or permit applications. Israel had declared a "general closure" of the West Bank and Gaza Strip six months before signing the Declaration of Principles, and had never lifted it once during the years that followed. Closure, at times stiffened to the point of trapping Palestinians in their towns and refugee camps, allowed Israel to dictate the movement of people and goods into, out of, and within the Occupied Territories. It also severely limited access to Jerusalem, blocking Palestinians' access to both its holy sites and commercial activity, and forcing them to take long and dangerous back roads in order to circumvent the city when traveling in the West Bank. Thus, even though the entire West Bank was smaller than the state of Delaware, my Birzeit University classmates could spend hours and hours on the roads each time they went home to visit their families. My friends from Gaza, on the other hand, could not get home at all. In spite of Israel's pledge to treat the West Bank and Gaza Strip as a single territorial unit, no Palestinian could move from one area to the other without prior authorization from the Israelis. Many Gazans working or studying in the West Bank did so illegally because Israel had decided not to renew their permits.

The fragmentation of the territories, to say nothing of Israel's control over and disproportionate use of water, had devastating economic ramifications for the Palestinians. Israel's regulation of the movement of people, products, and the means of production rendered Palestinians a captive market for Israeli goods and a pool of cheap labor for its least desirable employment sectors. As the Palestinian economy became ever more dependent upon and subservient to the Israeli one, Palestinians' standard of living deteriorated. According to the CIA *World Fact Book,* real GDP per capita declined by 36 percent between 1992 and 1996. Unemployment, less than 5 percent during the 1980s, had risen to over 20 percent by 1995. An easing of Israeli closures and security procedures led to some economic recovery after 1997. Notwithstanding, 20 percent of Palestinians were living below the poverty line at the time I arrived in the West Bank. In the Gaza Strip, where 78 percent of the population were refugees and over half of all refugees lived in U.N.-administered camps, a full third of the population was in poverty. Palestinians' belief that peace would improve their lives had been turned upside down and inside out.

In the end, the seemingly unremitting train of interim agreements had brought the accoutrements of change without any of its substance. For the first time, Palestinians were serving as their own police force and voting for members of their own parliament. Nevertheless, the outward trappings of Palestinian self-rule disguised Israel's enduring domination of Palestinians' lives. As anyone who filed a paper with a Palestinian ministry knew, PNA functionaries were empowered to act on inconsequential matters but had to forward any issue of substance on to their counterparts in the Israeli bureaucracy, where real decisions were made. Israeli policies both arrested Palestinians' political autonomy and riddled their daily existence with hardships and humiliations that one would be hard-pressed to excuse on the grounds of security. Meanwhile, resolution of issues striking the core of the Palestinian national movement, such as the plight of the Palestinian refugees and the sharing of Jerusalem, were yet to come to the table.

The more time I spent in the Palestinian Territories, the more I appreciated that Oslo's contradictions were untenable. There were surely some who benefited from this arrangement, such as those whose privileged access to power enabled them to create commercial monopolies or whose V.I.P. badges exempted them from the travel restrictions that strangulated everyone else. Regardless of personal advantages that Oslo offered some in the Palestinian leadership, Palestinian people, who were never consulted about Oslo, were being forced to pay the price.

On the other side of the Green Line, many Israelis also felt like they were paying the price for a failed peace. Less than a year after the September 1993 signing of the Declaration of Principles, the Palestinian Islamic resistance movement Hamas detonated a car bomb inside Israel, claiming to revenge the killing of Palestinians in Hebron a few months prior. The bombing, ushering in a new era of terrorism targeting civilians, was the first of fourteen such attacks that would kill more than 120 Israelis and wound over 550 during the Oslo years. As Israelis came to live with the fear that terror could strike anywhere at any moment, many charged that they had upheld their agreement to withdraw from Palestinian cities, but the Palestinians were failing to fulfill their promise to relinquish violence. Stories accumulating about Arafat's support of terrorist groups and anti-Semitism in Palestinian textbooks exacerbated Israelis' doubts that the Palestinians truly wanted peace. While many Israelis continued to labor in the peace camp, others came to believe that the critics of Oslo had been right when they warned that the Palestinians did not and would never recognize Israel's legitimacy. It seemed that, far from being satisfied with the West Bank and Gaza, the Palestinians were using the negotiations in order build a base from which they could fight for all of the land that they continued to covet as theirs.

Given Israelis' long history of war and on-going struggle against terror, it was not difficult to empathize with their fear that the Palestinians did not truly want peace. Given a window into the human dimension of the Palestinians' struggle, however, it was difficult to believe otherwise. In the West Bank, I spent hours upon hours just listening to my Palestinian neighbors, colleagues, and classmates tell me about their lives, and what I heard helped me to appreciate who they were, where they were coming from, and what they were fighting for. The personal stories and heartfelt reflections that I encountered did not expose a hatred of Jews or a yearning to push Israelis into the sea. Rather, they painted a portrait of a people who longed for precisely that which had inspired the first Israelis: the chance to be citizens in a country of their own. Palestinians were fed up with having to obtain Israeli permission before they could attend a conference abroad, launch a business, build a home, or make any one of the myriad choices that remained subject to Israel's whims. They were sick of the searches and delays, of the checkpoints, of hostile demands for their identity cards, and the constant fear that they could be beaten, shot, or arrested. What they wanted was to exercise genuine control over their own fates; to be able to plan for the future and provide for their families; to be free from the unremitting awareness that some Israeli action, executed without warning, explanation, or accountability, would block their way or obliterate what they had worked so hard to create. Regardless of their political affiliations, the Palestinians I met were ordinary people who were denied the right to live ordinary lives. Simply put, they wanted to be respected as human beings and as a nation.

I completed my term in the West Bank and moved to Cairo, Egypt, on a yearlong fellowship for advanced Arabic language study. The situation in the Occupied Territories continued to deteriorate as the months passed. In July President Bill Clinton brought Arafat and Israeli prime minister Ehud Barak together at Camp David in a hasty attempt to piece together a quick fix to the Israeli-Palestinian conflict.

When Camp David failed, the American and Israeli press quickly praised Barak's generous offer of some 90 percent of the Occupied

Territories and blasted Arafat for demanding more. The media did not mention that this charitable chunk of Palestinian territory was to be divided into four separate cantons, each surrounded by Israeli-controlled territory. Under this scheme, Palestinian citizens and goods would require Israeli permission in order to move from one part of their own country to another. They did not mention that Israel would retain control over water, borders, and airspace, as well as a "security zone" along the Jordan River valley. They did not mention that Israel refused to acknowledge any moral responsibility for the expulsions and intimidation that precipitated the flight of over 700,000 Palestinian refugees from the land that became Israel in 1948. They did not mention that Barak's willingness to spin creative simulations of Palestinian sovereignty over select neighborhoods in Jerusalem was bound by his unwillingness to relinquish its essential status as Israel's "eternal and undivided capital."

Most fundamentally, they did not mention that Palestinians had already compromised when they accepted Israel's existence on 78 percent of historic Palestine, and now were expected to compromise again by giving up more from the remaining 22 percent. The rhetoric about Barak going further than anyone before him failed to note how much further he had to go before his plan would recognize Palestinians' independence and sovereignty in a land free from Israeli settlements, roads, and intervention. The fact that Israeli negotiators were able to put forward a better package at the Taba conference several months later countered the myth that Camp David proved that the Palestinians do not want peace.

The Palestinians bore their share of responsibility for the breakdown of talks at Camp David, as well. Some critics charged that, in rejecting Barak's proposal without putting forth a counterproposal of their own, the Palestinians failed to signal a way out of the impasse. Others argued that the Palestinians failed to appreciate that, given the deep rifts in

Israeli society, Barak had genuinely ventured to the limits of what his national consensus and own fragile political coalition would allow. Still others argued that the Palestinian public's demands were simply unrealistic, especially with regard to the refugees' right of return.

Regardless of shortcomings in either Barak's plan or the Palestinians' rejection of it, the crux of the failure Camp David may have been most attributable to its overriding conditions. Barak put his proposal on the table as the ultimate, all-or-nothing end of the decades-old struggle between Arabs and Israelis. It was not simply another step forward on the path towards eventual achievement of two independent states and a just settlement of Israelis and Palestinians' remaining needs and fears. Rather, it fixed the ceiling of Palestinian national liberation at establishment of a pseudo state with fragmented access to parts of Jerusalem, and no recognition of Israeli responsibility towards those who lost their homeland in 1948. Had Arafat accepted Barak's proposal, he would have been agreeing to surrender all of his peoples' unresolved legal, political, or moral claims. When he refused it, neither side knew precisely how they would pick up and move forward with negotiations once again. Two months later, Sharon made his historic visit and the second *Intifada* erupted. The rest, as they say, is history.

I was in Egypt at the time, and for the next three months I watched the violence unfold on my TV screen. As I became immersed in hour-to-hour updates about the situation raging in Israel and the Palestinian territories, it is difficult to say what made me more distraught: the news of deaths, injuries, and destruction, or the way in which the American media reported them. Again and again, the media appeared to condemn Palestinian violence and justify Israeli retaliation, validate Israeli suffering and blame the Palestinians for all that befell them.

Even more frustrating, the press reported endless assertions about what Palestinians thought and desired, but hardly an interview with actual Palestinians. Palestinian mothers were accused of sending their children out to die on the front lines, yet given few occasions to express their own points of view. Palestinian civilians trapped under closure and curfew were berated for putting Israel under siege, yet denied the chance to describe the misery of their own lives. The Palestinian voices that had provided me with such a clear awareness of the political situation while I was living there were simply absent from the news being broadcast in the U.S.

Given the strength of the U.S.'s economic and political support for Israel, I believed that Americans had a right, if not an obligation, to hear the silenced Palestinian side of the story. As few Americans had sat down and chatted with actual Palestinians, it was little wonder that they viewed them more as terrorists than as human beings. If they had the opportunity to listen to them speak their minds as I had, however, they might understand things differently. If they had contact with real Palestinians, they might see through the false allegations that Palestinians were against peace or that the engine of their conflict with the State of Israel was anti-Semitism. If Americans were able to put themselves in Palestinians' shoes, they might even be able to comprehend how victims of military and structural violence could come to take up violence themselves.

I finished my semester in Cairo and took the first bus back to the West Bank with the goal of recording some of the Palestinian voices missing from American media reports. Coming from Egypt with a backpack filled with blank tapes, I spent my winter vacation interviewing Palestinians about their experiences during the Intifada and under the Israeli occupation in general. Laura Junka, a Finnish photography student based at the Hebrew University in Jerusalem at the time, accompanied me to take portraits of the interviewees and the environments in which they lived. Together we spoke with people at hospitals, offices, and the sites of homes that had been bulldozed. We sipped endless cups of tea in family homes and breathed in a fair share of tear gas in our visits to military checkpoints.

The informal route that brought me to each of the interviewees resembled a series of fortuitous encounters more than a scientific methodology aimed at identifying a representative sample. I conducted interviews in Arabic or in English, at the interviewee's discretion. While I approached some of the interviewees on my own, I reached others with the help of an acquaintance, or the acquaintance of an acquaintance.

In seeking people to interview, I had five objectives in mind. First, I wanted to talk to "ordinary people," not political spokesmen. Second, I hoped to speak to those who had been personally affected by some of the major incidents being reported in the news at that time, such as shootings and house demolitions. Third, I sought people whose backgrounds rendered them especially situated to speak about topics of general social concern, such as health, the environment, the economy, the impact of violence upon children, and the psychological dimensions of life under occupation. Fourth, I sought people who lived in areas that had been sites of unique conflict, such as Beit Jala, Hebron, and Rafah. Fifth and most importantly, I wanted to maximize the multiplicity of voices in the collection as a whole. While I knew that I could not depict the full diversity of Palestinian society, I aspired to capture as wide a range as I could in the month I had. As such, I made every effort to speak to both men and women; the young and the old; Christians and Muslims; working professionals and the struggling unemployed; and residents of various cities, villages, and refugee camps in the West Bank and Gaza Strip.

Nearly all of the interviews that I recorded appear in this volume. A handful of interviews were excluded because they lacked the breadth of personal and political commentary of the others. What made a good personal narrative, I discovered, had as much to do with whether or not the person liked to talk as with the substance of what he or she had to say.

The men, women, and children whose voices appear here, therefore, were good talkers. They were people who received me with the utmost openness, sharing their stories at length with a minimum of involvement on my part. I began my interviews by asking them how the first three months of the *Intifada* had been for them, and ended by asking if there was any message that they wanted to address to the outside world. Between these opening and concluding queries, I usually kept conversation rolling with clarifying questions and such penetrating interventions as "uh-huh" and "then what?" The interviews resembled free-flowing monologues more than structured question-and-answer sessions. As an interviewer, my most difficult task was to keep changing the batteries in the hand held tape recorder I had bought at Wal-Mart years beforehand. I learned the hard way that batteries have to be changed frequently if they are to get the job done.

After a month of speaking with people throughout the West Bank and Gaza Strip, I headed back to Egypt with my backpack filled with tape recordings. I transcribed and translated some interviews myself, and recruited friends and teachers to help with others. I took responsibility for reviewing all transcriptions for accuracy and editing the final versions for length and cohesion. The following summer I returned to work at a human rights organization in the Gaza Strip. On a weekend when I was not in the office at the Jabalia Refugee Camp, I traveled to southern Gaza where I recorded two more interviews to add to the collection.

That was now two years ago, and a tremendous amount has happened since.

The suffering of people on both sides increases daily and the violence shows few signs of abating. Observers in the West, horrified by suicide bombings, often ask why there is no Palestinian Gandhi. They question why the Palestinians have failed to develop a nonviolent liberation movement more capable of winning the sympathy of the international community and liberal Israelis alike. They wonder what kind of society this is in which young men and women in the prime of life line up for the chance to kill themselves and innocent civilians in suicide attacks, and the majority of the public supports their deeds.

Here, I believe, it is vital to return to the first three months of this *Intifada*. We cannot discern the nature of the present hostilities, no less how to end them, unless we know how they began. For Israelis, the period from the outbreak of the *Intifada* until the end of the year 2000 was a period in which Palestinians threw rocks at Israeli soldiers at roadblocks and shot at settlements, military installations, and settler roads throughout the Occupied Territories. Palestinians turned out in mass for demonstrations and funeral processions in which they called for resistance in the name of statehood and the right of return. Coming on the wake of Arafat's rejection of Barak's famed generosity at Camp David, the eruption of unrest seemed clear proof that the Palestinians did not want peace. Moreover, many in the Israeli public feared that Palestinians had interpreted Israel's withdrawal from Lebanon the previous spring as proof that Israel could be made to submit to violence. Feeling afraid and besieged, an increasing number welcomed the army's pledge to deliver a hard and swift blow that would teach the Palestinians, once and for all, that terror does not pay.

As virtually no Israeli civilians ventured into Palestinian areas, however, few had a clear idea of what this hard and swift blow meant for the ordinary Palestinians who absorbed it. With the press rallying around the flag, it was easy to disregard the human rights reports that documented how the Israeli army was shooting at Palestinian ambulances and journalists, using heavy artillery against civilian neighborhoods, firing live ammunition at unarmed protestors, and giving cover to armed settlers roaming the Palestinian countryside. It was tempting to excuse the uprooting of thousands of trees and the demolition of hundreds of homes as necessary for security. And it was difficult to appreciate that Palestinians were complaining about closure not because it was inconvenient, but because it was resulting in an educational, health, economic, and commercial collapse of crisis proportions. For those who wanted to know what was happening on the ground in the West Bank and Gaza Strip, reliable information could be hard to come by. And for those who did not, it was sufficient to insist that Palestinians had started this mess and thus Palestinians would have to bear the consequences.

According to B'Tselem, the Israeli Center for Human Rights in the Occupied Territories, 279 Palestinians were killed during these three months, of whom eighty-two were children. During the same period, 41 Israelis were killed, of whom none were children and all but four were killed inside the West Bank and Gaza Strip. One hundred and forty Palestinians were killed before the *Intifada*'s first suicide bombing took place inside Israel on November 2, 2000. It was the first suicide bombing in Israel in two years. This, and two other such attacks before the end of the year, would claim a total of four Israeli lives.

I conducted interviews in the Occupied Territories throughout the month of January 2001 and the voices in this book thus capture this moment. But they go beyond it, as well. In describing the how and why of the current *Intifada,* the Palestinians with whom I spoke could not but make reference to Palestinians' long history of dispossession and occupation. Their testimonies therefore give expression to the enduring ache of the loss of historic Palestine in 1948 that displaced over three fourths of the Palestinian population from their homes. They portray life under Israeli rule since 1967, the sacrifices and spirit of the first *Intifada,* and the disappointment that characterized the Oslo years. They provide commentary on key political questions while illustrating their significance upon the lives of real people. Thus, although the second *Intifada* is the springboard for the voices in this volume, the issues and experiences that render them "occupied voices" go much beyond current events. Their words provide one slice of the larger Palestinian experience, and thus offer important insight into the struggle of years past and of years to come.

Of course, these conversations with Palestinians show only part of the story. They do not claim to offer a comprehensive portrait of the social, ideological, and religious diversity of Palestinian society. Nor do they pretend that this conflict can be understood without earnest exploration of Israeli points of view. Interviews with Israelis are necessary to express their experiences, and many books should be composed to present their voices. That I have not done so here is a reflection of my own academic and linguistic background, which has brought me into contact with Palestinians and unique stories of the injustices that they have suffered.

Furthermore, it is my belief the widespread misrepresentations of Palestinians and the general dearth of materials allowing them to tell their own stories makes a collection of exclusively Palestinian interviews crucial at this time. For reasons of common culture and political history, Westerners tend to be more familiar with the Israeli narrative than its Palestinian counterpart. Palestinians deserve a forum in which they can speak freely. We in America, in Europe, and even, if not especially, in Israel stand to gain tremendously if we stop and listen.

I do not doubt that there will be those who read these interviews and quickly retort, "Yes, but Israelis have suffered, too." They will be absolutely right, but they will have missed the point. In presenting Palestinian voices, I am not trying to argue that Palestinians' miseries trump those of Israelis. If there is a contest to be the nation that has endured the most anguish, both Israelis and Palestinians have performed so spectacularly that it is senseless to declare a single first-place finisher. There is an imperative, however, for each side to hear the other side express itself in its own terms. In this sense, no one stands to gain more from this book than do Israelis and their supporters.

Others will read these interviews and say, "Yes, but given the suicide bombings, Israel must act to defend itself." They too will be absolutely right and they too will have missed the point. These interviews paint a portrait of the kind of political and societal context that nourishes extremism. Anyone who reads them should appreciate why making Palestinians miserable is not a viable counter-terrorism policy. History has proven that Israel cannot pound the Palestinians into submission. No amount of military force can restrain a people committed to the justice of their cause. Neither security walls nor checkpoints will stop those who feel that they have nothing left to lose and no other way out of intolerable oppression. This book's stories of Palestinian suffering should be a distress signal for all who care about Israel, as the more Palestinians are made to suffer the more Israelis will be made to suffer in turn. The sooner that both sides understand each other's needs and fears, the more lives can be saved.

The aim of this book is to help foster this understanding. It is my attempt to bring Palestinian voices to audiences that have had little opportunity to hear Palestinians speak for themselves. Not all the occupied voices in this volume are Palestinian, however, as the voice that interweaves the others is my own. In including introductory essays that explain how I came to meet each person whom I interviewed, I invite readers to discover the Palestinian story as I did: one life at a time. Beyond offering anecdotes from my own experiences in the West Bank and Gaza Strip, these bridging introductions provide the background information necessary to appreciate these interviews in their broader historical, political, and social context. They show that the Palestinian stories recorded here are not idiosyncratic sketches, but rather illustrations of a dehumanizing political situation that entraps the entire population of the Occupied Territories.

This book is divided into three parts, each consisting of six sets of interviews. Some of the interviews feature the monologue of a single speaker, while others contain the voices of two or more individuals grouped together because they are relatives, colleagues, or friends speaking on common themes. Part One, entitled "Generations of *Intifada,*" presents three generations of Palestinians whose stories situate the Al-Aqsa *Intifada* in a long battle against dispossession and occupation. Here we meet a grandmother-activist who fondly recalls having Jewish neighbors when Palestine was a British Mandate, and a mathematics professor who became a refugee when his family fled its home in 1948. We meet three thirty-something friends who describe life under Israeli military rule following the occupation of the West Bank and Gaza Strip in 1967, and two young professionals who explain how their coming-of-age during the first *Intifada* shaped their identities. Finally, we meet two schoolchildren whose frank descriptions of their encounters under the military assaults of the second *Intifada* illustrate how violence has become the taken-for-granted backdrop for their daily lives. These individuals' tales of pain and courage, in conjunction with bridging introductions that chronicle the trajectory of events from the 1940s until the present, show how every generation of Palestinians bears the mark of its own suffering. The history of struggle will continue, these stories tell us, until Palestinians at last fulfill their right to live with freedom and dignity on their own land

Part Two, entitled "Loss and Longing," offers interviews with a handful of Palestinians whose lives have been transformed by the violence of the current chapter of the Israeli-Palestinian conflict. Their testimonials give expression to overwhelming losses of life, property, health, freedom, and possibility, as well as to profound longings for a just peace. Here we meet the mother and sister of a child killed by Israeli soldiers, and their plainspoken grief illustrate what is often missing in the Western media's portrayal of Palestinians' praise of martyrdom. We meet a family whose home was shelled in a nighttime assault from an Israeli settlement, and a man whose house was bulldozed by Israeli soldiers. We meet one young man injured during the first *Intifada,* another during the second *Intifada,* and a doctor who has witnessed thousands of other such individuals lose and recuperate life on his operating table. These voices, prefaced by introductions that profile the nature of developments during the first three months of the second *Intifada,* reveal the impact that the violence has had on the lives of ordinary people.

Part Three, entitled "Faces of Everyday Resistance," takes us from these devastating instances of violence to the more veiled, everyday cruelties of life under military occupation. These voices of men and women from different walks of life demonstrate how the denial of Palestinian self-determination impinges upon nearly every aspect of what they are able to do, dream, and become. Here we meet a filmmaker who describes how politics penetrates and envelops Palestinian art, and an agricultural engineer who explains how even the land, water, trees, and natural environment of the West Bank and Gaza Strip bear the scar of occupation. We meet a clinical psychologist who analyzes Palestinians' day-to-day traumas, and a college student who searches in her own study of psychology for strategies for coping with the violence that has shaped her life. We meet two shop-owners who describe the economic crisis that has locked the overwhelming majority of Palestinians in a battle to feed their families from one day to the next. Finally, we meet two members of a theater troupe whose mission is to reach out to Palestinian children and inspire them to believe in a better future. These everyday stories, as well as bridging introductions that discuss a range of related political, social, and economic issues, paint an image of the Palestinians that is as honest as it is uncommon in the Western media; that of regular people whose quests to live regular lives are blocked by an endless chain of hurdles and abuses.

Every Palestinian man, woman, and child in the West Bank and Gaza has a story to tell about how his or her life has been affected by the Israeli occupation in general and the present *Intifada* in particular. These are some of the accounts, ranging from the heart wrenching to the uplifting, that I encountered. Any other person with a hand held tape recorder and a good supply of batteries can visit the Occupied Territories and record other voices. While the particular stories will vary, I am confident that the core message will be clear for all who, in good faith, allow it to be heard.

PART ONE

Generations of Intifada

1. SAMIA, *community volunteer*

2. SABER, *professor*

3. SULTAN, NARIMEN, AND JAMILA,
three friends in a village near Bethlehem

4. OSAMA, *financial adviser*

5. SUZANNE, *TV reporter*

6. SANA' AND SAMI, *schoolchildren*

Samia, at Rawdat Al-Zahour school

1 . SAMIA, *community volunteer*

I WAS FORTY-FIVE *minutes late to my appointment with Samia. "Couldn't find the front door?" she asked when I finally arrived at the East Jerusalem elementary school that she supervised. I had followed Samia's directions precisely, but found only an Israeli courthouse and its parking lot where the school was supposed to be. It never occurred to me that the building in the middle of the lot could be the school.*

"Everyone gets lost trying to find us," Samia smiled. "When the school was established fifty years ago, this was all open field. Then the Israelis annexed Jerusalem and the courthouse next door, and turned our front yard into a parking lot. We wrote the Jerusalem Municipality and said that it was unacceptable to make the children walk between all these cars to get to school, but they never responded. So here we are today."

She shrugged and added, "Of course, this is the least of our problems."

With hazel eyes no less vibrant than her silver hair, Samia exhibited the poise of a woman who has borne witness to historic struggles. When her parents were born, Palestine, the historic land on the eastern Mediterranean shore, was under the control of the Ottoman Empire. About 92 percent of its population was Muslim and Christian Arabs and the other 8 percent were Jews. When the breakup of the Ottoman Empire became imminent during the course of World War I, however, Great Britain set its sights on the area. Adherents of Zionism, the movement to establish a state for the Jews in the land that had once been theirs during antiquity, pressed the British to be mindful of Jewish interests should it acquire a mandate in Palestine. In the 1917 Balfour Declaration, the

3

British government promised to "favor the establishment in Palestine of a national home for the Jewish people . . . it being clearly understood that nothing shall be done which may prejudice the civil and religious rights of existing non-Jewish communities in Palestine." British officials simultaneously reassured Arab leaders that the indigenous inhabitants of Palestine would be granted their independence, as well.

By the time that Samia was born in 1933, it was clear that the British authorities' contradictory promises embodied an impossibility: Palestine could not be transformed into a Jewish state without violating the rights of the Arabs already living there. As the Jewish community in Palestine gradually created its own social, political, and economic institutions, Arabs protested what they saw as newcomers intent on stealing their homeland. The rise of Nazism and then the Holocaust brought tens of thousands more Jewish immigrants, and clashes between Arabs and Jews intensified further. Exasperated and unable to mediate the conflict, Great Britain at last decided to hand the "Palestine Question" over to the newly formed United Nations. In November 1947, the General Assembly voted to partition the area, designating 55 percent of the land for a Jewish state and the remaining 45 percent for an Arab state.

For Palestinian Arabs, this was unthinkable. Jews represented 35 percent of the total population of Palestine at the time, and no more than a 60 percent majority in the portion designated for the Jewish state. While it could not be denied that Jews had endured the most horrific of atrocities in Europe, the indigenous Palestinians protested that they should not be forced to pay the price. As David Ben-Gurion, Israel's first prime minister, himself admitted, "If I were an Arab leader, I would never sign an agreement with Israel. . . . We have come and we have stolen their country. Why would they accept that?" [1]

On May 14, 1948, Jewish leaders in Palestine declared the establishment of their new state and war broke out between Israel and the armies of several Arab countries. By the time a truce was reached about a year later, Jews had not only

1 Quoted by Nahum Goldmann in *Le Paradoxe juif (The Jewish Paradox)*, p. 121

secured a political entity in the Holy Land for the first time in two thousand years, but had conquered half the territory designated for Arabs as well. The Palestinians, meanwhile, found themselves with neither a state nor sovereignty over any of the land. The estimated 725,000 of them who fled or were expelled in the course of the fighting became refugees. Palestinians who stayed within Israel's still-unofficial borders became an Arab minority. Much of their land was confiscated and the population was placed under military government, where they would remain for the next eighteen years. Palestinians who found themselves on the "West Bank" of the Jordan River became subjects of the Kingdom of Jordan. Those who found themselves in the Gaza Strip, the rectangle of land on the southern Mediterranean coast, came under Egyptian rule.

For Israelis, this watershed would be revered as the War of Independence. For Palestinians, it became mourned as Al-Nakba, "the Catastrophe." In 1967 Israel and the neighboring Arab states went to war again. In six days of fighting, Israel not only defeated the combined armies of Egypt, Jordan, and Syria, but also annexed Arab East Jerusalem and occupied the West Bank, the Gaza Strip, Egypt's Sinai Peninsula, and Syria's Golan Heights. While Israel withdrew from Sinai in accord with the 1979 peace treaty with Egypt, it has yet to relinquish control over other territories conquered in 1967, counter to United Nations Resolutions 242 and 338. The Palestinians of the West Bank and Gaza, now 3.5 million in number, remain stateless.

Samia's life bears the impact of these events. She has lived in various parts of Palestine under British, Jordanian, and Israeli rule. She was president of the Jordanian YWCA when the West Bank was under Jordanian control, and then became the first president of the Palestinian YWCA when it established itself independently. She is currently a board member of the Sabeel Ecumenical Liberation Theology Center, an organization advocating justice and peace through nonviolent means in the quest for Palestinian independence.

When I met her, however, Samia's chief duty was overseeing the Rawdat Al-Zuhur elementary school and its 250 mostly low-income students. Touring the school grounds, I was struck by the doves and rainbows painted on every wall. The *struggle for independence infused the school's stated mission "to build a new Palestinian generation committed to moral values, discipline, and public welfare" and "to empower them to meet the challenges of peace, democracy and state building." Indeed, even the school's name, Rawdat Al-Zuhur or "Garden of Flowers," declared its steadfast defiance of the Israeli parking lot obscuring its front door.*

It was at the school that Samia told me her story, not at all dismayed that I arrived forty-five minutes late.

* * *

My name is Samia. I was born in Jaffa and brought up in Ramle. My family lived in other parts of Palestine too. I am president of Rawdat Al-Zuhur, which is a women's organization that runs an elementary school in East Jerusalem.

I'm also on the executive of the Sabeel Ecumenical Liberation Theology Center. Sabeel is a venue that gives you an opportunity to affirm your own faith during these days in which faith and hope tend to be shaken. They call this land the Holy Land, but unfortunately it is one of the places where religion has been used to justify injustice.

For us Palestinians, religion and religious tolerance is part of our culture. Of course, you will always find fanatics, among Christians just as much as among Muslims. But religion is not a source of conflict between Palestinian Christians and Palestinian Muslims.

We local Christians were the first Christians. We became Christians when Christianity started here two thousand years ago. We exported it to where it has been exploited and split up and returned to us in shambles. And then Christians in the West ask us when we converted to Christianity. Many Christians in the West have no idea that there are Christians in the Arab world. To them, all of the Arab world is Muslim.

Although our faith is Christian, our culture is Arab. Here Christian culture and Islamic culture overlap, and we all influence each other. For example, 90 percent of the students in Palestinian Christian schools are Muslims. But we don't see these schools as serving one religious group or another. We are serving our community. We are teaching children. Whether we are Christians or Muslims, we are one people. We are all Palestinians struggling together for independence. In fact, some of the most radical factions of the Palestinian Liberation Organization happened to be Christians.

So it hurts to see how much religion has been abused. The State of Israel was established as a Jewish state. When you identify it from the start as a Jewish state, non-Jews simply can't have the same rights.

We were living in West Jerusalem in 1948, and we evacuated our house and moved to Birzeit, which was my father and grandfather's hometown. We left out of fear. People were so afraid after they heard about the massacre at Deir Yassin.[2] Members of the *Irgun* and Jewish underground came in trucks to the Palestinian areas and announced, "Look at what has happened! Leave the country! This can happen to you, too."

Every family has its own story to tell about what it was that made it leave. My husband was a boy at the time. He says that he was out in the field picking almonds when bullets flew right over his head. Then one of his neighbors got shot. So his family decided that it was no longer safe, and it left.

So, many of the refugees left because they were afraid. Of course in some areas, like Ramle and Lydda, they were driven out at gunpoint. I

---

2 Between April 9 and April 11, 1948, about a month before the end of the British Mandate, members of Menachem Begin's *Irgun* movement and the Stern Gang attacked the Palestinian village of Deir Yassin. They killed over 100 men, women, and children from among the village's 750 residents. Word of the massacre spread quickly, and is credited with greatly fueling the flight of the Palestinian refugees.

was in boarding school in Birzeit when Ramle and Lydda were attacked, and I saw the refugees coming on foot. They were walking after being evicted from their homes, and Birzeit was the first town they reached. The boarding school and both the Anglican and Catholic churches opened their doors to provide the refugees with shelter and food. After a while the Red Cross put up tents for them. Things dragged on and on, and they had to find better shelter. So they built shacks and so on until UNRWA was created and took charge of them.[3] Nobody ever thought that this would go on for over fifty years, and we're still not finished.

But it wasn't enough that the Palestinian refugees ended up living in refugee camps. On top of that, Israel even razed their original villages. It wanted to obliterate history completely. You go to where these villages used to be and you won't find anything more than a cactus or a few rocks. That is all that is left to show that there was once a Palestinian village there.

And then came the '67 War. I remember after the war, when those of us in the West Bank made contact again with the Palestinians who had stayed inside Israel. They really suffered in Israel after 1948. So much of their land was confiscated. They were under military rule until the 1960s, and they needed permits to travel from one city to another. Their educational system was so bad, there was no way they could qualify to go to university.

---

3 In 1949, the United Nations General Assembly established UNRWA, the United Nations Relief and Works Agency for Palestine Refugees in the Near East, as a temporary specialized agency. In the absence of a permanent solution to the Palestine refugee problem, however, the General Assembly has voted to renew UNRWA's mandate every three years since then. Today UNRWA offers education, health, relief, and social services to 3.9 million registered Palestine refugees in Jordan, Lebanon, Syria, the West Bank, and Gaza Strip. Its services are located in or near the fifty-nine recognized camps that house about one third of the total refugee population.

After the occupation began they told us, "You're still in a honeymoon stage. Just wait and see what's in store for you."

You don't know what occupation means unless you go through it. It puts an end to your freedom, even your freedom of thinking. You get up in the morning wishing that you could get in your car and drive somewhere. But this can't happen when you're under occupation.

What does occupation mean? I remember something that my mother said when we were kids. There was a curse that people used to say: "*Ye'ifel Sidrik;* may your chest be blocked." When the occupation began my mother said, "You know, I never used to understand what that curse meant, until now."

You feel that there is a heavy, heavy thing just there, as if it is embracing you. You just can't get out. You can't do anything about it. You can't move, you can't imagine. You start thinking, "I'm going to do this, or do that." But you know very well that you can't. You can't just pick yourself up and go to Jordan to see your cousins overnight or go to Egypt to attend a seminar. No, you have to stand in line for hours at the Israeli Ministry of Interior to get a permit. That is, of course, if you are lucky enough to be able to get into the Ministry of Interior or if it isn't closed, like it is today.

But beyond the closed borders, occupation is the everyday harassments; the army stopping you at the checkpoint, checking your ID, and so on. And these days you cannot even reach from one town to another because of the roadblocks all over.

It is the loss of human dignity that is the worst part of occupation. We are treated like a herd of sheep. For example, see how we pass through Israeli security in order to cross the Allenby Bridge to get to Jordan. At one time, the Palestinian branch of the YWCA was part of the Jordanian YWCA. I was national president, and the general secretary and I had to go to Amman often. We were treated like dirt when we used to cross the border. We were stripped and searched so thoroughly that it just made you sick. You know, they have these handheld machines that they could just wave in front and back of you, and they serve the same function. But they choose to strip you, simply in order to humiliate you.

One day the security policewoman even removed my sanitary napkin. Can you imagine? She said, "I'm sorry. I have to do this."

I said, "I'm sorry for you."

I think that they are more dehumanized in the process of occupying us than we are. Because at least we know that we are occupied. They're supposed to be the conquerors. They're supposed to be the strong ones and the only democracy in the Middle East. But what they do certainly must dehumanize them. Take the soldier who goes around shooting young children. How is he going to behave when he goes home and looks at the eyes of his own children? He is probably going to see the eyes of those little children that he shot. It is little wonder that they say that domestic violence is increasing in Israeli society.

It is sad, very sad. Because we are destined to live side by side. We're not going to throw Jews into the sea, and they're not going to get rid of us. I always say that it is like a Catholic marriage: no divorce possible. So, the earlier this occupation comes to an end, the more lives will be spared. And then there might still be a possibility for reconciliation. So much animosity and so much hatred have already been created. There isn't one Palestinian home that hasn't been hurt or touched in one way or another.

Now, who doesn't want peace? Every human being that has any sense wants peace for his children, for his family, for future generations. We have had enough struggle in this land. And as I said before, nobody is going to get rid of the other. We have to live together.

But will the Israelis ever be magnanimous enough to say to the Palestinians, "We have done you an injustice?"

I think that the occupation must end, even for the sake of the Israelis. I always tell my American friends that if the United States really likes

Israel and really wants to support it, then it should support it in dismantling the occupation. Because if you like somebody and you favor his well-being, you support him in what is good for him and in what he should do; not in what he wants to do but knows is morally wrong.

There is a double standard that puts Israel above the law. It lets it get away with everything. It allows it to defy all United Nations resolutions and human rights charters. Now, we saw what happened to Iraq for noncompliance with United Nations resolutions. They still haven't heard the end of it. Until today they continue to bombard Iraq. Israel, on the other hand, hasn't complied with one United Nations resolution since 1948.

It looks like a hopeless situation, unless Israel comes to terms with reality. To start with, the Israelis have to admit that they have committed a grave injustice against the Palestinians, and they have to be willing to do something about it. And then we can start negotiating. The only solution to Israel's security problem is justice. The prerequisite for security is justice. It is like a thief on the run. If he carries the loot with him, he is never going to feel secure. He is always going to keep running. But the moment he hands in the loot, he is a free man again.

We are not talking about 100 percent justice; we're talking about relative justice. We're talking about something that will be acceptable. We announced that we are willing to establish our state on the territories occupied in 1967. And we are ready to establish it alongside the State of Israel. Of course, the ideal situation is that all historic Palestine would stay as one entity, a secular democratic state for all people: Jews, Christians, and Muslims, both Palestinians and Israelis.

But we have come to terms with the new situation. In a changing world you come to terms with certain realities and live with them. But Israel does not accept the fact that the Palestinians, in Algiers in 1988, made a real compromise for the sake of peace. We said that we're willing to accept Israel as a state in the region and willing to establish our state on the Occupied Territories.

If Israel is genuinely interested in peace and wants to guarantee its security, it will start from this premise. It will end the occupation so we can all move on.

Sometimes I wonder how we have been able to maintain our faith in these times.

I have been very, very scared during this *Intifada*. I am a grandmother. I have children who go to work and grandchildren who go to school. And of course, we have this school and the children here. The worry! You can't believe the worry I have every day when the children leave the house. Every day when my daughter takes the kids to school I am on the edge of my nerves, waiting to make sure that they arrive safely.

It is just so scary. At the beginning of the *Intifada* the Israelis would announce every now and then that they were going to bombard the headquarters of the Palestinian Authority. Both my sister and a close friend of mine are living in that area. I am so worried. We are on the telephone all the time checking up on them. The *Intifada* has affected all normal ways of life, not that life was so normal to start with. But even the normal of the abnormal was at least partly normal.

My children and grandchildren don't know a Jew except as an Israeli military occupier. But I will always cherish the years in which I lived in Palestine before 1948, when Jews, Christians, and Muslims lived side by side. I am privileged to have lived during that era.

We had Jewish neighbors when we were living in Safad. I remember that on Easter my mother would give me a plate of special Easter cookies to take down to our neighbor, Hannah. She would in turn send her daughter back with a plate filled with something special that she had baked.

You know something. In the early 1940s, the Second World War was still raging. We didn't know if Germany or the Allies would turn out to be the winners. Mrs. Eisenberg was so scared for her daughter. So she came to my mother and said, "Linda, if Germany comes into this country, will you consider Batia your daughter?"

My mother used to repeat this story always, and I am telling it to you to show you what kind of relationship we had with each other. Our neighbor had enough trust to let her daughter be in the hands of an Arab family to protect her from what might happen to her under Germany.

Years after my mother passed away I was clearing some of her papers. In her address book I found an address with the name Batia and then another last name. I said to myself, this must be Batia Eisenberg, who has taken on a new married name. She and her parents had visited my parents once after 1967.

You know, I kept that address on my desk for days and days and months. And finally I said, I must contact Batia. After all that has happened, maybe people like us could do something to set things straight and make things make sense.

So I finally wrote her a letter. Unfortunately, the letter came back saying "Address Unknown."

I didn't say much in my letter. I didn't know if she would be interested in corresponding. Maybe she has lost a son or her husband. You never know. We have all had our share of suffering. My brother was expelled from the country for almost twenty years. My cousin, a poet and the PLO spokesman at the time, was one of the Palestinian leaders who Barak assassinated during his raid on Lebanon in the '80s. My son is a musician, and he spent six months in jail for recording music during the first *Intifada*. He was charged with promoting incendiary material.

But this is part of the struggle for liberation. Eventually, many people have to pay a high price. But what is important is not to lose hope and not to become bitter. Because if you're bitter there is no way that you can communicate. And, it is important to keep moving forward. That is basically what we try to do here in this school. We try to keep rekindling hope in the hearts of these children. We do this so that everything we do will have meaning. We try to give them hope in the future. And I hope this succeeds.

Saber, rushing a wounded child to an ambulance at the City Inn checkpoint

2 . SABER, *professor*

IN THE TWENTY-SEVEN *refugee camps in the West Bank and Gaza Strip, as in the other thirty-two Palestinian refugee camps located elsewhere in the Middle East, ask children where they are from and their answers might surprise you.*

These kids, and there are sure to be throngs of kids wherever you turn your head, may have never seen a world beyond the cement blockhouses and narrow dirt alleyways where they were born. Ask them where they come from, however, and they will likely name this or that town or village inside what is now Israel. They'll tell you how their family had land and how they raised the sweetest oranges, tomatoes, or olives that you have ever tasted. They'll tell you about how their grandparents fled in 1948 with nothing but the clothes on their backs. They'll tell you that they ran because of the killings and the stories of killings, and they never thought that it would be for good. And even the little ones, playing barefoot with whatever they find in the street, will be able to tell you that United Nations General Assembly Resolution 194 affirmed their right to return over fifty years ago, and they're still waiting.

The families in these dismal and overcrowded camps hold on to their dreams and the keys to their former homes, knowing that most of these homes no longer exist. No sooner had the Palestinian refugees fled than the new State of Israel made their exodus irreversible by confiscating property, establishing new settlements, and shooting Arabs caught trying to "infiltrate" back to their homes. Over four hundred Palestinian villages were depopulated, destroyed, and expunged from the map as if they had never existed. As historian Gabriel Piterberg argues, the ongoing debates about why the Palestinian refugees left evades the more essential question of how they were blocked from coming back:

> *The form that this 'population transfer' was to take did not need a pre-meditated plan of expulsion by the Israeli government. . . . Rather, the crucial decision was to prevent Palestinian Arabs at all costs from returning to their homes, regardless of the circumstances in which they had 'left' them, and no matter how plainly their departure had been envisaged as a temporary move made under duress, in the midst of war.*[1]

A generation later, the 1967 War displaced another 300,000 Palestinians, many of them made refugees for the second time. Today a total of five million Palestinians, two thirds of the total Palestinian population, are refugees or the descendants of refugees. They represent the oldest and largest refugee population in the world. Over one million of them live in refugee camps.

The refugees have suffered wherever they have found themselves. In Lebanon, over 376,000 registered Palestinian refugees are denied not only citizenship, but also the right to own property or to work in over seventy professions. In Syria, Palestinians have neither Syrian passports nor the rights to vote or hold public office. In Egypt, even those Palestinians born in the country possess no automatic right to stay, but rather hold residency documents that must be renewed periodically. In Jordan, where Palestinians constitute over half the total population, Palestinians often suffer discrimination that renders them second-class citizens. In the oil-producing Arab states, hundreds of thousands of Palestinians are unprotected laborers entirely vulnerable to governmental whims: over a quarter million Palestinian workers were expelled from Kuwait after the Gulf War and some five thousand were expelled from Libya in 1994. Memory of the massacre of one thousand men,

---

1 Gabriel Piterberg, "Erasures," *New Left Review* (July–August 2001), p. 34.

women, and children in Lebanon's Sabra and Shatila camps in 1982 admonishes all refugees of their ongoing vulnerability.

I have always found it strange when critics call attention to Arab regimes' abuse of the Palestinian refugees as if it absolves Israel. The fact that the refugees' suffering has been unremitting during a half century of exile in Arab countries, it seems to me, only accentuates the extent of the devastation that the Zionist project brought for the native people of Palestine.

In his proposal at the July 2000 Camp David summit, Prime Minister Barak demanded that Yasser Arafat agree to the statement that Israel bears no legal or civilian responsibility for the displacement of the Palestinian refugees. On humanitarian grounds, Barak offered to allow 100,000 refugees to return to Israel, and suggested that the United States and Europe help finance compensation for the five million others. Had Arafat accepted this offer, it would have become the permanent and definitive termination of the Palestinian refugee problem. Any other claims—moral, material, or legal—would have been waived forever.

In the enduring tragedy of the Palestinian refugees, Saber is an exception to the rule. He is one of the fortunate ones who was raised in a refugee camp but has been able to raise his children elsewhere. Expelled from his home in the Negev desert in 1948, he was raised in Gaza, was educated in Egypt, and spent years as a stateless resident in the Persian Gulf. It was not until he settled in Texas as a university professor that he acquired citizenship for the first time.

I met Saber a few months into the second Intifada at one of the "confrontation sites" where Palestinian rock-throwers clashed with Israeli soldiers. At first glance, I would not have taken Saber for either a Professor of Mathematics or a resident of the proud state of Texas. Wearing a cheerful smile and a vest that identified him as a Red Crescent volunteer, he was engaged in lively chitchat with the boys. When I saw him I couldn't help but notice that his first-aid kit contained, in addition to the usual supplies, something that seemed more appropriate for a Houston cosmetic counter than for medical relief in Palestine.

"Excuse me," I said, approaching him. "Why the bottle of perfume and cotton balls?"

"Perfume wards off the effects of tear gas," he responded in perfect English. "When the Israelis fire gas we spray perfume on cotton and pass it out to the kids."

Intrigued by the perspective that a fellow American citizen might be able to offer about doing duty at a West Bank checkpoint, I asked if I could interview him. He happily obliged. And when I asked him where he was from, he replied matter-of-factly, "Beersheba."

·◈· ·◈· ·◈·

MY NAME IS SABER. I was born in Beersheba in 1943, five years before the creation of the State of Israel. My parents and family were forced out in 1948. At that time, some people were shot by the Israeli forces. We didn't know who they were at the time, but since then I've read about it and now I know that this was the *Haganah*.

We left Beersheba and kept moving south until we hit the Gaza Strip. Eventually, in 1950, my family moved to a refugee camp called Al-Maghazi. I was raised there. I went to the only high school for boys, which was a joint school for three different refugee camps in the area.

It was very hard growing up in a refugee camp. We were very poor. Everyone was very poor. I remember that my clothes were always worn out and patched. I used to put my hands over my elbows to cover the holes. At school I got free lunches from UNRWA, the United Nations committee set up to help the refugees.

My parents used to talk about Beersheba all the time like a kind of paradise lost. They would say that everything there was green, that there was a lot of land and fruit trees. And there was space in Beer-sheba, not like in Gaza, which was small and crowded. As a child I would dream about going back to this lost paradise.

This place, Palestine, was not lost because of anything we had done. It was stolen from us. This feeling of injustice will always be with me. It will never go away. I will never be able to forget it. I see the same thing in the kids today, this longing for Palestine.

I went to Cairo for college and studied mathematics. I went with just 40 Egyptian pounds in my pocket. The whole family had to sacrifice, selling gold or goats or whatever in order to pay my tuition. The 40 pounds ran out before the last week of the semester. I remember that I didn't eat for the whole week of final exams.

When I finished college I went to Kuwait to teach math in a middle school. I was in Kuwait during the 1967 War. After the Israeli occupation began, I was considered "nonexistent" according to Israeli law. This was the case for hundreds of thousands of other Palestinians as well. Israeli law prohibited me from returning to Gaza. I wasn't able to go back until I became an American citizen and could travel on an American passport.

I stayed in Kuwait teaching math until 1973. Then I went to Emporia, Kansas, to get my master's degree at Emporia State University. By that time I got my Ph.D. in 1978, I was married and had three children. I went back to Kuwait and stayed another five years, and then my family and I decided to move back to the United States. One of the reasons we returned was that my kids and I were stateless. We had no passports; no Palestinians had passports except for those living in Jordan. I wanted my children to get some sort of citizenship so they would not face the same difficulties that I had faced, always having to move around.

Now I'm a professor of mathematics at Trinity College in San Antonio, Texas. But I've always thought about coming back to Palestine to help my people. I felt an obligation to do so. So I applied for a Fulbright Grant to come to Birzeit University to teach a course and give a seminar to the faculty here. I got it and came here last summer.

You know the rest of the story. The *Intifada* started and the university closed during October and November. Still, I wanted to do something. I felt that I had to do whatever I could to help the *Intifada*. So my niece Rolla and I enrolled in a workshop on first aid. We were trained and then started going every day to the checkpoint, where the clashes are between Palestinians and Israelis. School was closed, so we dedicated all of our time to being first-aid volunteers.

We've developed a lot of friendships with people of all ages at the checkpoint. It's nice to be doing something worthwhile, even if it is a very little thing.

Once when we were at the checkpoint a small boy, probably twelve years old, fell down after inhaling a lot of tear gas. He was on the ground unconscious and I went to pick him up. He was so light, like a baby. I thought that he was going to die before I could get him to the ambulance. I almost fell myself as I carried him. If I hadn't gotten to him, he probably would have died. But we made it. Now I see that same little kid back at the checkpoint all the time. I tell him, "Go home! Don't come here anymore, please!" But he keeps coming back.

Another time my niece Rolla fell and was injured. I was worried that she might pass out, and I tried to carry her but I couldn't do it. We took her to a nearby hospital and after about fifteen minutes she was OK. She had inhaled too much gas. She was just so close to the frontlines.

I've seen some very terrible things, too. Once someone about five meters away from us was hit in the head. His brains were shattered. That is a sight that will stay with me forever: the first time I saw brains shattered in front of me. After a while, all the people you know get shot. It's painful. Almost everyone I know has been hit. Some hits are severe and some people have been killed.

Palestinians are just tired of dealing with all of the humiliations of the occupation. They're sick of the checkpoints, of being asked to show their identity cards, etc. But on top of these difficulties, the settlers make this a double occupation. On the one hand, you have a traditional military occupation with an army that wants to exploit the country. On the other hand, you have the settlers, who want to take the land and want the indigenous people out. They consider you to be a resident and not a citizen in your own country. So you feel that you are just surviving, with all of these settlers everywhere, on every hill.

I want to compare our situation to the American Revolution. The Americans wanted to be free from the British and the Palestinians want to be free from the Israeli occupation. It is an occupation. You have a military with tanks. They are surrounding Palestinians' villages and cities, and most Palestinians can't move from one town to another. It is much worse than even the British occupation of America was.

I want Americans to look at the situation from a different angle than that which they hear in the news. Here you have an underdog people, the Palestinians, who are really suffering. The only thing they want is to live their lives on whatever is left of Palestine. In 1948, they lost 78 percent of Palestine. They lost their country so that a new country called Israel could be established. The Palestinians, with no crime on their part, had to suffer the consequences of the massacres of Jews in Europe. There was a crime committed by Israel in 1948, uprooting Palestinians from their country. And now Palestinians are supposed to forget about that.

So I want to ask Americans to have a new perspective. From 1948 until now, Israel has been trying to cover up what happened to the Palestinians. And worse than that, Israel is still occupying them, oppressing them, and killing them. So the killing continues from 1948 until now, with the support of the U.S. government. The U.S. government gives its full support—with billions of dollars pouring into Israel every year—to help Israel suppress the Palestinians.

If any other country of the world except Israel had committed these crimes, there may have been an invasion of American forces, such as in Kosovo. Or there may have been an embargo and an invasion, as in Iraq. But Israel can now do no wrong. Even Israel's own citizens of Arab descent are being killed. At least thirteen of them were killed in the first weeks of the *Intifada*.

The media always show the Israelis as the good guys and the Palestinians as violent. But the violence of rock-throwers against Israeli tanks cannot be said to be equal violence.

I think that most of the kids at the checkpoint are really proud. They think that this is their *Intifada*. This is for young people; it is their creation. They are at the front lines and the older people are in the back. This is their uprising.

It does seem that every generation of Palestinians has its own *Intifada*. If one generation gets tired, the next generation acquires a fresh look and new blood. This Palestinian nation will never be conquered. It will never submit. The only way out is a fair share of the land, of historic Palestine. Nothing short of a just solution will end the conflict.

From left to right: Sultan, Narimen, and Jamila, in Batir

3 . SULTAN, NARIMEN, AND JAMILA,
three friends in a village near Bethlehem

BY THE TIME I *got to Batir, a village just outside Bethlehem, I had switched taxis five times, walked through three checkpoints, and was covered in mud from the January rains. The leg of the journey from Ramallah to Bethlehem was the worst part. Only sixteen miles as the crow flies, the driver of my shared taxi had to take the torturously winding back roads because he lacked a permit to travel directly through Jerusalem. As a result, we spent an hour and a half trudging through* Wadi An-Naar, *"Valley of Hell," the only route from the northern to southern West Bank for those compelled to circumvent its central transportation and economic hub.*

Once out of the taxi, I asked for directions to Jamila's house. Batir, once an ancient city and site of a Roman castle, is a Palestinian village of fifteen hundred people. On its outskirts lie the remains of a sixth-century Byzantine church and springs thought to be Saint Philip's fountain mentioned in the New Testament. Not too far beyond the springs sits one of the twenty Israeli settlements built on land confiscated from the Bethlehem District since it was occupied in 1967.

The day that I visited Batir the rain had turned its paths from dirt to mud. As I made my way to Jamila's, I wondered how Israel was able to rule over these narrow paths and each of the families in these stones houses. In the months following the Six-Day War, U.N. Security Council Resolution 242 called upon Israel to withdraw from territories occupied in the course of the fighting. Israel did not comply. Rather, it developed a system by which it absorbed the land without the people. And so the Palestinians of the West Bank and Gaza Strip, allowed neither to become Israeli citizens nor to create a state of their own, came to live under military rule.

The military occupation government combined security measures such as curfews, house raids, and surveillance with a web of administrative regulations that left no aspect of daily life untouched. As "resident aliens," Palestinians could be forced to obtain Israeli permission for everything from buying a refrigerator to building a new porch. Books and newspapers were censored, the gathering of ten or more Palestinians outlawed, and such incendiary behavior as holding one's fingers in the form of a "V" reprimanded by patrolling soldiers. Display of anything resembling the Palestinian flag—be it a child's sketch or red, white, and green laundry drying together on the line—was prohibited.

According to the military orders that served as law under the occupation, any Palestinian leaving home without his or her Israeli-issued identity card was liable for a year in prison. This created a dangerous dilemma for those whose IDs had been confiscated at checkpoints or in house raids. Military orders also granted all Israeli soldiers the authority to arrest any Palestinian without specifying a reason. Once detained, Palestinians could linger for months in jail without counsel or trial. As the first Intifada *took root, arrest campaigns sweeping entire villages induced many young men to flee to the hills in an effort to escape indefinite confinement in an Israeli prison or desert internment center.*

Palestinians not only had to obey military rule; they also had to fund it. Israel collected $1 billion in taxes and deductions from Palestinians, some 2.5 times the amount that it invested in the Occupied Territories. The tens of thousands of Palestinian workers who awoke before dawn in order to do menial labor in Israel likewise had to pay a fifth of their wages to Israeli national insurance, even though they were legally ineligible for some of the benefits enjoyed by Israeli workers.

In a call for independence, Palestinian nationalists triumphed in West Bank municipal elections in 1976. In response, Israel discontinued free elections and created a system of "village councils" by which a puppet local leadership collaborated in carrying out Israeli-occupation policies. Nevertheless, as the years of occupation dragged on, Palestinians became more strident in their strategies for protesting it. The unifying force for resistance was the Palestine Liberation Organization, which had been established by 420 leading Palestinian figures in 1964 and had come under the control of Yasser Arafat's Fatah *movement five years later. Based in Jordan and then Lebanon and then Tunisia, the PLO both provided social services to refugees and sponsored kidnappings, hijackings, and other armed operations against Israel. In the mid-1970s the PLO began signaling its willingness to negotiate with Israel, and in 1988 it formally renounced terrorism and recognized Israel's right to exist.*

It was around this time that Jamila's brother-in-law was killed by Israeli soldiers and her husband was imprisoned for his suspected activism. During the six years that he spent in jail, Jamila studied, worked, and cared for two young boys on her own. She would be the mother of three before she achieved what had long been her dream: to finish college.

Jamila received her bachelor's degree in social work in the spring of 2000. A few months later the second Intifada *began, and a few months after that I arrived at Jamila's door with my tape recorder in hand. Greeting me with kisses, she sat me down at the wood-burning stove that heated the house and gently wiped away the mud that I had somehow gotten on my nose. Narimen and Sultan—a married couple who were both relatives of Jamila's husband in the multistep way that people in villages always seem to be relatives—had also come in anticipation of my visit.*

In the hours that followed, tea glasses were filled, emptied, and filled again, and conversation took on a life of its own. Jamila, Narimen, and Sultan's rapid-fire political debate and affectionate teasing put me in such stitches that I almost lost sight of the burdens that each one bore; Sultan had been tortured in prison, Narimen was out of work, Jamila's children couldn't sleep because of the bombing at night, and so on. The three of them referred to their life trials nonchalantly, as if they were hardly worth mentioning at all. They were nothing more than ordinary people in an ordinary village, they insisted, like any other village in Palestine.

·◆·　·◆·　·◆·

Narimen

My name is Narimen. I work in Bethlehem in a souvenir shop that sells to tourists. I'm married to Sultan.

Sultan

I'm Sultan. I own a small factory that produces ceramic souvenirs and gifts for tourists.

Narimen

The shop I work in depends on tourism, but now there is no tourism whatsoever. The roads are closed because of the *Intifada*. I guess the tourists are afraid to come to Bethlehem because they think that we're all terrorists.

So the guides that lead tours don't bring tourists to Bethlehem anymore. The souvenir shops are all closed. Every shop employs twenty to forty employees, who rely on it for their livelihood. In addition to them, many other people depend on tourism to make a living. Like all the people who carve olive wood or are in the ceramics business, like my husband.

Sultan

Two years ago I started my own factory to make ceramic souvenirs. It was a little factory, not a big one. Not too long after that, everyone began planning for the Bethlehem 2000 celebrations. It was supposed to be a huge event that would bring tens of thousands of tourists to Bethlehem. Or maybe millions. I decided that this was going to be my big opportunity, so I started to build up the factory. I invested millions of shekels to buy machines and materials. I spent everything I owned. I even bought some special equipment from abroad. I hired workers and I trained them. This was last February. Then the *Intifada* started in September. And now it's all gone. Gone. There are no tourists, so there's no business in making souvenirs. I'm bankrupt. All I can do now is to try to search for an investor to come and provide some new capital.

Narimen

Of course the Israeli tourist sector has also been affected. But the difference between them and us is social security. In the end, if you're out of work, is there someone there to look out for you? Is there someone to cover your expenses for a while or to help you pay a hospital bill? We have no social security whatsoever. It just doesn't exist for us because we don't even have a state. They have a state and services. We don't have anything.

Sultan

As for me, I don't have a cent to my name. I can't even buy a tomato.

Narimen

When you live under occupation it's like you get squeezed from the pressure. Before the *Intifada* I used to go to Bethlehem without any problems. But I had to think it over one hundred times before going to Jerusalem, which is just eight kilometers farther away. I was just scared that a soldier would stop me and make me get out of the car and prevent me from going.

But now I don't even feel safe going to Bethlehem, no less Jerusalem. I'm even scared to go to Al-Khader, the next village over.

So how am I supposed to think about moving forward with my life, when I can't even move forward to the next village? How am I supposed to think about continuing my education? How am I ever supposed to live like normal people do?

What does Israel want to accomplish? Do they want us to leave our houses? That's not going to happen very easily. It would take a lot to make me abandon my house.

How am I supposed to love Jews when they deny me a life of peace?

Sultan

Listen, the problem in Palestine is that we Palestinians are backward. We were backward in 1948, and that's why it was so easy for the Zionists to waltz right in from Europe and take everything away from us. If we'd been more developed, that wouldn't have happened.

In the world there are two kinds of people: those who work and those who sleep. The Israelis work and we Palestinians are sleeping. The whole Arab world is sleeping. That's why this is happening to us.

Narimen

Wait a second, that's not right. Israelis don't have all of that power just because they work for it. They also have support from all the other countries of the world.

Jamila

And they steal our land. They build settlements and treat our workers like slaves.

Sultan

It's all about money. The land should belong to whoever makes it flourish.

Narimen

When Sultan was young he was active in supporting the PLO.

Jamila

And now he's a capitalist.

Sultan

People just want to be able to eat, to earn their daily bread. The real peace is the peace of business, like Shimon Peres said.

Jamila

I disagree, Sultan. We tried peace negotiations but they didn't bring us anything.

Sultan

So you're against peace!

Jamila

Be quiet and listen to me, Sultan! The question is what kind of peace do they want?

Sultan

Five years ago the Israeli prime minister said that he could accept the existence of a Palestinian state with Jerusalem as its capital. Israel has changed.

Jamila

Yeah, and what about what Israel is doing now? And all of the refugees who are still scattered all over the world waiting for their rights? Israel hasn't changed at all.

Forget it, Sultan, this conversation isn't going anywhere. Here, let me tell you about my job. As Narimen said, nobody has work during this *Intifada*. Sultan, Narimen, my husband, Billal . . . they're all unemployed. I'm the only one with a job.

I'm a social worker. I wasn't working before the *Intifada*, but when the *Intifada* began a crisis emerged, and with it programs to help people. I was watching all of the terrible scenes on TV, and I wanted to do something. I applied to volunteer for a crisis-intervention project in Bethlehem. Before I even had an interview, they made me coordinator. It was an emergency situation and everything was happening so fast. It is just a temporary project, but at least it's something.

Through our intervention in the field we've seen how terrible the situation is for people. We go to the refugee camps and see how frightened the children are. There are children who wet their pants day and night out of fear. Children are afraid, and they don't think anyone can protect them. When they bomb at night, children don't go to their parents. Instead they hide under the table.

Narimen

I get scared when the planes and helicopters come and bomb, and I'm an adult. How is a child supposed to sleep at night?

Jamila

That's my situation. As a social worker, I have work when things get bad. If everything were OK, I'd be out of a job.

Sultan

Ha! Jamila has a job so she wants the *Intifada* to continue! The *Intifada* has ruined me, so I'm totally against it!

Jamila

Listen, Sultan, I support the continuation of the *Intifada*. But not in the bloody form that it's taking now. I want the *Intifada* to achieve real gains. But regardless of whether or not the *Intifada* stops, my work will continue because we have to cope with the crisis and post-crisis problems. The worst could be yet to come. In the future we'll have to cope with all of the effects of trauma on children, the injured, the families of those who have been killed, and so on.

The situation is very, very bad. This *Intifada* is having an impact on the entire society. If someone is shooting and Israel bombs, it doesn't just drop a bomb on the person who is doing the shooting. It drops a bomb on the entire area. It bombs the children and the mothers and everyone living there.

A part of this *Intifada* is the clashes between Palestinians and soldiers. But a big part of the *Intifada* is completely arbitrary violence. There is a four-year-old from the next village over named Ismael. He walked outside and got hit by a bullet in his eye. I have his file in my office. The bullet took his eye out. His mother just came out of the house and found him on the ground covered with blood. Now he has only one eye. The strange thing is that he keeps searching for the eye he lost. He keeps trying to touch it. He is only four years old and he is looking for his eye. He was such a beautiful child, but he has changed a lot. It's very strange.

And there are many children like that. The soldiers shoot at children as they're leaving school. Where is the justice in this? Where is the human conscience? Where is the democracy? There is no equivalence in our power. I work with children in this area, and some of them throw stones at the cars on the Israeli bypass road. Let them throw stones. The cars drive at 80 km per hour. They have weapons with them and protected windows. The children can't do anything to them.

Still, the army has responded by shutting down the schools. Here we had to set up an alternative school in a very old building that was being used as a barn for sheep and chickens. There are six hundred students and they have to study in three different shifts because there is not enough room for all of them to be there at the same time. The first shift of students comes at 7:30 and finishes at 10:00. Then they go home and another group starts at 10:30 and finishes at 12:00. Then they go home and other students come in.

During this *Intifada* Israel has had two main targets: young men in armed factions and children. There is no peace in this. There must be international protection for our children.

Sultan

The *Intifada* is wrecking everything. Hundreds of people are under the ground and thousands are injured. Enough *Intifada* already.

Narimen

During the first *Intifada*, Sultan was wanted by the Israelis. He had to go into hiding in the hills.

Sultan

Somebody told the occupation authorities that I had been throwing stones. So I became a "wanted person." If I stayed at home they would have come for me. So I ran off into the countryside. I was on the run. And I was hungry all the time. More than anything else, I just wanted to eat.

I couldn't afford to buy a chicken, so I would go to the butcher shop and ask them if they had any dead chickens lying around. But you know that it is forbidden in Islam to eat the meat of a dead animal like that. An animal has to be butchered according to Islamic law. You have to slit the throat in the way that brings the least amount of pain and say "in the name of God." But I didn't have any money to buy a live chicken. So I'd get some chicken that was already dead, and I'd go ahead and slit its throat anyway and say "in the name of God." And that is what I would eat.

I was in hiding and I had no money. What could I do? I lived like that for two months before they finally caught me.

Narimen

That was about the time that we got engaged. They put him in jail for three years. That was the situation for almost all young men at that time.

Sultan

My situation was completely normal. Some guys spent ten years or fifteen years in prison. There is practically no guy my age who didn't go to prison for some time during the first *Intifada*.

Do you know what it's like in Israeli prisons? Do you know how they torture you? Do you know the *Shabah*? They make you sit in a tiny chair so your knees are up by your ears. They tie your hands behind your back. You sit in that position, not for an hour or two, but for four days or five days in a row. Or they make you stand against the wall with your arms tied behind your back.

On top of that, after you're released they give you an identity card with a different color. They give you a green ID, which means that it is forbidden for you to work inside Israel and forbidden for you to move. That is the ID that I'm stuck with now.

I spent three years in jail. And do you know what my crime was? I was asked if I liked *Fatah*, and I said yeah, I like *Fatah*. That's it. I didn't do anything more than that.

Jamila

At that time everything was prohibited for us. Listening to a Palestinian nationalist song? Prohibited. Reading a nationalist book? Prohibited. Having a picture of Yasser Arafat in your house? Prohibited. It was even prohibited to wear a *kuffiyeh*. If you wore one they'd shoot you.

I got beat up by soldiers once during the first *Intifada*. That was when my husband was in prison. I had been throwing rocks and they came and beat me and also beat my father, who was an old man at the time.

There is no humanity in occupation. And there is no occupation as bad as the Israeli occupation. This is why the *Intifada* must continue. I don't want anyone to die. But there is no solution to our conflict. Sometimes some people must die so that others may live.

Osama, on a visit home to Jenin

4. OSAMA, *financial adviser*

ONCE DURING MY COLLEGE *semester abroad in Morocco, my American classmates and I were treated to a performance of traditional Berber songs and then asked to perform something that represented our culture. At a loss for a song to which we all knew the words, we finally belted out the theme to* The Jeffersons. *One of the things that most connected us as a generation of twenty-something Americans, we were disconcerted to discover, was 1980s sitcoms.*

Five years later, when I was studying with Palestinian twenty-somethings at Birzeit University, I discovered one of the things that most connected them as a generation: the first Intifada. *On any night in the coffee shops of the premier Palestinian college town, students' heated political debates inevitably conjured up recollections of the popular uprising that consumed the Occupied Territories from 1987 to 1993. Witnessing a fair share of these impassioned exchanges, I could not help but wonder how I would be different, had I grown up with episodes of curfew, shootings, and house raids rather than episodes of* The Jeffersons.

The first Intifada *began in December 1987, when an Israeli truck collided into Palestinian laborers from Gaza's Jabalia refugee camp, leaving four dead and seven injured. As a Jewish salesman had been killed in Gaza two days earlier, many Palestinians viewed the crash as deliberate. Riots ensued in Jabalia, ending in the Israeli authorities' killing of three Palestinian teenagers. As unrest spread throughout Gaza and the West Bank, it took on the name "Intifada," a grassroots effort to "shake off" the occupation and create an independent Palestinian state.*

Guided by political communiqués that circulated through towns and refugee

37

camps, Palestinians formed popular committees to organize a variety of kinds of resistance. In an effort to decrease economic dependence on Israel, Palestinians boycotted Israeli goods, held commercial strikes, and fed themselves from their own gardens. In confrontations with Israeli soldiers, young men threw rocks, burned tires, and set up roadblocks. The uprising was overwhelmingly nonviolent: Israeli army figures reported that 80 percent of Palestinians' forceful protest consisted of stone-throwing, while 15 percent involved petrol bombs and 5 percent firearms.

Israeli defense minister Yitzhak Rabin vowed to restore order, first by crushing the Intifada with an "iron fist," and then by breaking protestors' arms and legs. As scenes of Israeli soldiers beating teenage stone-throwers became televised throughout the world, however, criticism mounted both inside and outside Israel. Meanwhile, the Israeli army was discovering that the technological sophistication and combat training that had enabled its triumph on the battlefield was of little help in chasing children through refugee camps or overpowering mothers intent on protecting their sons and grandsons.

As the Intifada dragged on, Israel came to appear less a "light unto nations" than an armed Goliath occupying a civilian David. More and more Israelis came to believe that the conflict demanded a political rather than a military solution. In the aftermath of the Gulf War's shakeup of the region, Israel agreed to attend the 1991 Madrid peace conference with neighboring Arab states and, for the first time, an independent delegation of Palestinians from the West Bank and Gaza. Shortly thereafter, Israel initiated direct talks with the PLO, culminating in the 1993 Declaration of Principles and the Oslo peace process. The Intifada, against the backdrop of a changing international political environment, had brought Israel to do what it had never done before: formally recognize the Palestinian people as a nation struggling for self-determination in its own right.

For Palestinians, however, the Intifada's achievements did not come without tremendous costs. According to B'Tslem, Israelis killed over 1,100 Palestinians during the period from the Intifada's inception until Rabin and Arafat's historic handshake on the White House lawn. Of these, about 250 were children. During the same time period, 160 Israelis were killed by Palestinians.

Israel's crackdown on Palestinian activists and suspected PLO sympathizers went well beyond these numbers. Over 100,000 Palestinians were wounded, almost 500 were deported from the Occupied Territories, and no less than one in five males between the ages of fifteen and fifty-five were arrested. The Public Committee Against Torture in Israel estimates that tens of thousands of Palestinian detainees were tortured, whether by being beaten, deprived of sleep or food, tied in painful positions for hours or days, or abused verbally, sexually, or psychologically. Torture remained legal in Israel until it was banned by the Supreme Court in 1999. Nonetheless, many human-rights groups charge that it continues until the present.

The Intifada's toll on Palestinian society at large was even more sweeping. Countless Palestinian families were forced to watch as Israeli troops stormed their homes in the middle of the night, ransacked their belongings, and beat their relatives bloody. A generation of children and young adults paid the consequences for Israel's closure of Palestinian schools and universities, notwithstanding teachers' willingness to assume the risks involved in carrying out lessons in their homes in secret.

Beyond this, the whole population of the Occupied Territories spent hours, days, or weeks trapped inside under curfew. During curfew, anyone daring to step into the street, or even to lean too far out the window, risked being shot. Some West Bank villages were under curfew for more than one third of the years 1988 and 1989, and the entire Gaza Strip was under permanent night curfew from 1988 to 1994. The combination of curfew and strikes, in addition to a standstill in exports, subcontracting, and eventually the inflow of remittances from the Gulf, resulted in a 40 percent decline in Palestinians' living standards.

These facts should speak for themselves. But they do not. In my experience, at least, it was not until I spent some time listening to Palestinians my own age that I realized the profundity of the first Intifada's place in their lives. The Intifada,

I came to appreciate over the course of many late-night conversations, was not something that young Palestinians had lived through. It was something that had made them who they are. Listening to their stories during the waning days of the peace process, I found palpable their frustration that so much suffering had borne so little fruit.

It was at one of these discussions, over a table of empty coffee cups and overflowing ashtrays, that I met Osama. Like many of his classmates, Osama received something of an education in Israeli jails years before he went to college, earned a degree in business, and landed a job with an American-sponsored project. Shortly thereafter he had married his longtime love, a European national who had come to theWest Bank as an exchange student and found in it a second home.

With perfect English and the cosmopolitan air of a young Ramallah professional, Osama struck me as the kind of guy who was going places.When he told me about his life, however, he made little mention of his own personal successes and aspirations. Rather, it was the first Intifada *that emerged front and center.*

* * *

My name is Osama. I am from Jenin and work as a financial officer in Ramallah. The current *Intifada* is painful, for me and for everyone.

The first *Intifada* was different, because the soldiers were not just waiting outside the cities. They were here; you could see them. They could stop you anytime they wanted; they could enter your house anytime they wanted. They would enter our house and break things and make everyone afraid. It was a way of saying, "We are here. We are the powerful ones."

It was scary. I mean, I spent seven years running. I remember very well that I never walked down the street. I was always running. I was a young guy, which meant that I was a target, whether I was participating in resistance activities or not. After all, it was the instructions of Yitzak Rabin, the "man of peace," to break Palestinians' bones.

This is my life experience. I will never forget it, and I will pass it on to my children. It was a huge stage in my life and it has marked me forever. I was a teenager; I was supposed to think about girls, about enjoying life and having fun. But I was running. It was not my choice.

My father is a refugee. He came from one of the Palestinian villages destroyed in 1948. My father would tell us that he had a house in that village and he still has the papers to prove it. But he never told me to hate.

He never even encouraged me to participate in activities in resistance to the occupation. But for me, the first *Intifada* was a golden opportunity to stand up. I spent many months of my life under curfew, and I lost very good friends during the first *Intifada*. I will never forget them. But still, I don't know anything called hate, because this is how I was raised. My mother and father never told me to hate.

When I was a child my mother told me not to be afraid because soldiers don't hit children. But then one time some soldiers hit me when I was coming home from school. I remember that I cried and came home and told my mother that she had lied to me. I wasn't doing anything and they hit me. I was so afraid that I was shaking. Do you think I am going to forget this? No. But not because of hate.

I got my strength from my mother especially. She had wanted to go to school but never got the chance. Her father was blind and she had to work to help her mother at home. They were refugees and very poor. She suffered a lot. History won't write about my mother, but in my eyes she is a very important person. She gave her life to us, and it has been her dream to see my brothers and sisters and me graduate from college.

We're not a unique family, but we have experienced a lot of pain. My brothers and sisters and I never had toys because it was just something that my father couldn't offer us. We all used to sleep in one room, and I was fourteen years old before I ever slept in a real bed. We all worked, which is something I'm very proud of. We all learned how to be independent.

I was seventeen when they arrested me for the first time. I spent eighteen days being tortured, and then they released me because I had nothing to tell except my name.

Then I was arrested again and taken to prison in the Negev desert. I spent six months in "administrative detention," which meant that they had no proof of any offense. They only had reports from collaborators who said that I was active. They tortured me to make me speak but I had nothing to tell. So I was released after six months. I never had a trial. The lawyer didn't come until the week before I was released.

They can do whatever they want to me physically. But they'll never touch my soul and my beliefs.

My father was the only one who sent me letters when I was in prison. He stood against me when I wanted to participate in the *Intifada*, but he was the one who wrote to me while I was in prison. He would put his cologne on the letters so I could smell it. I received the letters late, after a delay of one or two months. Still, the letters showed me that he was alive and that he cared about me.

When I was finally released I discovered that I had lost one of my best friends. He was sixteen years old and had been shot. He was not threatening the soldiers in any way. He was running, and they killed him.

I don't hate. I don't want revenge. I don't want to kill a child because my friend was killed. But at the same time, I cannot forget this. It was not a toy that I lost. This was a human being.

No, I don't want revenge. On the contrary, all of this has given me the strength to believe. I am not a terrorist as they describe me. I am not a monster, and I never hated anyone.

I have brothers who were also put in prison. One of my brothers was a sophomore in college when he was arrested. He was imprisoned for four years. Another brother was arrested when he was eighteen years old. They came with a tank and turned the house upside down. I was nine years old and was crying and shaking. After that he was always being transferred from one prison to another because they didn't want him to make friends or feel stable. They released him after a year and a half. He was tortured and almost lost his vision. He has had surgery but still has a lot of trouble seeing.

After my brother was released he got a scholarship to study in the States. At his graduation ceremony all of the flags were hanging except his flag. There was no Palestinian flag.

Now during the current *Intifada*, there are people who want revenge. It is difficult. We have a saying in Arabic, "Speak when your hand is in the fire, not when your hand is in the water." In other words, the situation is completely different when you have lost someone close to you. This time I have not lost a friend or my brother or father, so it is easier for me. I'm calm.

I don't want to kill them. I don't want to throw them in the sea, as some Israelis claim. I want them to leave me alone. I don't want them to use my oxygen, my water. These are my resources; please leave them to me. If you go to the refugee camps here, you'll see that they have no water to drink. A few meters away the Israeli settlement has swimming pools. Is this fair? Where is the international community? Where is America? Where is Europe?

I respect all religions, whether I believe in them or not. Muslims, Christians, and Jews all worship God. And I want to be very clear. There is a big difference between Judaism and Israel. I have no problem with Jewish people living in Iraq, or in the United States, or in Russia. But I have a big problem with people who come here and confiscate my water and land.

In the Palestinian constitution of the 1940s, it is written that Jews, Muslims, and Christians can all be Palestinians. That is, they can all be residents of Palestine. Why do Jews have to have their own country? Does it make sense for all Christians to get together and have their own Christian state, or for all Muslims to have their own Muslim state?

This region will never be stable unless there is a real solution, from the roots. And the Palestinian negotiators know that they cannot sign an agreement that does not offer a fair solution for the refugees. I remember that I was twelve years old when Ariel Sharon ordered the massacres in Sabra and Shatila. The children of Sabra and Shatila will never forget this, and neither will I.

I don't think that the Israelis are going to allow the refugees to return to their homes inside Israel. At the same time, I don't see how the refugees can come to live in the West Bank and Gaza Strip. It is not that they are not wanted. On the contrary, they are most welcome. They can share my house—they've had enough suffering. The problem is that there is no space. If they came here, how long could it last? We are a very small country. It will be a time bomb waiting to explode. This is the situation in Gaza now. There is barely enough air for people to breathe there.

This reminds me of the other day when I went to Nablus for work. There was a checkpoint on the main road and then there was a detour to a back road. The soldiers told me, "Don't continue on the main road, take the back road instead." Why? They know that I'm still going to make it to Nablus. They aren't going to close the roads completely, because they know that people will explode. But they want us to suffer. They want us to think only about how to survive day to day. If you have a secure life, you'll start thinking about other things. And they don't want this.

Why should Americans care about what is happening here in Palestine? Why do I care about what goes on when people die in Africa, for example? I have enough problems in my own country. But I care. I care because I'm a human being and I have feelings. When you suffer, you know what it means to suffer. You care about other people who suffer, too.

I'm not asking for the moon. I'm just asking for my freedom.

My role as a Palestinian is to keep standing. You have to live your life. I went to a party this New Year's Eve. Everyone was dancing and having a good time, but I could hear that there was shooting going on outside. That is what they want, to make our lives so difficult that we'll leave. I'm committed to this message: Keep going because it is your right.

Occupation is a cancer. The Palestinians have been occupied throughout history, but I go to sleep at night content because our history is clean. We've never occupied anyone else.

I'm sure that there will be an end to all of this injustice and unfairness someday. That is history.

Suzanne (right), with her sister Jehan in Ramallah

5. SUZANNE, *TV reporter*

I ADMIT THAT WHEN *I first arrived in theWest Bank, about eight months before the collapse of the Camp David summit, I didn't fully understand why people were so fed up with the peace process. Living in PA-controlled Ramallah, I felt like I was witnessing the long-awaited Palestinian state take shape. Palestinian flags waved freely, new businesses had sprung up, and there was not an Israeli soldier to be found on the streets. If there was still occupation as everyone claimed, why couldn't I see it?*

I decided to ask my political science professor at Birzeit University. A stern man known for his forthright criticism and low tolerance of mediocrity, he often remarked that he did not know which contributed more to his high blood pressure; his students' laziness or the dismal political situation.We, his lazy students, revered him.

One afternoon I caught him in his office and asked the question that had been bothering me:What was so bad about Oslo? I remember that he looked at me dismissively and boomed,"Must you Americans be that naive?"

As I fumbled to regain my composure, he told me that I had fallen into the trap of mistaking the façade of Palestinian independence for its substance. Oslo allowed Israel to disengage with the Palestinian population and wash its hands of the everyday oversight of Palestinian cities.Thus the Palestinian Authority, my professor continued, built and filled its prisons. Israel, meanwhile, continued to confiscate Palestinian territory and build a network of settlements and roads that cut Palestinian cities off from one another.The doubling of the settler population since Oslo, he explained, convinced Palestinians that what Israel gave with one hand it took away with the other.

47

I was still not completely convinced. My professor shook his head scornfully and tried again. Take the American Revolution, he said. Imagine that the British said that they would grant you independence gradually. During that time, they took snatches of your land and established colonies. They gave British citizens benefits to move there and sent British soldiers to protect them. They built British highways all over your country, and wherever their highways crossed your roads they set up checkpoints and could prevent you from traveling. As the colonies underwent "natural growth," they took even more land to accommodate their needs.

"What would you Americans do if the British offered you this kind of independence?" he asked.

I paused before replying. "We'd declare war."

My professor nodded, as if to say that maybe I wasn't so dense after all. And then he gave me a look that told me to get out and let him get back to work.

I scuttled out of his office before I had a chance to ask for some concrete examples of this façade of independence with an essence of occupation. But when I thought about it, I realized that I did not have to think further than my own experience. Like anyone who wanted to reach the Palestinian territories, I had crossed Israeli borders and passed through Israeli security. As Israel did not recognize Birzeit as a university, I was residing there on an Israeli tourist visa rather than a student visa. When it came time to renew my three-month visa, I went to the PA Ministry of Interior to fill out the requisite forms. Although I spent several hours shuffling from office to office, both the clerks and I knew that the routine was a farce. The Palestinian Authority had no power over travel, family reunification, permits for Palestinians' foreign spouses, or any other matters relating to residency. All it was authorized to do was collect forms and send them to Israel, which alone decided who was allowed within its borders and who was not.

My professor was right. Behind every façade of Palestinian sovereignty lurked continued Israeli control. Even laws passed by the Palestinian Legislative Council, after all, were subject to Israeli approval. The only realm in which Israel wanted the Palestinian Authority to be truly authoritative, it seemed, was that of cracking down on Islamist opposition groups.

I was mulling over these thoughts as I wandered from my professor's office to the student cafeteria. Like college cafeterias everywhere, this one was abuzz with laughter and the clatter of dishes. Many students were cramming to finish (or start) their reading before class, and many more were flirting. I saw Jehan, a girl in my political science class, sat down beside her, and began to recount the conversation that I had had with our professor. Yet as I went on about Oslo and façades and realities, I noticed that she was looking at me very oddly.

"Don't you agree?" I asked

"Of course I do," she responded, "but who are you?"

And this was how I met Suzanne, my classmate Jehan's identical twin. I fumbled for an apology, as I would do again and again as I continued to confuse them throughout the semester. Born and raised in Jenin, both sisters were quick-witted, hardworking, and exhibited plenty of the strong will for which their hometown was famous. My unyielding professor, after all, was a Jenin native as well.

The second Intifada began the following autumn. Birzeit, like the other five Palestinian universities in the West Bank and East Jerusalem, was forced to shut its doors for several weeks and lost yet another semester to political unrest. In subsequent months Israeli bulldozers destroyed the Birzeit-Ramallah road. When Palestinians came together to repair it, the army established a checkpoint that allowed it to open or close the road as it wished. The status of the university, as well as the thirty-five surrounding villages that similarly depended on the road, vacillated from day to day. My professor's blood pressure, I feared, did likewise.

It was a few months into the Intifada that I fortuitously came back into contact with Suzanne. I had come to the northern Ramallah clash point to talk with the teenage stone-throwers when I spotted her in the crowd. Freshly graduated, she was on location in her new job as a TV reporter.

"Jehan!" I exclaimed, running toward her.

"No, it's Suzanne," she replied.

As I began to fumble for an apology, gunshots rang out and ambulance sirens announced another sprint to Ramallah hospital. Suzanne gathered her equipment and rushed off to catch the story, but not before she agreed to let me put her on the other side of the microphone. We met a few days later at the place of her choosing: Checkers, Ramallah's premiere hamburger joint. Worried about the volume of the American Top 40 tunes blaring in the background, I placed my tape recorder directly on her tray, between her French fries and Diet Coke. And after insisting that I share her fries, Suzanne told me about what the Intifada had been like for her.

·◆· ·◆· ·◆·

MY NAME IS SUZANNE, and I'm twenty-three years old. I work as a reporter for a local television station here in Ramallah. I am originally from Jenin, in the northern West Bank.

I was hired for my first job as a reporter on a one-month trial. But after a few weeks, this *Intifada* started. All of a sudden we had all of these events going on around us and we were running from place to place. So I guess you can say that I joined the profession of journalism just when everything was getting big. It was sort of like a crash course in TV reporting.

The first days of the *Intifada* were a mess. Everything was happening so fast and nobody knew what was going to happen next. There were clashes everywhere and demonstrations and people getting shot. We were working day and night. At first we thought that the situation would be over in a matter of a days. But then it spread and spread just as the first *Intifada* had done.

And then people gradually formed a vision of what they wanted to achieve. I suppose the time was right for Palestinians to stand up and say that we had had enough of all of these bad deals. We tried. For the past seven years of negotiations, we tried. But we just can't take it anymore. We are occupied and we are fighting against this occupation. We are fighting in order to live. Nobody likes killing, nobody likes blood. But we can't just stand back and watch the soldiers and the settlers march in forever.

Israel still controls us, but now in a more awful way because there is the mirage that they've given up some control. I don't want to live this sham anymore. They control the borders and water. They can close the roads between cities whenever they want. They can still confiscate any piece of land and we can't do a thing about it. Anyone who would consider this to be peace is crazy.

You can't just launch an *Intifada* like this every day. It isn't easy. Some people think that violence is nothing more than a game for us because we like to annoy the Israelis. But this is far from the truth. I hate to use the word *violence* anyway. It isn't violence. It's struggle. And it's hard. It affects everyone in all aspects of their lives.

Since the *Intifada* began, the people get down when there is talk about resuming negotiations again. They feel like, "We are giving all of this, and in the end they are just going to go back to the drawing board and negotiate as if nothing ever happened?" This is impossible for the people to accept.

As a reporter, my time has been divided between going to the hospital to interview injured people, going to the cemetery to bury the dead, and going to the checkpoints to run after boys throwing stones.

Our camera crew used to report from the Israeli side of the checkpoint. But I would just stand there and watch the soldiers shooting and shooting for hours. Maybe some little stones would come over the barricade, if anything came over at all.

So then we started reporting from the Palestinian side, where there are loads of things happening. There are older women who break big rocks into small stones. They gather in their dresses and carry them to the guys. There are guys handing out slingshots, and people hovering around them saying, "I want one, I want one." It's like a beehive of activity.

Sometimes at the checkpoints I ask the guys why they are protesting, especially when there is news about new negotiations. I tell them, "They are out there negotiating, and you are here. Why? What are you trying to accomplish? What is the message that you are trying to give?" They always say that they will keep struggling. They say that it is time for all of us to stand up.

I can tell you that I've never been surprised by what people tell me. I'm not surprised, because I myself am also part of this struggle.

It has been really hard interviewing the mothers of people who have been killed. Sometimes I even start to cry before they do, and they end up comforting me. Sometimes I get lost in what they are saying and then I'm just not with them anymore. My feelings overwhelm me. It hurts me so much to think that this could happen to my little sister or to my brother. I just keep thinking, "What if?" There are some moments when I start thinking and I forget the interview and lose all the questions that I wanted to ask.

Some Israelis say that the Palestinian media are propagandist and that they incite violence. But it is silly to call this propaganda. The pictures talk for themselves; they don't need manipulating. Of course Israel calls what we are doing propaganda. How else can they defend what *they* are doing?

I do what I do as a person, as a Palestinian, and as a journalist. I try to be with people and to make their voices and ideas heard. I try to provide a real image of what is going on, especially its human side.

I've tried to talk to Israeli soldiers sometimes. I know that a journalist is supposed to try to be objective. But for me the whole conflict is not objective, so why must I be? What is happening doesn't make sense at all, so why should I treat it as if it made sense? Besides, this soldier is wearing a military uniform and is in an army jeep. He introduces himself as an occupier. What am I supposed to ask him?

So it is silly to go and talk to the soldiers. But sometimes you can't avoid arguing with them. They say, "You are not allowed here." I say, "Why?" They say, "We're doing our job." I say, "I'm doing my job." For example, last week I was at the checkpoint on the road to Jerusalem, and I was trying to talk to Palestinian men who had been pulled out of their taxis. The soldiers stop cars when they cross the checkpoint and look inside. Sometimes they ask for ID cards or choose guys and make them get out of the car. A group of these guys had been pulled out from different taxis and they were being made to wait there at the checkpoint. I wanted to go and interview them. But the soldier told me that I had better leave or else.

Perhaps the most difficult thing for me as a reporter covering the *Intifada* has been seeing people who've been killed. I've covered so many funerals. I never thought that I would walk five kilometers next to a dead body. The corpse is right there, where you can see all of the bruises and everything. For a while we were going to the cemetery every day, like it was going for a walk or something.

And at the checkpoint I've seen guys get shot right in front of me. It's like watching a movie. One minute he is in front of you throwing stones, and the next moment he falls to the ground, and there is blood all over and the ambulance comes. You just can't believe it's real, but it is.

Once the cameraman and I were at the checkpoint when I heard this whizzing sound. I touched the top of my head and my hair was filled with dust and debris. Then I saw that the bullet had hit the rocks right behind me. I just looked at the cameraman and he looked at me, and neither of us could say a thing. I kept thinking, "The bullet was that close to me." It was shocking. You never know when you might get shot. The bullet had just missed my head.

But I am less frightened than the foreign journalists. I have the passion inside me to do something. This is also my cause. I am not just a reporter who goes to cover the scene. I have something to say. These people are giving their lives, and I should do something along with them.

When I was in elementary school, there was never any mention of Palestine in our schoolbooks. It was never in any of the maps in our geography books. We would draw the maps of all the countries in the world—England, Germany, France—but never our own. Our teachers were prohibited from mentioning Palestine. If they risked it, they could be reported.

I was in the fourth grade when the first *Intifada* started. So you can say that my whole childhood was spent during the *Intifada*. And I suffered as all Palestinians suffered.

Because I was a child at the time, most of my experiences during the first *Intifada* revolved around school. I can still remember how it felt to sit in class and hear all of the shooting and screaming coming from outside. You just tried to close your eyes and concentrate on the lesson, but it was so hard to do.

From time to time you would smell the tear gas, and the kids would start crying and running here and there. We were so afraid. Sometimes the Israeli soldiers would storm the school and start looking for young men. And sometimes men would come to the school with their faces covered and tell all of the children to leave because it was too dangerous to stay. As a child, this would make me panic. It was all very scary.

There is something else that I will never forget. My school was in an area where there were a lot of confrontations, so the Israelis set up barriers to block the road that led to the school. We were able to move the lower barrier but we couldn't move the top one. This made a little open space, sort of like a tunnel.

The only way to get to school was by passing underneath this tunnel. So every day we got down on our hands and knees and crawled through. It was so humiliating. Can you imagine? You and your teacher and your classmates—everyone who has to get to school—crouching on their knees. Everyday we had to do it. Our hands and knees would get dirty. Our uniforms and socks would get dirty.

This is something I will never forget as long as I live. I had to get on my hands and knees every day, twice a day, in order to go to school. What more can I tell you than that?

It was hard being a kid during the first *Intifada*. It was an atmosphere in which there was no place for the kinds of feelings you begin to have as you grow up. Everything was serious and you were just too busy struggling. As kids, we always talked about politics and the situation going on around us. It was shameful to play silly games. It was shameful to listen to a love song. How could you listen to a love song while people are getting killed? You couldn't have a birthday party. What if you had a party and played music and your neighbor heard, and someone in your neighbor's family had been killed? You just couldn't do it. And for many years, our lives just stopped at 5:00 because it was too dangerous to go out after that. This was suffocating for me.

Because of all of this I have a hurt inside of me, and I don't think it will ever go away. The hurt is called Palestine. Even if someday we have peace, the hurt will never disappear. I wished I could have had a chance to be a kid. But I can't be ten or eleven anymore. The time has passed.

But because of all of this I also have a lot of spirit inside of me, as well. It's in my blood.

So seven years ago, when they said that all of a sudden there were peace negotiations, I felt like it was betrayal. I thought, "Oh no! All of the years of bloodshed and all of the terrible things that we endured, and then nothing." I couldn't believe that some form of settling would be enough.

With time, I accepted the hope that negotiations could bring us a better life. But it turned out to be nothing but disappointment. We heard all of the words about peace but never felt it. Nothing really changed. We were essentially living a big, fake peace. Everyone else in the world was happy about the peace, just smiling and saying that this was finally the end to the Palestinian problem. The world was thinking that they had done something for us. But they hadn't actually done a thing.

When Jehan and I were in college we participated in these encounters with Israeli youth. We wanted to know how they thought. The exchanges were sponsored by some organization, but I can't say that it was a peace organization. It wasn't about peace as much as it was about taking photographs. They would bring us together in a restaurant and then snap one hundred photographs so they could say, "Look! Here are Palestinians and Israelis sitting together and eating!"

Once we invited the Israelis to Ramallah, and we went to a restaurant decorated in traditional Palestinian style. We were looking at all of the Palestinian tapestries and pictures, and then we came to a map. I remember that there was a guy named Ben, and when he saw the map he said, "What is a map of Israel doing here?" And I said, "This is not Israel, this is Palestine!" We were both looking at the same thing and he said this is mine, and I said this is mine. And he wasn't wrong and I wasn't wrong.

You know what else the Israeli youth would tell us? They would say, "We might give you the right to live like everybody else, but every time we give you something you want more. So if we give you a little, how can we guarantee that you will be satisfied?"

What they don't see is that they've never given us enough. Never. That's why it continues like this. Until they give us a fair share of the land, the water, the borders, it will continue like this forever. The people might get tired and it might stop for a while, but then it will all build up inside and we'll stand up again.

I have to say that as a Palestinian raised during the first *Intifada* and having experienced everything that I've experienced, my dream is for all of Palestine. When I was little we would visit Haifa and Jaffa and Akko and walk through the Arab neighborhoods and see the Arab houses. This is Palestine for me. It might seem extreme, but when I think about Palestine it starts at the Lebanese border and ends at Egypt.

I have the dream inside of me, but I also have a realistic side. I also have to live according to the circumstances that I find around me. So I think of Palestine as being the Gaza Strip and the West Bank—without any settlements. And we share Jerusalem. Of course I wish that we could have all of Jerusalem, but we can't kick them out. We have to think about the things that we can actually achieve with some time and some struggle.

So this is the realistic settlement that would be acceptable to me. All of the settlements out, we share Jerusalem, and we get free borders. As far as the refugees, my ideal solution would be for all of them to return. That's what I think is right. But I'm also realistic. If they won't allow these people to return, they at least have to recognize that they kicked them out of their homes. They should recognize that it was wrong, and then we can negotiate on how every Palestinian refugee can be compensated for his losses.

Many years have passed in which Palestinians were not really living. What we need is a huge change. And maybe then there will be peace.

Sana' and Sami, at home in Hebron

6. SANA' AND SAMI, *schoolchildren*

THE SECOND INTIFADA BEGAN *with an outburst of violence that took both Israelis and Palestinians by surprise. As Palestinians armed with rocks and rifles faced off with the Israeli army, the death toll registered like a perverse scorecard: day one, five Palestinians and one Israeli dead; day two, another eight Palestinians and no Israelis dead; day three, yet another eight Palestinians and one Israeli dead. And so on and so forth.*

On day four, the Israeli air force joined Israeli ground troops, undertaking its first combat mission in the Occupied Territories since the 1967 War. Dozens upon dozens of such missions would follow. While Israel lauded the surgical accuracy of its strikes on Palestinian installations, Palestinian civilians listened to the roar of helicopter gunships, felt the jolts of cannons and missiles exploding, and feared the worst. Anticipation of the bombings was nearly as traumatic as the bombings themselves. In preparation for one impending raid, a single guy I know went to his corner market and bought everything on the shelves. Among his purchases were a five-pound canister of Nido baby formula and a thousand-count box of tampons.

On day nine, Prime Minister Barak addressed the Israeli people. "This is one of the most important struggles in the history of the State of Israel," he said, "a struggle for our very right to live here in this difficult and tormented region as free people." At that point, five Israelis had been killed, all of them inside the Occupied Territories. Palestinian deaths, meanwhile, totaled sixty.

And so days turned into weeks and months, and Israelis and Palestinians made out the best they could. When Israel closed Palestinian roads, Palestinians improvised alternative routes through fields, villages, and refugee camps. Travel on the unpaved back roads was time-consuming and treacherous. Worse yet, one woman explained to me, was its effect on people's thinking:

> *The terrible thing about the situation is that you begin to find alternatives to cope with the difficulties, and the alternatives gradually become fine. This road is blocked. Fine, I'll go from here. This road is also blocked. Fine, I'll go from there. When they open the roads, you feel better, even though you're still worse off than when things started. You got used to it taking two hours, so when you are able to get there in one hour, you feel better. You forget that it should take you no more than ten minutes.*

Nevertheless, Palestinians kept traveling hours on the back roads and, in one opinion poll after another, voiced their support for the Intifada. *The situation thus came to resemble something of a test of wills in which both Israelis and Palestinians vowed to withstand adversity rather than capitulate to force.*

Perhaps nowhere was this daily battle seen more dramatically than in the city of Hebron. Located eighteen miles southwest of Jerusalem, Hebron is home to the sacred tomb of Abraham, the patriarch of Jewish, Christian, and Islamic monotheism. The single structure erected at his burial site is divided into the Ibrahimi Mosque, the second most holy Islamic site in Palestine, and the Cave of the Patriarchs, the second most holy site in Judaism.

In 1929, riots broke out in Hebron and Arabs murdered sixty-nine Jews. While 435 Jews found refuge in Arab homes, the British evacuated the remainder of the city's Jewish community shortly thereafter. Jews returned to build settlements when Israel occupied Hebron in 1967. In 1994 an American-born settler named Baruch Goldstein entered the Ibrahimi Mosque and opened fire, leaving twenty-nine Palestinians dead and 150 wounded. Since then, Israeli soldiers and metal detectors have controlled access to the mosque, and no worshiper enters without passing a security search.

With a population of 120,000 Palestinians, Hebron is the West Bank's second largest city. About six thousand Israeli settlers live on the outskirts of town and another four hundred live in the heart of the Arab Old City. In a deviation from the Oslo scheme for Israeli withdrawal from Palestinian population centers, Hebron was not ceded to the Palestinian Authority without a sizable condition: the settlers would stay and Israel would retain power over the Old City in order to ensure their comfort and safety. The snag in this special arrangement was that the 20 percent of Hebron falling under Israeli control encompassed more than just Israeli settlements. It also contained the main Palestinian marketplace, the Ibrahimi Mosque, and the homes of thirty-five thousand Palestinians—approximately nine Palestinian residents for every one Israeli settler.

I visited Hebron for the first time in the spring of 2000. Walking down a single street, one moment I was in the area under Palestinian authority and a few steps later I faced a roadblock regulating entry into the Israeli-controlled sector. Passing through to the other side, I saw Israeli settlers, both young and old, toting Uzis and assault rifles along with their groceries and book bags. No fewer than fifteen hundred Israeli soldiers were on duty in the area, and everywhere I looked I saw them pointing their guns and stopping Palestinians to check their IDs. One had only to look up to see more armed soldiers looking down, monitoring the streets from rooftops and guard towers.

This was ordinary life in Hebron during the calm of the peace process. Then the second Intifada *began. The* Intifada *was less than a week old when Israeli army officials ordered Palestinians in Hebron's Old City to stay inside their houses. While the fifty Jewish families continued to move about freely, thirty-five thousand Palestinians remained under complete or partial curfew every day until the end of the year 2000, for a total of eighty-two consecutive days. In and around the Old City, thirty-three Palestinian schools serving thirteen thousand students were forced to close. Four of these schools were ordered shut by the Israeli army and transformed into military bases.*

Sana' and Sami are sister and brother growing up near Abu Sneineh, a Palestinian-controlled neighborhood bordering the Israeli-controlled section of the city. When the Intifada began, the neighborhood became the site of constant gun battles. During those early months, Sana' and Sami's days were dictated by the uncertainty of whether school would be open or closed, and their nights were dominated by shelling. Israeli tanks reoccupied Abu Sneineh about a year into the Intifada, withdrawing and reinvading intermittently in the months that followed.

Since then, Israel's reincursions into most West Bank towns have rendered the Oslo distinction between Israeli- and Palestinian-controlled areas hollow. Hundreds of thousands of kids have thus come to share the experience of their peers in Hebron: direct occupation by Israeli troops and days on end under curfew. All Palestinian children now understand that Israeli soldiers can return to the streets at any moment, their gunfire and tear gas filling the neighborhood and megaphones ordering everyone to get inside or else. At least twelve Palestinian children have been shot and killed when they disregarded this warning and ventured out their doors.

Perhaps ten years from now, when Sana', Sami, and other Palestinian schoolchildren are twenty-somethings, some American exchange student will come and speculate about what binds them as a generation. It should not take her very long to figure out.

•◆•   •◆•   •◆•

Sana', *ninth-grader*

MY NAME IS SANA' and I'm a student at the Al-Ya'koubia school in Hebron. I'm in the ninth grade.

Our house has been hit by shelling. It got hit once at the beginning of the *Intifada*. We were all sleeping in our rooms when bullets started coming through the walls into the house. So we left our rooms and moved to the one room that was farthest away from the shelling. My sisters and younger brothers got really scared and my mom took them away so they wouldn't see the bullets anymore. I was really scared, too. The whole thing was so frightening.

The shelling was coming from the Osama school, which is not far from our house. The Israelis took over the school because it is the tallest building in the neighborhood. From there you can fire down at everything else.

The bullets entered inside our house and wrecked some things. My two sisters and I share a bedroom and it faces the school directly. So our room was the one that got hit hardest.

Now we try to sleep during the day instead of at night. At night you hear all of the shelling and it's impossible to sleep. It's too scary to sleep, anyway.

Now with the *Intifada* and all of the shelling, I've started to dream about really scary things. I dream about bombs. I dream about how they slaughter people and how they kill them right in front of us. On TV you see a lot of really scary things.

My school is located between the area controlled by the Palestinian Authority and the area controlled by Israel. It is near Shellalah Street, which is where all of the clashes are. If we want to watch the confrontations, we can see the Israelis fire and the Arabs get shot. There are settlers living in the houses surrounding the school. They go up on the top floors and fire dumdum bullets down from above. Some people get shot.

So we're really scared when we get trapped in the school and there is all this shooting going on outside. The principal will go and try to reach an agreement with the Israelis so they let us go home. She'll ask them to stop shooting long enough to let us get out and cross the street. If they don't let us pass, then we end up trapped at school for a long time. If they do agree to let us go, then they won't shoot at us while we're crossing the street. But as soon as we get to the other side, they start shooting again. Then we just have to run.

Before the *Intifada* started, I walked to school. It wouldn't take more than ten minutes. But now the road is closed and this path is cut off. So we have to go all the way around the long way to avoid going through the Israeli part of the city. We go through Abu Sneineh and stop where Israeli control begins. Then we take the car on the back roads. It's very difficult because they're dirt roads with potholes and everything. Anyway, we drive for about half an hour. Then I get out and walk up the hill toward the school. Then I have to stop at the checkpoint. If the Israelis let us, we pass on through to school. If they don't, we go to the mosque, which is located on our side of the checkpoint.

When they don't let us into the school, we have classes there at the mosque. Classes will last for a half hour, even though they're supposed to last a full hour. We're supposed to have three classes, but we never know if we'll have them or not because of the situation. Half of the girls can't come to school because they can't get out of the areas where they live. Some of the other girls got really scared when the Israelis fired tear gas on our school, and now they're too frightened to come back.

It's kind of hard to learn anything anyway, whether there are classes or not. Even when the Israelis let us into our school we just can't pay attention in class because of all the shooting going on outside.

When there are confrontations, the principal and the teachers will have a meeting to decide whether or not we should continue on with classes or just go home. In the end they usually decide to cancel class. The principal and teachers try to act normal, like there is nothing going on. But inside they're scared, too. They worry about how we're going to get out of the school and go home.

Sometimes someone from the PA Ministry of Education will come to school and put on some sort of recreational activity for us. Once we had games and recreation for the whole day. They'll give lectures or do first-aid training or something else for fun.

My most frightening experience at school was once when we were trying to cross the street to get home. The settlers were shooting at Mohammedia, the boy's school that is right next to our school. It was curfew and nobody was on the streets. They started firing tear gas. The minister of education called our principal and told her that she should send us all home. We left and they started shooting and firing tear gas at us, and we all just ran. It was very scary.

Another time we were driving in a neighborhood called Takroury. It is between the area controlled by the PA and the area controlled by the Israelis. We were in the car and I was so scared that the soldiers and settlers were going to start shooting at us.

Other schools are dealing with the same sorts of things. There is a school near the Kiryat Arba'a settlement, and then there is the Osama school that they seized, the one that they use when they shell at night. Then there is the high school where my brother is a senior. He's supposed to take his secondary-school completion exam, but none of the students are really learning anything. Besides, a lot of teachers can't make it to school because of the closure. They have to drive around and around on the back roads in order to get anywhere.

Two of our neighbors have been killed. One was killed in confrontations on Shellalah Street. The other was killed in the shelling. He was in his room sleeping. A tank fired a shell and it hit him and he died.

I know people who have been injured, too. Once one of my friends was coming to school when they lifted the curfew for an hour or so. She was walking all by herself and they shot her. She got shot in her leg and her hand. She went to the hospital. Now she walks with a limp.

Another friend of mine lives near a settlement. She was just sitting in her room when they started shooting. She got hit by five bullets, three in her stomach and two in her hand. Now she is . . . well, she's not in very good shape. She was injured a month ago. She has started to come to school again, but her injuries haven't healed yet. She's still recovering.

Before the *Intifada* I liked to draw scenes from springtime and people playing. I love to draw those sorts of things. But now that the *Intifada* started, I just can't draw pretty things anymore. So when I draw now, I draw the *Intifada*. For example, I'll draw Mohammed Al-Durrah or Shaker Al-Hassuni.[1] After Shaker Al-Hassuni got killed, the Israelis grabbed him from the right and the left and dragged him on the ground. And his blood spilled out there on the ground. Also, I'll draw Deboya Street, which is where all the settlers are.

I also get scared from TV. For example, there was a Christian doctor who died when they fired on him. On TV they showed what happened to his body and how it was all blown up into many pieces. I got really scared when I saw that. I started to dream about it and then I wasn't able to sleep.

As far as our financial situation at home, my dad used to go and work inside Israel. Now it is prohibited for him to go and work. So he's out of work and we have no money at home. A charity has started helping us, and that's what we're living on these days.

I love to draw and I also love journalism. So in the future I'd like to work for a newspaper and draw caricatures. I'd like to draw about the situation so people outside can know what is happening here in Palestine.

•◆•   •◆•   •◆•

---

1 Twelve-year-old Mohammed Al-Durra was killed by Israeli gunfire in Gaza on the third day of the *Intifada*. Captured on film, pictures of Mohammed crouching with his father for safety and then being fatally shot were shown widely throughout the world.

SAMI, *seventh-grader*

MY NAME IS SAMI and I'm in seventh grade at Hebron Primary School.

My mom and I keep a garden next to our house. We grow all sorts of vegetables and flowers. We grew radishes, lettuce, spinach, mint, and a flower called "crazy." Once one of the foreign volunteers in Hebron passed by while I was working in the garden and asked me, "What is the name of that flower?" I said, "Crazy!" She was shocked and said, "What did you say about me?"

My granddad's house is right below ours. I always go and spend time with him. I love to listen to his stories because he has a lot of stories to tell. For example, when he was young he was a great swimmer. Once a man fell in a well. People thought he was going to die, but my granddad jumped in and rescued him.

He has another story from when the Jordanians were here. There was a field that nobody used because everyone thought that it was filled with mines. One day a donkey got loose and walked through the field. Nothing happened to it, and that is how they learned that there were no mines in the field after all.

Before the *Intifada* began, we would go to the Ibrahimi Mosque. The mosque is the most beautiful thing in Hebron. The stones are so big, no person could possibly lift them. They say that they were placed there by angels.

My friends and I used to ride our bikes down from our neighborhood to the mosque. We used to talk to the soldiers there. It was normal. Once a soldier took my bike and rode around on it a little bit. He gave it back to me, and he even said thanks!

Things were different then.

The *Intifada* started because Sharon entered Al-Aqsa Mosque and Muslims don't want nonbelievers to enter the Al-Aqsa Mosque. So

Sharon caused the start of the *Intifada*. This made the citizens really mad so they rose up in protest. And this led to confrontations.

This changed how I go to school. When the *Intifada* began, there would be curfew for a day or two. One hour they'd lift the curfew and then the next hour there would be curfew again. We weren't able to get to our school, which is in the area under Israeli control. So instead we had to start going to a different school that is in the part of the city under the control of the Palestinian Authority. It is called Al-Nahda school. Sometimes when we're coming home from school the Israeli soldiers fire tear gas at us. This makes you choke and suffocate.

Our school is next to the Ibrahimi Mosque, which is near the settlements. Once Israelis came and attacked the school. They told us that if we didn't come out right away, they would fire tear gas on us. The principal came to our class. He asked the army if they could please give us just fifteen minutes because we were in the middle of class and he wanted us to finish up. The soldiers didn't respond and after a little while they fired tear gas on us. Thirteen students breathed in too much gas and had to go to the hospital. We were all really scared.

On days when the Israelis lift the curfew, we go to our school like normal. On the days when there is curfew, we go to Al-Nahda school. And on those days when it changes from hour to hour—when they impose curfew and then they lift it and then impose it again—we also go to Al-Nahda school.

We don't have the same classes at Al-Nahda school. We don't have drawing or gym or computers or art or anything. We just have Arabic, math, English, and stuff like that.

These days it takes longer to get to school. There are soldiers and settlers on the road and they block our way.

Before the *Intifada* we used to go to the market and go shopping. We used to go out and do lots of things. Things were normal. But now we're scared to go to the market or go downtown. It's dangerous. The settlers can attack you and beat you up. That's what happened to my brother. He went to the market one day when there wasn't curfew, and the settlers beat him up.

Life is scary now that the *Intifada* has started. One of my relatives got killed. He was in his car at the time. He was driving home one night when the Israelis started shooting. He stopped the car and turned off the lights so they wouldn't see him and wouldn't fire on his car. So he was just parked on the side of the road, waiting for the shooting to stop so he could drive the rest of the way home. Then another car came up behind him and its headlights shined on his car. Then the soldiers were able to see him. They opened fire on him and he died.

There has been a lot of shelling in our neighborhhood at night. All the shooting makes a lot of noise. We're usually sleeping when the Israelis start to shoot artillery, and we hear all the bullets whizzing by over our house.

When they first started shelling at night we got really scared. But then we got used to it and now we aren't scared anymore. They say that during the first *Intifada* there wasn't shelling like this. Maybe the soldiers would shoot someone in the streets, but they didn't bomb everyone like they do now. At night I dream that they are shelling on our house, either with tank shells or with 800mm or 500mm bullets. I dream about people being slaughtered, like in the massacre in the Ibrahimi Mosque.

We go to bed early so we can get some sleep before they start shelling. But then we'll hear a plane come and we'll hear it drop bombs. We'll all crowd together and hide in the safest place and just listen to the shelling. Maybe we'll hear Arabs shooting, and after that we'll hear the Israelis. Then a surveillance plane comes and maybe it sees some Arabs shooting off their guns. So the surveillance plane calls a helicopter to come and then it starts to bomb the houses.

People have been killed during this *Intifada*. Abdel Aziz Abu Sneineh and Arafat Atrash were both killed. Everybody knew them. Arafat was a friend of my brother Mohammed.

Some of my friends have gotten injured. One of my friends was playing with a group of other kids. Then he saw a cat. He started calling to the cat and tossed stones at it. A soldier was sitting near there and he saw my friend throwing stones. So he opened fire and shot him. My friend got hit with five rubber bullets in his leg and two in his face. He had to go to the hospital.

There is another boy in my class named Saad. He was in the doorway of his house when the soldiers shot him with rubber bullets in cold blood. He also went to the hospital.

There is another boy in my class named Hatim. They fired on his house at night and a bullet went right over his head.

They've also fired on my granddad's house. My dad was sleeping over there because my granddad was sick. Some bullets flew right over my dad's head. He slept on the floor so he wouldn't get shot.

My hope for the future is that the Israelis leave Palestine. Then the future will be nice for us here.

When I grow up I'd like to be a doctor or an engineer or an accountant or a lawyer, anything. It doesn't matter, but I'm going to be here and I'm not going to leave and go someplace else. I just want the Israeli soldiers to go away, like when Lebanon was liberated. In Lebanon *Hezbollah* carried out lots of operations. The Israeli settlers there had to hide in trenches. They got really scared, so they finally gave up and left.

My dad used to work in construction. Sometimes he worked in the area of the city under Israeli control. Now there isn't any work anymore. But then, he wouldn't be able to get to the area with the construction anyway because of the curfew. Sometimes if there is some small job to do, the men who work with my dad will come to our house and they'll help him get to the Israeli area. They have to go very early in the morning. But in general, there just isn't any work.

I used to get a shekel and a half for allowance. Now I just get a shekel.

PART TWO

Loss and Longing

7. MUNA AND SOHA, *mother and sister of a child martyr*

8. MOHAMMED, *surgeon*

9. MOHAMMED, *injured in the second* Intifada

10. ISSAM, *injured in first* Intifada

11. AHMED, AMAL, MANOA, AND IBRAHIM, *members of a family in Beit Jala*

12. MAHMOUD, *owner of a demolished home*

Muna, with her husband and some of Mohammed's possessions

7. MUNA AND SOHA,
mother and sister of a child martyr

WHEN I WAS IN *Egypt during the first months of the* Intifada, *I read so many reports about Palestinian demonstrators clashing with Israeli soldiers that I imagined these confrontations taking a form akin to the Battle of Gettysburg as dramatized in the PBS videos we used to watch in high school. I was unprepared for what I discovered when I visited an actual "clash point," the hub of what the Israeli army was then calling unprecedented "violence in the territories."*

One of the main clash points during the early months of this Intifada *was the northern entrance to Ramallah's sister city, Al-Bireh. Israelis referred to this site as the Ayosh Junction, where a settler bypass road marked the edge of the area under PA control. Palestinians referred to it as* seettee-een, *the name of the once-pristine thirty-three room hotel located at that intersection. In 1997, Abdel Hamid Kased had given up his successful supermarket in Brooklyn, brought his family back to the West Bank, and sunk $1.2 million into the building of the "City Inn." He was one of two thousand Palestinian-American "returnees" who, trusting that peace had come and statehood was on its way, had left their homes in the United States in order to invest in the land of their birth. At its prime, Kased's City Inn was a hotel and conference center with a staff of thirty-four employees. By the time I arrived, it was a scorched wreck, its walls cracked with bullet holes and its roof seized as a base for Israeli sharpshooters.*

Walking to the City Inn from downtown Ramallah, I found it difficult to say where the residential neighborhood ended and the frontlines began. A crowd of several hundred people milled in the general area and a vendor had set up a stand to sell kebabs. Grandmothers chopped large boulders into slingshot-size stones, gathered them in the skirts of their traditionally embroidered dresses, and distributed them to the boys. A gaggle of reporters was on hand, and people said that the clash point appeared on TV so often that merchants had started to hang advertisements there in the hope of catching free publicity.

Cutting through the crowd, I approached the barricade of burnt car parts that separated Palestinian- and Israeli-controlled territory. On the Palestinian side, young men flung stones and, less frequently, Molotov cocktails. On the Israeli side, soldiers in armored jeeps fired shock grenades and tear gas, and snipers stationed on rooftops shot rubber bullets and live ammunition. Hardly a half hour could pass without the blare of ambulances announcing that another Palestinian had been hit.

There were Palestinian "gunmen" as well, but they played relatively minor roles in this drama. Monitoring the clash point for ten days, B'Tselem recorded Palestinian use of firearms in only half the demonstrations. According to B'Tselem, Palestinians opened fire for less than five minutes, and only then in response to Israeli fire:

> In all the cases, Palestinian gunfire began after the demonstration had lasted at least an hour and after the soldiers had already fired "rubber" bullets and live ammunition. In fact, after Palestinians fired the soldiers stopped firing and did not respond, except in one instance. [1]

My Gettysburg visions had been, to say the least, erroneous. The clash point was not a battleground for two armies as much as a site for civilian demonstrations. The force employed by Israeli troops, however, was often more appropriate for the former than the latter. As Amnesty International wrote:

> In a demonstration or riot involving the use of stones, or even sling-shots or Molotov cocktails, a well-trained police force should be able to contain and defuse the demonstrators without loss of life. The

1 B'Tselem, *Illusions of Restraint: Human Rights Violations During the Events in the Occupied Territories, 29 September- 2 December 2000* (Jerusalem: December 2000), p.9.

international standards for law enforcement officers are quite clear: they should respect and preserve life and minimize injury and damage. Israeli security forces have persistently breached international standards; they have also breached their own rules of engagement.[2]

A visitor to a clash point did not have to be an expert in international law in order to sense that something was awry in the fact that Palestinians were getting shot left and right while their stones hardly reached far enough to scratch an Israeli jeep. As Amnesty International's investigations confirmed, "Israeli security forces have repeatedly resorted to excessive use of lethal force in circumstances in which neither the lives of the security forces nor others were in imminent danger, resulting in unlawful killings."[3]

From the start of the Intifada until the present, not a single Israeli has been killed in confrontations at the Al-Bireh clash point. On the third day of the Intifada alone, however, three Palestinians were shot dead. One of those who was killed was a fifteen-year-old Boy Scout named Mohammed Nabil Hamed Daoud, or Hammouda, as his family called him. He was hit in the head by a live bullet and died instantly.

A friend and I decided to go to Mohammed's family and request an interview. They lived in a middle-class neighborhood in Al-Bireh, about a half mile from Yasser Arafat's compound. It was not difficult to find their house. We simply wandered among the white stone houses and well-stocked supermarkets and asked the first group of children we found playing soccer in the street. Every one of them could point out Mohammed's house with precision.

2 Amnesty International, *Broken Lives: A Year of Intifada* (London: Amnesty International Publications, 2001) p.17; available online: http://web.amnesty.org/ai.nsf/ 4e5be749f06b3e4880256af600687348/64f59dc0b44c5fef80256aff0058b1b8/$FILE /ch2.pdf.

3 Amnesty International, *Israel and the Occupied Territories: Excessive Use of Lethal Force* (Amnesty International Report MDE 15/041/2000, 19 October 2000); available online: http://web.amnesty.org/ai.nsf/Index/MDE150412000?OpenDocument&of= COUNTRIES\ISRAEL/OCCUPIED+TERRITORIES.

Mohammed's father answered our knock at the door with a knowing nod. Inviting us in, he did everything one must do to welcome guests. His eyes, however, could not disguise an all-encompassing exhaustion. Three months had passed since he had buried his youngest child, and he appeared as though he had not known real sleep since. And now he was being asked to put his grief on display for yet another journalist.

Struck by something I can only call shame, I realized that I had no idea what I could possibly ask this man about having lost his son. Instead I asked if I could come back another time. "Whenever you wish," he whispered. "Our house is your house."

I returned several days later, and this time Mohammed's mother, Muna, answered the door. As drained as her husband had appeared, she appeared even more so. Each word she uttered seemed to pull upon some inner reserve of faith and stamina.

Muna sat me down in the veranda and waited for me to begin. I again found myself at a loss for what to ask. After several moments of silence I mumbled, "Tell me about Mohammed."

Her eyes, still a perfect expression of weariness, showed a flicker of life, and she began to speak. Before long Mohammed's sister Soha joined our conversation as well.

I filled several tapes that afternoon. When I listened to them later, I was amazed to hear that my voice was absent. Muna and Soha talked for hours, but I had hardly asked a single question.

—◆— ◆— ◆—

MUNA, *mother*

MY NAME IS MUNA. My family is originally from Abbassia, a village near Lydda. We used to have a lot of property near what is now Ben-Gurion Airport. The documents and the key to the house, they're all here. When my family was expelled we moved to the Jalazun refugee camp, and then eventually to Al-Bireh. We also lived for a long time in Kuwait, where I got married. I had Mohammed in Kuwait.

We used to come to Palestine once every summer when we were living in Kuwait. The kids loved Palestine and the freedom they had here. It was different than in Kuwait, where we always stayed at home. Here, you are in our own country. Your child can go to school by himself and come home by himself. There the school was far away and strange to us. Here everyone is family, neighbors, and friends. Here you know everyone, because you are one of them.

The only problem in Palestine is the Israelis. When my children leave the house I'm only afraid for them because of the Israelis. I'm not afraid that they'll get into trouble because we all know each other, and people here are good people. The kids can play and have fun because it's our house and our land.

Mohammed was four years old when we moved back here from Kuwait. He was the baby of the family and the spoiled one. He used to like to know about everything. He was about seven or eight when he joined the Boy Scouts. He learned many values from scouting, like kindness, helping others, love of country, strength, and courage. He would wear his scouting uniform and he seemed older than his real age. He used to love to do the things that the older kids did. He understood things that even adults don't get.

He would tell jokes and make us laugh at home. When someone new would come to the house, Mohammed would stand in front of everyone and imitate him. Even the person being imitated would laugh. When we were upset, he would come and change the atmosphere . . . it's difficult to describe someone like him. Without him, the place is empty. There's no activity. Everyone is silent.

When he ate, he would say, "Mom, your food is delicious. I love your cooking." He would give me a kiss and say, "Your cooking is terrific." He loved pizza and grilled meats, and I always used to make these things for him. And also hummus; hummus was his favorite. I would put some meat and pine nuts on it for him. And all summer he used to drink grape juice like water. He would go to the grape vines in our garden and fill the basket, and we would wash the grapes together. Then we'd make the juice, the two of us together. He loved it all. He was a beautiful, energetic boy.

Last December 22 he turned fifteen. He was fifteen when he died.

Because he was the youngest, he liked to learn from his older brothers and sisters, from his uncles, from everyone. He loved to talk with older people and visit them. He liked to help people. He'd help people in the neighborhood carry their bags, for example. And there were about six sick people that he used to like to visit. If someone didn't have family or children, he used to visit him or her, too. He would come home and tell me, "Mom, one of our neighbors is sick. Why don't you go and visit her?" This one wants to travel, this one is sick, this one's son is ill.

He used to find out all of the news in the neighborhood and come back and tell me. I didn't know any of these things because I was always busy with work in the house. But he would go out, see his friends, walk around, play, and ride his bike. He would tell me about whom he saw and what he heard. He would come and say, "Mom, can I tell you a secret?" I would say, "OK, go ahead and tell me your secrets." And he would tell me that this friend smokes cigarettes, or this or that . . .

Mohammed was everything to me. When he died, I almost went crazy.

He loved his brothers and sisters, and he liked to show them that he loved them. One day he would say to this one, "Your clothes are nice or your hair looks nice or you look great." He was always worried about getting a haircut. I would tell him, "Your hair is still short. Why do you want to get your hair cut again?" He would tell me, "No, it's not nice like this," and he would use gel and fix it up.

The week before he was killed he went to get his picture taken. He wore the same clothes he was wearing when he was killed, the same shirt. He'd gotten a haircut the day before and he went to get his picture taken. I asked him, "Did anyone ask you to get your picture taken?" And he told me, "No, I just wanted to do it." He didn't have a small personal photo other than this one.

He had a good life and he loved people. He never hated anyone and he never really got angry with others. When he did get mad, he wouldn't express it. I would say to him, "Is something wrong?" and try to get him to talk about it. He was a dear spirit, and he had pride in himself. If someone asked him to do something for a little money, he would say, "I don't want your money, but I'll help you if you want."

He never told me, "I want to go and become a martyr and die." He was a normal kid and never thought about dying. He loved life and growing up, and he wanted to stay with his mother and his brothers and sisters. Who wants to die? Impossible. I still can't imagine that he's dead. I feel that he's here with me in the house. Even now I can't believe it. It's like he has just gone on a trip. I just can't believe that he won't return home again. I don't want to feel that Mohammed is dead, that's it. I feel as if he is still alive. Whenever you love someone, it is hard to believe that he has died. Maybe if it were someone else I could believe it. But because he's my own son . . .

When he had to study, he would go to his room, study for five minutes and then come out again. I would tell him, "Why are you doing that? Stay in your room and at least let us think that you are studying!" Studying was like jail to him. He didn't like to be by himself, he always wanted to be with us. It was tough to get him to go to sleep or to study. He wanted to stay with us. I didn't know that he would be killed.

One time there was a new girl in the neighborhood, about his age. She came from the U.S. but had family here. The other boys in the neighborhood wanted to talk to her, but she wouldn't talk with anyone except Mohammed. He told me, "I want to tell you a secret," and I said, "What is it?" He said, "A lot of people think that she is not a nice girl, but that's not true. I know that she's a nice girl." I started to laugh, and said, "Of all the kids of the neighborhood, why has she decided to befriend you in particular?" She told him, "I like to talk with you, Hammouda, because you understand. The other kids are rude. They just want to flirt with me, but not you." She talked with him as if he were a man, a man who understands. He didn't behave like other kids his age, like a teenager.

One time he came home from school very upset. I asked him what was wrong and he said, "These two guys were harassing some girls. That's not a nice thing to do. Don't they have sisters? They shouldn't do that." I laughed and called his older brother and said, "Listen to what Hammouda said!" He spoke as if he were . . . as if he were a grown-up who would never do that sort of thing.

There was just one thing I used to worry about. He was more daring than he should have been. He liked adventures. I used to worry about this because I knew him. He wasn't a weakling, and he might take risks. That's what would always make me worry. I used to tell him, "Don't go to this place or that place." For example, he used to want to go to Ramallah on his bike. I told him that it was difficult for me to see him go alone, even when it was just to go to school on his bike. At first I used to hold on to the bike because I was afraid he would fall off. I wasn't able to let him be on his own.

He also loved trips. For example, he loved the swimming pool. Once his brother went to the pool in Birzeit. He went with a buddy of his and didn't want to take Mohammed along. But Mohammed was determined to go anyway. Mohammed let his brother leave, and then he took some money and went by himself. His brother was surprised when he saw that he had come by himself, and he started to teach him to swim. Later I asked his brother, "Why didn't you let him come with you?" and he said, "I wasn't expecting that he would learn to swim so quickly!"

He also liked to make the trip to Jerusalem. He would save the money and go by himself. He would go to the Al-Aqsa Mosque and would pray. Then he would go to visit the Church of the Holy Sepulcre. Once he brought back with him one of the thin, brown candles from the church. He went there on his own about ten days before he was killed.

What more can I tell you? The stories are endless . . . I'll never forget them.

He was killed on a Sunday. That Saturday, we worked together in the little garden behind the house. He helped me prune the trees and tend the crops. We worked all morning. I made him the breakfast that he liked, *fatat al-hummus*. I made the food that he loved and I made it as a surprise. When I was preparing it, I said, "Please, God, don't let Mohammed come into the kitchen and see me," so that it would really be a surprise. I don't know why, I just had this sense. And it was a surprise, because Mohammed was just sitting in front of the TV. So I came in and put the plate in front of him and he was so happy! He said, "You made this dish that I love, *fatat al-hummus*. It's so delicious!"

His dad had left for Kuwait the week before in order to renew his residency visa. He called on Sunday because there were clashes going on here and he wanted to know how the kids were. I said, "Thank God, Hammouda is here, and so are his brothers and sisters, and they're fine. Don't worry about them. Everything is OK." Mohammed asked his dad to bring him new pajamas, a jacket, and clothes for school. And later that day, Mohammed was killed. He was killed before his dad got back, before he saw his presents. His dad came back the day after Mohammed was killed and on the third day we buried him.

On Sunday he went out, because on Friday and Saturday I wouldn't let him leave the house. That Sunday there was no school, so he had breakfast with us, took a shower and got dressed, and then went out to play with his cousins who live nearby. When he came back I told him, "Why are you playing in the street? You are going to get your clothes and shoes dirty." Hammouda said to me, "I won't be long. Don't worry." I asked him, "Why don't you study for your exams?" He told me, "Tomorrow, tomorrow."

And he left the house again. All of his friends were going to the funeral of a boy his age who had been killed the day before. When they were coming back from the funeral they ended up near the City Inn checkpoint, which is close to our house. Some of his friends wanted to go back home, and he said, "Are you guys afraid? You're free to do what you want, but I'm going ahead to throw stones." Maybe they thought that they could improve the situation by throwing stones. So he went ahead. He was an energetic kid, maybe too energetic. He stood out at the checkpoint because he was active. He never just waited behind. He always wanted to be in front. In Boy Scouts he was the leader of his group. He used to hold the cane and walk ahead of all the other boys. He didn't want to be just like everybody else.

At the checkpoint he got hit with rubber bullets in his leg and his hand. His friends said, "That's enough, Hammouda. Let's go back now." He was the only one who got hit, but he said to them, "Why are you scared? Don't be afraid. If anything happens to me, my name and address are in my pocket." He put his picture and his ID card in his pocket. Then an exchange of fire began. All the kids fled to a hill nearby. There was also an exchange of fire coming from there, and someone next to him was shot. He was in critical condition, nearly dead, and Mohammed went to pick him up and carry him away. Mohammed didn't leave him and run, he wanted to save him. Mohammed was not just any person. He screamed for the ambulance to come and help the young man who had been shot, but then the man died right in front of him. Mohammed became hysterical. Finally an ambulance got through and took the man away. Someone came and tried to help Mohammed get over the wall to escape from that area. When he lifted him up, the Israelis saw him and shot him in the head right away. He was shot in the head, on the right side of his head.

Mohammed wasn't scared of anything. He was on the front lines, not in the back row. He didn't know that there was an enemy who wanted to kill him. He never imagined that he would be next. He was throwing stones, and he had rolled up his shirtsleeves and pants legs so that they wouldn't get dirty. That way, when he came back home, no one would know where he had been.

When he fell, he was in his friend's hands. When he was shot, his friend had to let go because he couldn't hold him anymore. Later his friend came and told me this. He said that Mohammed died instantly. The last words he said were, "I'm Mohammed Nabil."

Meanwhile, I was at home and was really worried. When I heard the sound of bullets being fired I felt that something was going to happen. I knew that Mohammed could not have been far from danger because I know him. He wasn't just anyone; it was impossible for him to have been far away.

So I went up to our roof, to see what was going on. I could see the scene at the City Inn and I saw the boys running up the hill. It was all very close to our house. Then I went back into the house to watch from the window. Something inside me told me that Mohammad was not coming home. I started to ask anyone I saw from the balcony. I started to talk to myself. My other children said to me, "Mom, why are you scared? Mohammed will come back like the other kids, for sure." I told them, "I don't know, I'm worried about him." I felt that Mohammed was in danger. The ambulances were going back and forth and the sound of gunfire was so loud that we could hear it from the house. Not a single one of his friends was in the neighborhood. They were all there with him. I called his friend's mother, and another friend's mother called me. We were all worried. Then I saw a young man get out of a car and run toward our house. He wasn't acting normal. I went to him right away, and asked him, "What's going on?" He said, "Where is the Nabil residence?" I told him, "What happened? Has Mohammed been killed?" I asked the question before he could even say it. I just felt that Mohammed was not alright. It was the first time in my life that I had those feelings.

I went out into the street and called for him, but he didn't come. All his friends came. I started to call him and to call his father, even though his father wasn't there.

Those snipers have to be brought to justice. Our children are not cheap, and we are not sending them out to be murdered. They knew how old he was. They could see that he was small and that he didn't have a weapon. And in spite of that, they shot him. They don't do it accidentally. They knew what they were doing. They could see that Mohammed was climbing the wall to get out of there and come back home. They knew that he was not a threat to them. He was trying to leave, and they killed him in cold blood. No mother in the world can cope with her son being killed in this way.

We talk and we speak our demands. If the world had a conscience, then it would stand with us. Our goal is to free our country so that there are no more settlers in our land, no more roadblocks, nothing to prevent us from going to Jerusalem, or from leaving to go to Jordan or to Egypt or any place in the world. We're not in jail and we want to live free.

We used to dream that our children would grow up, and we would teach them, and they would become soldiers for the country. But we have not raised them so that they would be killed while they are still children, before they know anything about the world. They're just kids. They want to live their lives. To the soldiers, Mohammed was just another number, not a human being. They didn't think that he has a mother, or a brother, or a sister, a family, future, friends, and neighbors. They didn't think of that. They just killed him.

According to our religion, our son is now with God in heaven. He eats, drinks, and lives his life. But he has been taken from me! If he had grown up and was a believer and prayed and knew God, then he still would have gone to heaven. They took away life, they took my son's life away. The hardest thing in the world is to lose a child. You want to demand from the whole world that those soldiers be brought to justice, because these children aren't dangerous. A ten-year-old child was killed just yesterday, here in Al-Bireh. What was he doing to the soldier? He was coming from school, with his back-pack on his back.

We are people. We are human beings. We raise our children, and we are tired. For the last ten years my husband has been working in Kuwait and I have been raising our children myself. We came here out of fear during the Gulf War. I was scared for my children, so we left and my husband stayed behind. Palestinian women love their children; they are dearer than anything. We Palestinians don't have anything else besides our children. They took our land, they took our country, and we don't even have weapons with which to fight. Our children are our land and our lives, we'd do anything to protect them. We have to because everyone takes the side of the Israelis. We don't have anyone.

I want to send a message to the whole world that our people must live. We have struggled and we're tired. Like any people, we just want to live and want our children to live. We protect them and worry about them. We want stability. The Israelis agreed to return to the 1967 borders. What are they waiting for? For over seven years they've been negotiating. What are they negotiating for? There's an agreement and it must be implemented.

So our children keep dying. Today there was a meeting of the families of the martyrs. What we've lost is no simple thing. There's nothing dearer to us than our children. And now they're gone. Everything has been taken from us. But even if there is only one Palestinian child left, he will keep fighting. No matter how much we forbid our children from going out, young people will not accept the situation. Our children are the ones who are not satisfied with the way things are. Their blood is hot.

I've talked a lot. The television reporters and journalists come and ask questions. I talk to them, and they don't print everything I say. Just a few words and that's it. But I keep talking. I must talk. My son, the most beautiful thing in the world to me, was killed. I have to talk, because if I didn't, I would explode.

• ◦ •   • ◦ •   • ◦ •

SOHA, *sister*

MY NAME IS SOHA Nabil Hamed. I'm in college majoring in finance.

I want to talk about Hammouda, because I was very close to him. He liked to come along with me wherever I went. He had an e-mail address and he would come with me to the Internet café downtown. He could fit in with any crowd, and my friends always used to ask about him.

I used to write poetry, but I didn't like to read it to anyone except him. He said he wanted to learn to write like me and once he wrote a poem for our mom. If he had lived maybe he would have been a great writer. He had a fantastic imagination. He would tell a story and you'd think that it had really happened.

He made each of us feel special. He was so appreciative of anything I got for him, no matter how small it was. I'd have to tell him, "This is nothing. Why are you making such a fuss?"

I went to Amman a month before he was killed and brought him back a shirt. He was so happy that it was from me that he wore it to get his picture taken the very next day. It was the same shirt that he was wearing when he was killed.

I was in shock when I first heard the news. I don't know what happened to me. At the funeral, I just sat there and didn't even notice the other people around me. I felt like it was all a dream and that I'd wake up and find that it hadn't really happened.

People we didn't even know came to the funeral. They would tell us, "Mohammed used to visit us" or "he did this or that." We didn't even realize how social he was until after he was martyred.

It's true that we let him go out with the others kids in the neighborhood. Once before the start of the *Intifada*, there were clashes on the anniversary of *Al-Nakba*. I was at school but I came home right away because I knew that he would want to participate. The kids always used to go and watch the clashes because they wanted to feel brave. So I went to where the clashes were and got him and brought him back home. When we got home, I said, "What are we going to tell Mom?" He said, "Don't be scared. We won't tell her that you were there!"

Even now, we can't really believe that Hammouda is gone. His room is next to mine and before I go to bed I still feel like he is going to come in and wish me goodnight. Yesterday, I watched the video of my graduation party. We saw him there, dancing in the video, and it felt like he hadn't died after all.

We know that Mohammed is in heaven. He died a martyr and I also want to die as he did. But I miss him and his company. He's far from me now. The person who made things fun and exciting has left, the person who used to mix with young and old . . . There are so many memories it's hard to discuss just a few. Every day I remember new things about Hammouda.

Whenever anything in the house broke, he would go and tinker around with it until he fixed it. And he used to stop at the mirror even more than me! He would put lotion on his face and cocount oil in his hair before he went to bed. He might be hanging around the house in shorts, and I would ask him to go and pick something up at the store.

He would say, "What, go in shorts, like this?" I'd tell him, "You're a kid. What's the problem?" But he wouldn't go out in shorts. He'd insist on getting dressed properly first.

You'd never think that he would be interested in throwing stones. He cared a lot about himself. But the kids all get mixed up together and encourage one another. They also have a kind of passion. When you see these things going on in front of you, you feel that you have to fight somehow. How can you express yourself other than going to the checkpoint and throwing a stone? You feel like you have to do something, even if you know that the stone won't even reach them—even if you know that, in the end, it's useless.

We follow the negotiations but we know that no agreement on Palestine has ever been concluded unless some massacre has taken place. It is only after a lot of kids die that they agree on a little piece of land. There are no agreements and no land without the shedding of blood. It's a tragedy.

If somebody just gave us weapons or took away some of the Israelis' weapons, then it could be a war between equals. But it's not. We have rocks and they have arms. When we started to get some guns, they retaliated with tanks. Any strength that we muster, they retaliate with four times the power. If we somehow got our hands on some tanks, what would they do, drop a nuclear bomb? They don't shoot Palestinians in the legs with rubber bullets. They aim for the head in order to kill.

Every generation has suffered. Still, there's not a single Palestinian child who doesn't know where he's from. In our family we know that we have a piece of land in Abbassia. I've never actually gone there and seen it, but it is important for me to know why we had to leave.

They call this the Al-Aqsa *Intifada*, but we're not all dying like this for Al-Aqsa. Everything goes back to what happened in 1948. All the people in the world have their own country except for us. My home in

Abbassia means more to me than Al-Aqsa. Yes, the Mosque is a holy place. But all of Palestinian land is holy.

Hammouda was killed, but thank God he wasn't mutilated or tortured. This is our tragedy, losing Hammouda. How much harder it must be for families who have lost two people. Here you can go from one house to another and find that each tragedy is more terrible than the last. Each family tells its own tragic tale. I guess now it's our turn.

There's practically no young man among us who hasn't been beaten or killed or wounded or spent time in Israeli jails. So we've stopped having mercy. In the past when there was a suicide bombing in Israel and innocent children died, we Palestinians might have said, "That's terrible. What have these children done?" But now there's no longer any mercy, even for their children. They've killed so many of our children. They're the ones who have pushed us to this point, making us do things that we don't want to do. We do these things against our will. Now, even if there were peace we would not be able to live together like we did in the beginning.

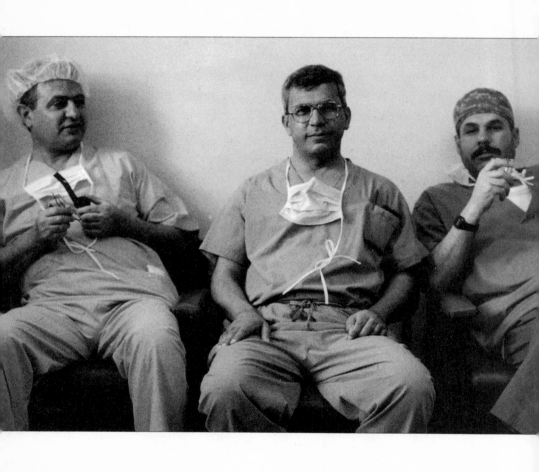

Mohammed (center), and colleagues on duty at Ramallah Hospital

8. MOHAMMED, *surgeon*

FOR MANY AMERICANS, MENTION *of Palestinian "martyrs" evokes the image of young men strapped with explosives, slaughtering innocents in busses and cafés. Hundreds of Palestinians have killed hundreds of Israelis in this way, and it represents a merciless use of violence. Amid the horror of terrorist attacks, however, it is often forgotten that the overwhelming majority of Palestinian martyrs did not kill, but were killed.*

Palestinians consider all those killed by Israelis—not just suicide bombers—to be martyrs. In fact, the second Intifada began with all martyrs and no suicide bombers. Israeli soldiers or settlers killed over one hundred-forty Palestinians in the first five weeks of the uprising before the Intifada's first suicide bomber struck inside Israel.

The presence of martyrs weighs heavily in the Occupied Territories. In the West Bank, streets are lined with glossy posters honoring those who have been killed. Together they form an ever-renewed exhibit of photographs of ordinary people. In the Gaza Strip, hand-drawn portraits of martyrs adorn the walls of many buildings. I once came upon a young man in the process of painting such a mural for his kid brother, who had recently been shot. Its paint not yet dry, the mural offered a rare splash of color in an otherwise gray refugee camp. While it too was bound to become gray with time, new murals would inevitably emerge to takes its place.

There is a Palestinian legend that white flowers planted at the graves of martyrs are nourished by their blood and turn red. I know of only one concrete instance of this phenomenon, at a memorial in Bethlehem's Manger Square. A few days before the first Christmas of this millennium, the stone plaza where Jesus was born was symbolically filled with ninety-four Styrofoam gravestones. Each gravestone bore the photograph of a child martyred during the first three months of the Intifada, and each was topped with an oversized plastic flower, its color blood red.

Some allege that such reverence for martyrs encourages people to become martyrs. Anyone who attended the memorial in Manger Square, however, could see that it was an experience in grieving, not hero worship. Others allege that people seek martyrdom so that their families will benefit materially. Anyone who watched that young man paint his brother's portrait on a wall in his refugee camp, however, could see that no amount of money would ever compensate his loss.

Perhaps no one has had more experience with martyrs than have Palestinian medical personnel, who day in and day out labor to prevent injured persons from slipping into martyrdom. A full 1 percent of the population of the Occupied Territories has been killed or injured during the second Intifada. These colossal casualties, combined with a surge of stress-related illnesses and malnutrition in line with the rise of poverty, have produced a medical emergency of mammoth proportions.

As grave as the overburdening of Palestinian hospitals has been is the health status of those prevented from reaching hospital in the first place. As the Israeli chapter of Physicians for Human Rights explains:

> *Israel has prevented the sick and injured from receiving treatment at medical centers, and has created many obstacles for doctors traveling to work or on their way to evacuate the wounded. This is in blatant violation of the Geneva Convention regarding the autonomy and immunity of medical personnel and medical institutions . . . Isolated villages have almost no access to central hospitals and basic medical services in cities, not to mention their access to pharmacies, food stores, etc. Dirt ramparts block the roads into and out of these villages, making it almost impossible*

for patients to receive medical attention. A healthy person would find it difficult to climb over these blockades, but for an ill, handicapped or elderly person it is impossible.[1]

My first personal contact with these issues came when my friend Nadia needed surgery. The closure presented her with one obstacle after another. First, she fell ill at school in the West Bank and found herself alone because no one in her family in Gaza could get permission to come to her side. Second, she had to reschedule her surgery several times because the army kept closing the road leading from her house in a village to the clinic in town. Third, when the troops finally opened the roads they allowed people to cross only by foot, not in cars.

Nadia could hardly walk by that time, but she decided that she could postpone surgery no longer. Somehow our group of friends managed to get her from her bed to a taxi, which drove us to the checkpoint. There we got her out of the car and held her upright as she took pained baby steps the obligatory quarter mile to where taxis waited on the other side.

Mohammed is one of the many health-care professionals who have been on call since this Intifada began. When I met him in January 2001, more than 10,500 Palestinians had already been injured in the hostilities. According to the Palestinian human rights organization LAW, 40 percent of those injured were children. As a cardiac specialist, Mohammed had attended to a fair number of these wounded people personally. As the Palestinian Authority administrator overseeing ambulance services, he was also carrying out one of the least enviable jobs in public health. During the first three months of the Intifada alone, the Palestinian Red Crescent registered 109 incidents in which Israeli soldiers blocked ambulance access, 101 incidents in which ambulances were attacked, the killing of one emergency medical worker, and the wounding of another sixty-five.

1 Physicians for Human Rights—Israel, *Annual Report 2000*; see http://www.phr.org.il

I met Mohammed at Ramallah Hospital. A forthright man with thick glasses and the sturdy tone of a public official, he answered my questions concisely. I tried to prompt him to recount personal stories, but he did not have much mind for frivolous anecdotes. His daily work, after all, was life and death. Mohammed's presence was so professional that when he talked about weeping over a certain child's body in the emergency room, I admit that I had trouble picturing it.

But the thought stayed with me. And eventually it clicked that the child who had died on Mohammed's operating table was one of the martyrs honored in the memorial in Manger Square. His photograph must have been there, taped to one of the ninety-four Styrofoam gravestones. Long before the white flower at that child's grave changed its hue, it was Mohammed's gloves that had been stained red.

And then I understood how the thought of martyrs could bring even the most reserved of doctors to tears. How could it not?

.•. .•. .•.

MY NAME IS MOHAMMED. I'm the director of Ambulances and Emergency Services for the Palestinian Ministry of Health and a specialist in heart conditions at Ramallah Hospital. I'm a refugee from a village near the city of Ramle. I grew up in a refugee camp.

What is happening now is not my first experience with *Intifada* because I also witnessed the first *Intifada*. And I saw similar incidents even before that, during all the years of occupation. I have lived this current *Intifada* from its very start and my experiences have varied in step with the number of injuries that we receive at any given moment.

The first three weeks of the *Intifada* were especially difficult. We received many, many injuries everyday, and these injuries were very grave and required immediate surgical intervention. The workday was continual and never-ending. I practically never returned to my own home at all. Here at the hospital we were so exhausted. There were times when I didn't even have the time to eat because the work just kept coming and coming.

But even at the times when I was most tired, I always remembered that the patient in front of me was a human being. He is suffering from his injuries and his family is also suffering for his sake.

The situation has been agonizing for each and every one of us. Nevertheless, we Palestinians have faith and dedication to the cause, so we are able to cope with all of the hardships and keep on going. This is particularly so when we receive serious cases in the middle of the night. I remember one night when we received a man who had been killed by a missile explosion. His whole body had blown up, and the only thing remaining was his chest. It was a sight that you can't even describe. A TV crew was present, but not even they could bear to look at the cadaver.

First and foremost, doctors are human beings. We've seen a lot of cases like this, and they've affected us very strongly. We can't help but cry. Also, many injuries come together at a single time. Recently, most of the injuries have been coming in on Fridays because that is when there are demonstrations and then confrontations. So on Friday afternoons, every hospital and every emergency room stands ready and prepared. We've learned how to distribute the work and cope.

At this hospital we've grouped all people with injuries related to heart and blood conditions in four rooms. As a doctor with this specialization, I have had to keep moving quickly between these rooms and do my best to keep all of the injured persons alive. During the month of Ramadan, all of the cases of injuries came to us just minutes before the meal breaking the daylong fast. As a result, it's not an exaggeration to say that I only broke the fast at home with my family five times during the whole month.

Of course, it's very difficult and exhausting. But this exhaustion is not worth a thing in comparison to the drop of the blood of someone wounded or killed in the struggle against the occupation.

There have been some terrible days, and some of the things we have seen are horrendous and tragic. I also have some memories that are very difficult for me personally. One day I was recalled to the hospital to attend to the arrival of a person wounded badly in both the chest and abdomen. He was in very critical condition. I went to perform the operation and only then discovered that the patient was a cousin of mine. He was just a boy. His name was Nizar Hidi, and he was sixteen years old. I was weeping while I performed the operation. I was weeping and my tears were dropping into his abdomen, which was open before me. He died there. I left the room and everybody wondered why. Only afterward they learned that this child was my relative.

I went to his funeral, but I wasn't even able to stay long enough to say good-bye to him because I got a phone call from the director of the hospital. He said that he understood the difficult situation I was in, but there was an extreme number of injured persons at the hospital and many were in critical condition. So I left the funeral and went directly to the hospital.

Of course, all martyrs are dear to us. But that child was especially dear for me. Even now, whenever I remember him, I start to tear up.

Anyway, since the *Intifada* began I have almost always been at the hospital. Every time I get home there is some other incident and more injuries that require immediate attention. During the recent holiday, *Eid Al-Fitr*, I wasn't even able to visit my family. We always go to my family's house at the refugee camp for the holiday, but this year I couldn't go. I was hoping to be able to visit my mother's grave, as well as the grave of Nizar, my cousin who was martyred. But it was impossible. I couldn't leave Ramallah for fear that something would happen and there would be wounded people who needed care.

As director of Emergency Services it is also my job to ensure that ambulances get to the injured and bring them to the hospital. But some areas are closed because the roads are blocked. Sometimes the ambulance picks up a patient and then gets stopped at a roadblock. The ambulance can't pass through, so nurses come and carry the patient on their shoulders until they reach the other side. Then a car takes him the rest of the way to the hospital. This happens a lot.

All the cases I see are difficult and distressing, but the ones that affect me most are those of children. When I see a child who is wounded or a child who has been killed, there is a moment when my heart aches. Really, there are times when I stop before the child and become paralyzed. I just can't do anything for him, and he passes away.

Behind every wounded person there is a story. Behind each martyr there is a story.

For example, last week an eleven-year-old boy was shot by an Israeli soldier near the checkpoint. He was all alone and he was just a kid on his way to school. If you could have seen his parents when they received his body . . . it was more than horrible. This was a child. What sort of threat did he present to an adult soldier three hundred meters away from him?

I also remember the case of an injured person who was shot while he was inside his own house. When he got to the hospital he was in a coma. He was almost dead. We really thought that we were going to lose him. We examined him and discovered that the arteries in his neck had been damaged. We performed surgery and the next day sent him to Amman, where he was treated over a long period of time. I saw him again not too long ago and was surprised to find that he has recovered remarkably. Now he is moving and talking.

But such cases are rare. Now the number of injuries has lessened a bit, but we are still in the midst of an ongoing state of emergency. Maybe this is our fate.

We've seen all sorts of injuries in this *Intifada*. All types of weapons have been used against civilians, from rubber bullets to explosives. We've had to pull all sorts of bullets out of the bodies of injured Palestinians. We've seen bodies that were turned to shreds because of the explosives used against them.

I wonder about the people who have been shot during demonstrations inside Palestinian areas. Isn't it their right to demonstrate? They didn't go outside areas under the control of the Palestinian Authority. Why have the Israelis come from outside to shoot these people in their own territory?

You can't even imagine the nature of some of the cases we've received. The number of dead and injured is enormous. Why were they killed? Why were they injured? Because they asked for their freedom? In this era there is no nation that is still occupied. No people would accept it if their country were occupied by a foreign nation and then they were forced to leave their homes. We are demanding nothing more than our freedom.

It is time that the American people look at the situation here differently than the way they perceive it now. It is time that they put pressure on their government to change its policies. Americans marched during the Vietnam War when they saw the pictures of the South Vietnamese soldier shooting one of the Viet Kong in the head. Why aren't they moved now when they see innocent Palestinian children shot everyday? What kind of rule of law would accept this inhumanity? As long as our people are denied their rights, there will be instability in this region forever.

Of course, we want the bloodshed to stop. But we also have our dreams. There must be a solution; there is no other choice. No people can rule another by force. Throughout history, no occupation has been able to last forever.

The *Intifada* broke out in defense of Palestine and in defense of the Al-Aqsa Mosque. God willing, it will achieve its goals—our goals, the goals of all Palestinians. As an Arab and a Muslim, I have a right to Jerusalem, too. And as a refugee, I have a right to return to my country. I have a right to have a country.

Mohammed, discussing politics

9. MOHAMMED, *injured in the second* Intifada

I WAS SURPRISED WHEN *I first learned that a friend of mine in Ramallah, a soft-spoken human-rights lawyer, had served several years as a Palestinian Authority policeman. When I told him that I could not imagine him carrying a gun, he laughed and said that had been the point. "As boys during the first* Intifada, *we saw Israeli soldiers with guns everywhere we went," he explained. "We dreamed about having guns of our own, and when the PA came we finally got our chance."*

During the Olso years, Palestinians procured firearms both legally and illegally, the foremost source for the latter being the Israeli black market. As the Al-Aqsa Intifada *erupted in violence, Palestinian protesters employed these weapons in exchanges of fire with Israeli troops or in armed attacks on military installations, settlements, and settler roads. Critics charged that Palestinians, whether affiliated with Security Forces or other political factions, were trying to win with violence what they had failed to achieve in negotiations.*

Most Palestinians believed that they had a right to use arms to fight occupation, as had national liberation movements throughout history. There were some, however, who expressed doubt about this strategy. As one Birzeit University professor argued:

> *The participation of "armed" Palestinian elements in popular demonstrations and shootings at soldiers and settlers must end, even though we know that it occurs within a context of self-defense. These shootings take place from a distance, and frankly speaking, are fruitless. While these people*

do not lack faith or the willingness to sacrifice, they do suffer from a lack
of appropriate weapons, a shortage of ammunition and more importantly,
a severe lack of experience, training and knowledge . . .

   It is understandable that young men publicly carry arms as a recog-
nizable symbol of a brave resistance for a people subject to the ugliest
kinds of oppression. In our present circumstance, however, this hands
Israel the excuse for crushing this resistance on a silver platter.[1]

If Palestinian gunfire revealed a lack of equipment and training, what
did Israeli gunfire reveal? According to Israeli journalist Ben Caspit, the
Israeli army had spent years preparing for the Intifada. "When it started,"
he wrote, "it unloaded its drawn-out frustration on the heads of the Palestinians." The army fired one million bullets in the West Bank and Gaza
during the first three weeks of the uprising alone. As one officer remarked,
this approximated "a bullet for every child." To illustrate the volume of this
fire, Caspit relays the story of a PA minister who toured Gaza with a European visitor:

He wished to demonstrate the degree of the IDF (Israel Defense Forces)
aggression to his guest. He asked his bodyguard to stick out his head
and fire a single shot from his handgun. The bodyguard fired once.
Upon hearing the shot, the entire sector came to life. The IDF fired from
dozens of weapons, including tanks, for two hours non-stop. Hellfire
came from guns, machine guns, heavy guns, anti-tank rifles, and what
not. Heavy, constant, never-ending fire was the response to a single shot
in the air.[2]

---

1 Saleh Abdel Jawad, "The Intifada's Military Lessons," *The Jerusalem Media and Communi-*
   cations Center Report, 25 October 2000. The article was published in an online journal
   after being rejected by Palestinian newspapers.
2 Ma'ariv, 6 September 2000. [FBIS-NES-2002-0913]

As the Israeli army's international law chief declared, "The Palestinians must understand that having instigated this thing, people will pay a price."[3] Later, Caspit observed, some Israeli political and military officials would come "to believe that it was the destructive IDF reaction and the heavy blow the Palestinians sustained over the course of the first few weeks that made the situation deteriorate and escalate the way it did."

In the hope of getting a better understanding of the militarized course of this Intifada, I decided to find out more about those Palestinians who had decided to take up arms. It was in this context that I spoke with Khallil, whose brother Mahmoud had been killed in an exchange of fire with Israeli soldiers.

Mahmoud had been twelve years old when he was shot while throwing stones during the first Intifada, and fourteen when he was arrested and sentenced to a year in prison. When the PA was established, he joined the Security Forces. At age twenty-two, he celebrated his wedding in a party with fifteen hundred attendees. Khallil said that he had never seen his brother happier. A few days later, the new Intifada broke out.

An impassioned nationalist, Mahmoud was visibly distressed by the early reports about the dead and wounded. Then, on the second day of the uprising, one of his closest friends was killed. As his brother put it, Mahmoud "decided to go out and do something." He and a few friends took their weapons to a hill that faced an Israeli army outpost some distance away. A gun battle ensued and before long both Mahmoud and a companion were fatally shot in the chest. Two ambulances approached and retreated under Israeli fire. Mahmoud bled for two hours before he finally made it to the hospital.

Khallil took me to the site where his brother was killed and pointed out the bullet holes piercing the concrete and iron doors of the houses nearby. "The fire that the Israelis unleashed on them was mind-boggling," he told me. "We're talking about thousands and thousands of bullets."

---

3 Press Briefing by Colonel Daniel Reisner, Head of the International Law Branch of the IDF Legal Division, Jerusalem, 15 November 2000; See http://www.mfa.gov.il/mfa/go.asp?MFAH0iaq0

Khallil's words about his brother offered one glimpse of those commonly referred to as Palestinian "gunmen." Wanting to know more, I went to the one place where I was sure that I could find a fair number of them: the hospital.

There, bound to their beds and wheelchairs, I found a motley crew of typical guys several years younger than myself. I tried to interview some of them, but they would answer my questions in no more than one or two words, as if dreading the teasing that they would receive from their buddies as soon as I left the room. They seemed terribly embarrassed to be the focus of the overt attention of a girl, no less a foreign girl. Figuring that their injuries were the source of enough suffering, I decided not to push it.

I had thrown in the towel when a friend suggested that I pay a visit to injured young men who had been discharged from the hospital and were staying at Ramallah's Merryland Hotel. They had all completed treatment, but could not make the journey to their homes in other towns due to lack of permits or fear of being apprehended by the army en route. At the hotel I met with a group of injured guys and explained my interest in interviewing them. They responded with a bashfulness similar to that which I had encountered earlier. And then Mohammed came forward.

On the one hand, Mohammed did not satisfy my search; far from using firearms, he had been shot by Israeli soldiers while simply coming home from work. On the other hand, he was not shy about talking. By that point, this was good enough for me.

Mohammed spoke with a maturity that belied his age. Perhaps this was because his first encounter with the Israeli army had come while he was still in primary school. He had spent six of his twenty-six years in prison, had been shot five times during the first Intifada, *and had been subjected to interrogation and torture at the hands of Israeli and Palestinian Authority police alike. All of this had happened before the second* Intifada *began and a new injury had brought him to Ramallah Hospital. Discharged to the Merryland Hotel weeks earlier, he continued to wait for an opportunity to return to his family in a Jerusalem suburb less than eight miles away.*

Regardless of its source, Mohammed's composure was to his credit and my relief. He talked to me about his injury and his life, unruffled by the guys who hobbled in and out of the hotel lounge on their crutches, exchanging giggles about the foreign girl, with the tape recorder.

•◆• •◆• •◆•

MY NAME IS MOHAMMED. I'm a Palestinian of Kurdish origin. I live in Jerusalem and have a Jerusalem identity card. This is like third-class Israeli citizenship with Israeli Jews being first and Israeli Arabs being second. One day during the beginning of the *Intifada* I was coming home from work and all of a sudden the soldiers started firing at us. We were just a group of people on the street, all unarmed. I was shot twice in the knee and once in the thigh. Other people were hit, too, including a journalist.

I was taken to Ramallah Hospital and now I have a steel rod in my leg. The injured here don't have medical care. There is no medication or good treatment. For example, when the clashes started, there was a man who was taken to the hospital after being shot in the leg. He could have been cured, but because of the lack of treatment he developed gangrene and they had to amputate his leg.

That was about three months ago. I've been here in Ramallah ever since.

The peace process never talked about those of us who are from Jerusalem and hold Israeli ID cards. There is no mention of us in any of the agreements coming out of Oslo or Madrid. Jerusalem was Arab and Muslim before Jews started immigrating here. They say that the Wailing Wall is theirs, but for two thousand years Jerusalem was Arab. Of course, Jerusalem has been a home for all faiths: Judaism, Christianity, and Islam. It is the place where all the prophets visited. We must protect it, but not through occupation. The doors of Jerusalem must be open to all who wish to pray. We are not against the Jews as people. We are against the occupation. As they say, Arabs and Jews are cousins. I am with the Jewish people, but against the occupation and the army.

I spent my early years in Jerusalem, but we moved to Nablus when I was ten or so. As a kid I went to school, and then worked two different jobs after school. My brother worked, too. This is what we had to do in order to help pay the rent.

I was thirteen years old when the first *Intifada* began. Early on, soldiers killed a little boy at my school. As I was in a higher grade, I felt a sense of responsibility for the younger ones. I started taking part in demonstrations and going to throw stones. My political awareness came from the street. I saw soldiers shooting and beating people and I knew that this was occupation. I was proud that I was doing something for my people.

It wasn't long before I became a wanted person. I left home and when into hiding in the hills and in the Nablus Old City.

I was shot for the first time when I was thirteen years old, and then was shot a second time a few months later. I was being treated in the hospital when soldiers came to arrest me. I was in and out of prison for most of the next seven years.

Prison is all about repression and oppression. There are the beatings, the *Shabah*, the attempts to brainwash you.

I spent almost a hundred days in interrogation. They would grab me by the hair and shove my head in a bucket of water. They would tell me that if I didn't give the names of this or that guy involved in resistance, they would kill me, or go after my mother, or sleep with my sister, or destroy our house. The Red Cross was officially responsible for my well-being, but it was prohibited from visiting me.

As prisoners, we were treated like less than animals. Forty people were kept in a cell for eight people. It was so crowded that we had to take turns sleeping. For food, they gave us rotten rice and some soup that was no more than colored water.

Israel deals with Palestinian prisoners as if there's no such thing as international monitoring or human rights. Where are human rights? Maybe you can find them in France or Italy or America, but not here.

In prison they try to kill Palestinians by making them empty from the inside. In the first *Intifada*, they did their best to produce a generation of Palestinians that was ignorant. But we studied in jail and proved that we had the ability to educate ourselves. When I was put in jail I was in seventh grade. By the time I got out I'd had the equivalent of a college education.

It was around the time that I was released from prison that the peace process began and the PA was established. Now of course I want peace. Who doesn't want peace? I want to be able to live. I want my kids to be able to go to school without getting scared when they see soldiers with guns on the street.

But I was against the peace process because it was peace without borders and without a country. It was a peace that brought a Palestinian Authority that was established in order to oppress. Israel didn't want to send its soldiers to die in the streets of Gaza and Nablus anymore, so it created the PA to do its work for them. What has the PA done for us? Instead of building schools, hospitals, or economic projects to benefit the people, it built prisons.

Not long after the PA was established, Israel sent an order for my arrest to the PA through their joint security coordination office. Then the PA came and arrested me. I was a member of a leftist opposition group at the time. The PA police told me that Israel had put a warrant out for my arrest, and that they wanted to protect me to make sure that the Israelis didn't come and try to kill me or something.

So they took me to a PA detention center. And once I got there they started to torture me like the Israelis used to do in their prisons.

I couldn't believe it. I said, "If you brought me here to protect me, why are you torturing me? Wasn't I one of the people who sacrificed in order to bring you guys back from Tunis in the first place?"

Time went by and then Sharon went to the Al-Aqsa Mosque and the Al-Aqsa *Intifada* began. The first *Intifada* was hard, but this one is much harder. Before, Israel assassinated activists. Israel still thinks it has the right to carry out assassinations; there was another assassination here just a few days ago. But now, there is no security for anyone anymore. I expect that someday I'll be walking down the street and they'll shoot me again.

Who is the one that doesn't want peace? One Israeli administration signs an agreement, but then there are elections and a new government comes to power and annuls the agreement. This has been happening for a long time. So with whom are we supposed to negotiate? With the United States? America treats Israel as if it were the fifty-first state. And as long as America fails to realize this, its own security is at risk.

We are a people with a cause. We're not the kind of people who like to die. We want peace, but a just and comprehensive peace: peace with self-determination, with the right to return, with a state and a capital in Jerusalem. We want Israel to withdraw from the Palestinian territories under occupation. The United Nations Security Council has recognized our legitimate rights. We are against violence, but we are following the only paths we see available to us. We use politics and we use rocks and we struggle. There won't be peace until the occupation ends and we can reclaim our land.

We want peace, and we want economic stability, too. You see how dead the economy is here. And you know the impact that economic pressure has on people. It can cause a lot of corruption in a society. This is not our way. We're a people with traditions.

We salute the American people, but we are against their government's policy of discrimination. In America they talk about racial discrimination against African-Americans. We don't have blacks and whites. We just have occupation. This occupation oppresses us every day. It kills us every day. Who is going to fight for our human rights? They say that we are terrorists because we are defending our country. But the terrorist is the one who bombs children who carry stones. The real terrorists retaliate with planes and missiles.

I want to live in a free country. I want to raise my children right, to put them through school and send them to college. I want peace, but a peace that protects our rights, a peace in which my mother will not be treated with disrespect. I want the kind of peace that will bring us back our honor.

Issam, at home in Rafah

10. ISSAM, *injured in the first* Intifada

I ADMIT THAT I had the jitters about spending the summer of 2001 in the Gaza Strip. Having lived in the West Bank, I felt like I had to see life in relatively more desperate Gaza in order to develop a fuller understanding of the Palestinian situation. Yet even Gazans, who are always calling the Strip a prison, told me that I was nuts for wanting to come. My father said likewise, but then threw up his hands, sighing that he had given up trying to talk sense into me back when I decided to get a Ph.D. in political science.

A five-by-twenty-eight-mile rectangle with an area about twice the size of Washington, D.C., the Gaza Strip is one of the most densely populated places on earth. Israeli settlers represent one half of 1 percent of Gaza's residents yet occupy one third of its land. Crammed into the rest are 1.2 million Palestinians, three fourths of them refugees and half under the age of fifteen.

Israel controls the Gaza Strip from all sides. Its Mediterranean coastline is patrolled by military boats authorized to shoot at any Palestinian fisherman venturing more than twenty miles from the shore. Its land borders are completely surrounded by an Israeli security fence, and no one or thing gets in or out without Israel's permission and extended searches. Any commercial product being shipped from Gaza to the West Bank must first be unloaded from Palestinian trucks, screened by Israeli metal detectors, and reloaded onto Israeli trucks. It is a process that takes hours with no guarantees that goods will make it through in decent condition, if at all. "If I had a shekel for every tomato that rotted at that crossing," one Gazan farmer told me, "I'd be a rich man."

Gaza is controlled from the inside as well as the outside. The one Palestinian-administered road running from north to south is intersected in two points by Israeli settler highways, in effect dividing the Palestinian thoroughfare into three parts. Israeli army installations at these intersections can subject Palestinian cars to long waits or block passage altogether. When travel is prohibited, as has been the case for much of this Intifada, *Palestinians have no way of leaving the one-third slice of Gaza in which they live. They are then trapped in a cage within a cage.*

During the summer of 2001, I lived in the northernmost of Gaza's three cages. I had come to do an internship at a human-rights group based in the Jabalia refugee camp. As our office's electricity went out several times each workday, however, I cannot claim to have been terribly productive. Lucky for me, I quickly found another vocation that gave purpose to my time in Gaza. I became a full-time roving houseguest.

Gazan hospitality is legendary. During the summer that I was there, over 75 percent of the population was below the poverty line and reliant on humanitarian aid. Still, everyone I met welcomed me home as a daughter or sister. Every day my officemates haggled with each other about whose turn it was to invite me to the midday meal. And in Gaza, a guest asked to lunch stays for dinner and then spends the night: anything less would be considered to eat and run.

One weekend when the closure eased a bit, I found myself a guest at my coworker's family home in a refugee camp in Rafah, Gaza's southern district. Upon arriving, I was treated not only to endless meals, but also to a full tour of the area. Issam, my coworker's childhood friend, had a car that he used as a kind of informal taxi service. As driving people around town was his main source of livelihood, he was the perfect guide.

Together we visited Rafah's key landmarks. We went to the Gaza International Airport and the Israeli crossing that was the major inlet for construction supplies. Both had long since been closed. We also saw where the Israeli army had bulldozed Palestinian houses, shops, and olive groves in order to clear a "buffer zone" the length of Gaza's border with Egypt. Israeli troops were patrolling the

wasteland of rubble, a few yards from the brink of a packed refugee neighborhood overflowing with children.

Everywhere we went, Issam pointed to the two Israeli observation towers that
loomed fifty feet high on the border. As it was impossible to avoid seeing them, I
couldn't understand why he felt it necessary to remind me of their presence. At last
I realized that Issam was not telling me to watch the towers, but rather warning
me that they were watching us. Israeli snipers stationed in the towers monitored all
movement in the area, and they could fire on anything within a wide radius. "Be
careful," Issam alerted me. "Everyone here knows someone who has been shot."

I knew from the human-rights reports I translated at work that the numbers
corroborated what he said. Just the previous week we had written a press release
about an eleven-year-old named Khalil Al-Mughrabi, who was shot from one of
these towers while he was playing with a kite. He was hit in the head with a
heavy-caliber bullet and died instantly. Two other boys were shot and wounded
when they tried to drag his body away.

I heard many stories of this type in Rafah. In fact, everyone I met had had
an experience with such gratuitous violence that I almost stopped recording
them, defeated by the thought that no one back home would ever believe me. As
the weekend progressed, I discovered that even Issam had a story of his own. I
had noticed his severe limp when we were first introduced. Yet it was only after
several hours on the roads, or on the side of the road waiting for his overheated
car to cool, that I learned their origin.

A soft-spoken young man, Issam was strikingly gentle; at one point in the
course of our circumvention of Rafah's gravel streets, he somehow came upon a
flower and presented it to Laura, who had accompanied us to take photographs.
He would glance bashfully in the rearview window when he addressed us in the
backseat of the car that earned him his daily bread. And little by little, he told
us about his life.

• ❖ •   • ❖ •   • ❖ •

My NAME IS ISSAM and I am a Palestinian from Rafah. I'm twenty-four years old.

When I was fourteen, Israelis shot me and I lost my leg. It was the last day of Ramadan, right before the time to break the fast. The roads and alleys were crowded and people were gathering in the market-place. Then the Israeli soldiers came. A group of young men tried to protect the area. They threw stones to prevent the soldiers from entering. The soldiers responded by opening fire on everyone. They killed four people and injured many, many more.

After they finished with the market area, they entered the refugee camp. I was at home and heard a gunshot, so I went out into the street. There was so much shooting going on. As soon as I stepped out into the street they shot me. It was at a close distance, they were no more than three meters away. I was hit with bullets in my right leg, bullets in my left leg, one bullet in my head, and two bullets in my back. I was knocked unconscious and didn't wake up again until I was in the hospital in Khan Younis. Later I found out that I was lying in the street for over twenty minutes before the Israelis left and someone was able to come and rescue me.

The hospital in Khan Younis had no facilities to speak of, so I was transferred to a hospital in Israel. That's where my leg was amputated.

One day while I was still recovering in the hospital, an American named Steve came to visit me. He offered to take me to America for treatment. I went with him. In America people took a lot of interest in me. I got a prosthetic leg and learned how to walk again. I spent eight months in treatment in San Francisco. The last two months I was in America they took me on a trip to see the country and to take my mind off the situation in Palestine a bit.

Americans welcomed me warmly. I would talk to them about how we live in Palestine . . . about the oppression, the daily curfews, and the deprivation at every moment. I had a video with me of incidents taking place in Palestine and I would show it to them. Americans would tell me that they didn't know about any of these things. They would say that the media show them that it is the Israelis who are being oppressed. I really like Americans. Those who know the truth understand our situation and sympathize with us.

I received medical care thanks to the generosity of the American people, not the American government. The American government gives Israel weapons that it uses to kill us. Americans pay taxes to their government, and the government uses it to send arms to Israel. So Americans are unintentionally causing the killing of children. I ask Americans to recognize this truth. I'm not asking for more than that.

Anyway, when I left America and returned here, the Israelis detained me in the airport for eighteen hours. They said that I had been instigating terrorism in the United States. Of course I had nothing to do with anything of that sort, but they were determined to keep me detained. The Red Cross intervened and finally got me home to Gaza. Eight months later I was supposed to go to the hospital in Jerusalem for a checkup, just to see if everything was OK. But they refused to let me into Jerusalem. They wouldn't give me a security pass. I had to go to court and sue Israel in order to get a permit. Arab-Israeli lawyers helped me until I finally got permission to go to the hospital.

Until this very day, I continue to have the same problem every time I need to go to the doctor for a checkup. Every time I'm due for a checkup, I have to go to court and raise another lawsuit just so I can get there.

And so I try to get on with my life. What else can I do? There is nothing else, not until the occupation ends and there is real peace for all.

This *Intifada* is necessary. It was inevitable. Throughout the past years, we have tried to place our trust in the peace process. We tried in all possible ways, without any violence or problems. But it has always ended in failure. They have always refused us. We are always turned away. And so we must do anything we can to bring the world to stand by our side and change this situation so that there will finally be peace and we can exercise our rights. Until then, until they answer the demands of the resistance, we will persevere.

During the first *Intifada*, we didn't know anything but Molotov cocktails and stones. Now we have hand grenades and weapons. We've created them ourselves, from all of the pressure. The more pressure they put on us, the more we try to do something in response. The oppressed always seek something, anything, no matter how difficult it is. The oppressed do the most difficult things to realize their goals and their dreams . . . to take back their rights. This *Intifada* has developed bit by bit. What is forced upon us is now also being forced upon them. They fired at us and shelled us with tanks and planes, and now they are also being shot at. If these activities continue, then we will continue to resist them and challenge them.

And so we support the *Intifada*. If there is any way in which I can participate, I will not hesitate to do so.

But it is difficult for me. All of my friends are able to walk on their own two legs and use stones to express all of the feelings they have inside them. I'm different from them. They walk, but I can only do so with a lot of difficulty. I can't go out with them. I can't leave the house because I'm scared that if the soldiers come after us I might not be able to get away. And if the soldiers cornered me someplace, they would either beat me or detain me.

The Israelis changed my whole life. They did this thing to me when I was a child, and I've grown up with it. They made me different from everybody else.

There was a bullet in my head. And the bullet in my spine left my back deformed. Now I don't even go to the beach because I don't want anyone to see me like this. Everything is difficult for me, so much has been taken from me. But I will never let anyone else do this to me again. They shot me, and I will not allow them to go on oppressing me on top of that. The Israelis have robbed me of everything beautiful in this world. They have taken my capacity to walk and lead a normal life. I will do anything to claim my rights.

If they keep oppressing people like this, and making them suffer, then they will reach the point where they strap dynamite to their bodies and blow themselves up among a group of Israelis. They put so much pressure on us that they make us think about blowing ourselves up. That is why we would be happy to know that we will die and that Israelis will die along with us. If we die at least we die on our land. They die on occupied land.

Israelis will never be secure until they give us our rights. We aren't asking for more than our rights. We want to be respected as human beings with homes.

The war and destruction will continue until the Israelis either kill all of the Palestinians or the world stands with us for truth. Otherwise, there will be war for as long as we live . . . and for many generations after that.

Manoa, with her youngest child in her home hit by shelling in Beit Jala

11. AHMED, AMAL, MANOA AND IBRAHIM,

members of a family in Beit Jala

FOLLOWING THE NEWSPAPER SALESMAN'S *directions, Laura and I walked to where the yellow taxis congregated in downtown Bethlehem, kept the big falafel stand on our left, and marched straight uphill. Ten minutes and a lot of panting later, we were in Beit Jala.*

At first glance, this traditionally Christian village struck me as something out of a fairy tale. Its silent streets were cobbled and its stone houses adorned with grand arches and wrought-iron balconies. Its Greek Orthodox, Catholic, and Lutheran churches housed peeling frescoes, flickering candles, and stacks of worn bibles.

A closer look, however, revealed the flip side of picturesque. House after house had broken windows and walls pocked with bullet holes. Several had gaping craters smashed into their roofs or façades. A mansion popularly dubbed "the Palace," the life investment of the richest man in town, had been destroyed and abandoned. I was surprised that none of the locals made cracks about the consequences of avarice. Avarice, apparently, had nothing to do with it. The tank shells could land anywhere, and every family feared that their house might be next.

Since the outbreak of the Intifada, *this quaint village had been the site of nearly nightly hostilities. Armed Palestinians, believed to be members of the* Tanzim *militia, were coming to Beit Jala to fire rifles at Gilo, a middle-class Israeli community situated a third of a mile away on the other side of a deep valley. The Israeli army was retaliating with heavy bullets, tank fire, and missiles dropped from helicopters and warplanes.*

Israeli spokespeople accused the Palestinian Authority of intentionally provoking Israel's retaliation against Palestinian civilians in an attempt to mobilize international and Christian sympathy. The residents of Beit Jala, on the other hand, insisted that Israelis shelled their houses even when there was no Palestinian gunfire.

The crux of the dispute, however, was not the source of fire as much as the status of Gilo. While Israelis regarded Gilo as a neighborhood of Jerusalem, Palestinians considered it to be a settlement. In this, they both seemed correct. When Israel seized control of East Jerusalem in 1967, it redefined the boundaries of the Jerusalem Municipality to encompass land expropriated from surrounding villages. Today, a dozen Jewish settlements constructed in the Arab neighborhoods of Jerusalem and its environs are home to some 200,000 Israelis. One of the largest of these settlements, established in 1970 on land originally belonging to the residents of Beit Jala and two other villages, is Gilo.

When the Intifada began and settlements emerged as a principal focus of Palestinian protest, Gilo came to be a representative target. As Uri Avnery, an outspoken former Knesset member, explained it:

An Israeli general said on television: "Gilo is a part of our capital. Would the British have tolerated shooting at London?" To which the answer could be: "If the British were to annex Belfast to the London municipal area, the IRA would probably shoot at it, too." [1]

And so Palestinians shot and Israel shot back. And the terrorized residents of Gilo were promised government funds to bullet-proof their houses. And the terrorized residents of Beit Jala prayed.

Curious about life in this village-turned-war zone, Laura and I walked

1. http://www.gush-shalom.org/archives/article160.html

the ten minutes uphill from Bethlehem to Beit Jala. Upon arriving, we called to the first person we saw sitting on a balcony and were promptly invited inside. It turned out to be the house of Farah Al-Araj, mayor of Beit Jala from 1972 to 1998. Unable to speak due to recent larynx surgery, the aging former mayor scribbled notes to us about his adventurous youth. As a young man he had traveled to Budapest, where he had come in first place in a running competition and had a Hungarian girlfriend. From there he went on to live many years in Latin America, and when he returned to Palestine he did so with the title "Consulado Honorado de Honduras." *When the second* Intifada *began and Beit Jala was shelled, his family hung the Honduran flag from the window in the hope that it would protect them from being hit. It had not.*

Leaving the house of the Honorary Consul of Honduras, Laura and I continued to meander through the cobblestone streets. We stopped when we heard a sudden "Heellloooo" from above. A small boy was poking his head out of a gaping cavity in the house next to us. Figuring we had found someone with something to say, we knocked on the door.

And so we met the family of Mr. and Mrs. Jameel Moslet and their many children. Their youngest was still in diapers, their eldest had a baby of her own, and every one of them old enough to speak could speak about the bombings in vivid detail. But the Moslet clan was eager to talk about other things as well. Thus, while I got buried in a debate on the merits of the newest Mexican soap opera dubbed in Arabic, Laura snuck up to the roof to share a clandestine cigarette with one of the teenagers. Then, while Laura took pictures of the boys playing soccer in the hallway, I listened to the girls' cassette collection and fumbled for an excuse to avoid dancing in the middle of the circle. Time flew, night fell, and dinner was devoured before Laura and I finally said that we really should be going.

"Going where?" the family looked at us perplexedly.

"Back to Laura's apartment in Jerusalem."

They shook their heads. Cars were prohibited from crossing the checkpoint separating Bethlehem and Jerusalem, and at this hour there were no taxis waiting on the Jerusalem side to take passengers to the center of the city.

"Just get us to the checkpoint," Laura suggested. "We'll walk from there."

The Moslets said that we were crazy, but we insisted. After all, Gilo loomed frighteningly close, and it was considered part of Jerusalem. Downtown could not be that much farther away.

Mr. Moslet reluctantly drove us to the checkpoint, bade us farewell, and watched as we walked across the threshold that separated PA-controlled Bethlehem from Israel proper. From there we kept walking. And walking. And walking. Technically we were in Jerusalem, but practically speaking we were on a highway far from any house or shop. At last we came upon a gas station and asked for directions. A middle-aged Israeli man filling his tank told us that we would be walking for hours before we reached downtown, and offered us a ride.

As we drove the remainder of the way the man told us that his children were about our age. One was graduating from the Technology Institute in the spring, God willing, and the other was preparing for his secondary-school examinations. I remembered what Mrs. Moslet said about worrying every time her children left the house, and imagined that this man felt likewise.

When we got out of the car, the man urged us to be safe in a voice filled with parental concern. We thanked him and told him to be safe as well.

· ✦· ·✦· ·✦·

AHMED, *brother, thirteen years old*

MY NAME IS AHMED. I'm thirteen years old. I live in Beit Jala.

The night they shelled our house we were all at home. We were in the living room, watching TV. Then they started firing and we all ran downstairs. A bullet came right through into the living room, but we'd already gotten out by then. So we all stayed downstairs. I started playing games with my little brothers and sisters so they would forget to be scared.

Then Dad said that we should turn off the lights because if they see lights, then they know that people are inside and they'll hit the place even harder. So we turned of the lights and sat down on the floor.

Then they fired the first bomb. My sisters and brothers started screaming and crying. My uncle came to our house and said that we should try to escape. He went back outside and we started to follow. But right then my uncle got shot in the chest with a bullet, so we all ran back inside.

Then they fired the second bomb. An ambulance came to take the injured people to the hospital and the soldiers started firing on them before they could even get the injured people into the ambulance. One of the nurses got shot. Our neighbor Marwa also got shot.

When things calmed down a bit some of my uncles and my cousins came over to our house. At that point there were seventeen of us in the house. They started bombing more and more. We were up all night together.

When it was happening, I kept thinking, "It's over. The whole city is going to be destroyed." The next day we went out and found that my dad's car and my uncle's car had both been ruined completely.

When they shell the bullets come in the house from all directions. Look there . . . and there . . . and there. You can see the bullet holes all over the place. Our house didn't look like this before. We're keeping a collection of all the different kinds of bullets and shrapnel that have landed in the house. Look here. You can see it all for yourself.

•◆•   •◆•   •◆•

AMAL, *sister, eighteen years old*
WHEN THEY FIRST STARTED bombing we were just scared. More than anything else, we were simply afraid. We kept thinking, "How will

we get out? When will they stop?" It was total confusion. You really can't think of anything else when they're bombing you. You think, "That's it. Tonight is our last night. We'll never make it out of here alive." Any one of these bullets flying around can hit you.

It's traumatic. You get hysterical and start shouting things like "No!" "Why?" "Stop!" You're trapped in the house. You can't open a window or a door. The pressure is so terrible that your nerves can barely handle it. Every action has a reaction, you know. So you just keep screaming because you have to let it out. The children are in a state of panic, too. And you can't calm them because you can barely even calm yourself.

When they first started bombing we would try to take shelter on the lower floor of the house. The truth is that it's not that much safer. But in this situation, if something can make you even 1 percent safer, you do it.

It was never like this before. During the first *Intifada* there were demonstrations and marches and maybe some shooting, but it was never as bad as this. Now they shoot to kill. It's clear that it's not in self-defense. No way. Maybe you've noticed, but most shots have been to the head or chest. When they aim at the legs it's to paralyze or hand-icap for life. They use dumdum bullets that get lodged in your legs and explode. Those bullets tear the body to shreds.

We've all suffered in the truest meaning of the word. Our house has been hit badly, but thank God it was only our house that was hit. The house is something that can be replaced.

But beyond this, the bombing has made us all feel so much anxiety. The pressure affects you profoundly. It makes you confused and dis-tracted all the time. You find that you can't concentrate on anything anymore. Whenever there is a calm and peaceful night you start thinking, "Maybe they'll bomb again."

They used to strike us with tanks, but it never scared us like this. It wasn't like seeing aircraft. Now the strikes are random. They shoot any object that moves, even if it's just some animal on the street.

That is what happened to Harry Fisher. Did you hear about him? He was a German doctor married to a Palestinian here in Beit Jala. One night when they were shelling, he came outside, not far from his house. They hit him with a missile and his body was torn to bits. Such cruelty. There are no words to describe the sight. You've never seen such brutality as a man hit by a missile. It's something you can't even begin to imagine.

In the end, a human being is just a bundle of feelings. So where are the feelings of these people? Do they have any feelings but hate?

You know, before there could have been some give-and-take between us. But now it's impossible. Now we've discovered that those seven years of peace were nothing but a façade. If you can even call it peace, that is, given all their acts of treachery throughout. Do you see how they disguised themselves during all of these years? And now, suddenly, their true feelings have been exposed. They don't want peace. They don't want us to have a homeland and to live with safety and security.

No, they want to annihilate us. They want one thing, and that's death to the Arabs. No tolerance. No compromise. They want to kill. A plane drops a missile on a car killing three or four or five Palestinians. If an Israeli dies, they want ten of us to die in return. They think that any Jewish life is precious but our lives are cheap.

No person on earth can accept this life of oppression and humiliation. They describe us as terrorists and criminals who want to steal their land, but the exact opposite is the case. They kill us, but they will never control our ideas or beliefs. We'll be saying "freedom" with the last breaths we take.

They have the most sophisticated weapons. We don't have anything but our refusal to give in. A situation like this forces you to react. It either reveals your weakness or makes you stronger. And it has made us stronger.

We might not be like other countries, but contrary to what you might expect, there is something in this that makes us happy. God has placed us in a land holy for all religions. What more could we ask for? In the West they may have luxury and security. But all of those luxuries can make people forget what "homeland" means. It can keep them from truly feeling for their neighbors or caring about their own people.

This is the land of our ancestors. No one came and planted us here. If we agree to give up our homeland, then we'll become scattered all over the world. So we remain steadfast.

We keep our eyes on the future. The morning after each nighttime bombing raid is like a new beginning. It is as if you are dead for several hours during the night and then you come to life again when the day breaks. That is how it has been for us here in Beit Jala. We die at night when they bomb, and then come to life again with each new day.

•-•-•   •-•-•   •-•-•

MANOA, *mother*

YOU CAN LOOK OUT our window and see how close we are to the Gilo settlement. It is on the hill there. They like to say that Gilo is a neighborhood in the southern part of Jerusalem, but you can see that this is false. It's a settlement and it's practically right in the middle of the town of Beit Jala.

You can see how much land the settlement takes up. And you can also see how well armed it is. There used to be tanks all around, but things have calmed now and they've withdrawn.

The children have finally started to forget the bombing a little. The pressure has tapered off. Still, whenever they hear an airplane overhead, they start shouting, "Planes! Bang, bang, bang!"

My youngest son was sitting here watching TV once when they

started shelling. I was in the kitchen cooking. He heard the shelling and came running to me crying, "Mommy, the plane is shooting." I asked him "Where?" and he said "Beit Jala." He understood the situation perfectly. I was astonished. When he heard the plane, he jumped up and cried, "They're bombing Beit Jala." The children understand everything that's going on.

So we all came here to the living room and huddled together. All fourteen of us were inside when the house was hit, and the children were crying the whole time. Bullets and shrapnel were coming into the house, so we couldn't move from where we were hiding. No one dared go out, not even after the shelling ended. We could hear neighbors outside calling our names to find out whether or not we were safe, but we wouldn't leave the house. We know that the Israelis can shoot anyone at any time.

Then an ambulance came and they started shooting at the rescue workers. One of the doctors was shot. It was terrible. More shrapnel came through our window and we thought, "This is it, we're done for." I mean, if the Israelis have gone as far as shooting ambulances, then what's next?

The ambulance left to escape the firing, but then came rushing back when the German doctor got hit by a missile. His body was blown to bits and parts of it flew everywhere. There were pieces of flesh stuck on the walls, stuck in the trees. Can you imagine? Where else in the world do such things happen? The Israelis will kill anyone: a little boy, a woman, an old man, it doesn't matter. If they feel so much for the loss of one of their own, can't they understand that the lives of others are precious, too?

We didn't dare go out the door after that. We wouldn't even go near it! Of course, if the roof came tumbling down on our heads, we would get killed just the same. Death is death. But we decided that we should just stay at home. We recited some verses from the Koran and told the children not to be scared.

Not too much later the electricity got cut off. When things gradually calmed down a bit we decided to leave the house for the first time.

You can't imagine the intensity of the strikes. They'll last from seven o'clock in the evening until three o'clock in the morning. That window over there got smashed by 500mm bullets. It wasn't until yesterday that we were finally able to fix it. But thank God, none of us was injured. It was really close. If the missiles hadn't missed the house, all of us would have been killed. All fourteen people would have died.

This is just a house, but it's our house and these are our things. We won't leave. Only death can take us away from our home, and we're prepared to die. This is our home, that's all there is to it.

Would America like it if the same thing happened to its people? Do you, the American people, like the fact that another people are being robbed of their land, their children, their honor? Americans are content in their homes and they're not interested in our situation. They're very far away and they don't understand the effects of their country's policies.

We have suffered under the Israeli occupation. Your son goes off to work and you don't know if he'll come back or not. You just sit there with your heart filled with worry. "Did they arrest him? Did they beat him? Did they kill him?" You can hardly believe it when he finally walks in the door alive.

How would you feel if you lost a father or a brother or a sister or any of your children? Would you just keep silent? How can there not be anger and violence after all of this? Children spend their nights in fear. My baby son will cry out at night, "Mama, bang!" My eight-year-old son is always coming down with a fever. Once he was so red all over that we took him to the hospital. The doctors said it was psychological, from stress.

Our lives have become miserable. We're trapped in here. No one comes or goes. No one sleeps. No one has any happiness. For three months now there has been no work. How are we supposed to live? We have no state to provide us services.

To top it off, the Israelis use people as agents and informants. So you don't even know if someone is your friend or if he's dragging you into a trap. It's just a miserable life.

All we want is to live with some freedom and security. We're just asking them not to bring our houses crashing down on top of our heads. People outside of Palestine can't imagine the pain and humiliation that we live through. To hear about something from a distance is not the same as seeing it with your own eyes.

We are asking every nation to try to sympathize with our pain and have mercy on the innocent children. Our children have nothing. There are no proper schools or parks for them. They have no toys, so they go outside and play with the remnants of missiles that they find lying around. There are one- and two-year-olds who die. There are children who lose an eye or a leg. There are children who are shot and their insides come out of their bellies right in front of their eyes.

A mother lives for her children. She worries if her child gets pricked by a thorn. So can you imagine what it's like for a mother in this situation? Maybe if the situation were safe I wouldn't have to worry so much.

All we're asking from the world, from the Arab states and all countries, is that they see our suffering and have mercy on our children. Just try to put yourself in our shoes.

* * *

IBRAHIM, *brother, twenty-two years old*
I WAS AT MY grandfather's house when the shelling started. When we heard the first explosion, we didn't think it was anything out of the ordinary. It seemed far away. But then a kid in the neighborhood came over and said that it was my family's house that had been hit. I couldn't believe it. I rushed like a madman from my grandfather's place to make

it home to see if everyone was OK. But the shelling was so heavy and they were shooting at the ambulances and everything in the streets. It was three in the morning before I reached the house.

The next morning I got a sense of the damage. Everything was ruined. The doors, windows, our schoolbooks, the television . . . everything was broken or burned.

Now anytime you leave the house, you know that they can kill you. They can kill you while you're inside your house, too. My mother is so frightened for us all the time. If I'm out for the day and don't pass by the house ten times to assure her that I'm OK, she goes crazy with worry.

I'm a resident of Beit Jala, but what is my crime? A few weeks ago some friends and I drove to Ramallah. Of course we couldn't go the direct route, because that passes through Jerusalem and is prohibited for us. So we had to go on the back roads through *Wadi An-Naar*. When we got to Ramallah we passed through the checkpoint and the soldiers didn't give us any problems. But on the way back there was a different shift of soldiers. They stopped the car and asked for our identity cards. When they saw it written that we were from Beit Jala they said sarcastically, "Well! Well! Beit Jala! Welcome! Welcome!" They made us get out of the car. There were a lot of other people waiting at the checkpoint, so they didn't do anything to us, thank God. If there hadn't been so many people around, they would have shot us. I could see that this is what they wanted to do. That's how it goes. They can just shoot anyone they want. It's like a game for them.

I used to work inside Israel, but now it's prohibited. If there were some other way to make a living, we'd never go to Israel for work. But we have no alternative. The Arab states aren't opening the borders to let us in. Everything is closed to us.

But now it's too dangerous to work inside Israel, anyway. You could get killed at the checkpoint or en route or in Israel. At any moment you can get shot and then it's all over for you. So for now I'm staying close to home and trying to get by with odd jobs here and there. Yesterday my father and I filled in at a bread bakery from twelve midnight to twelve noon. My father has diabetes and gets tired easily, so he couldn't do as much. But I worked until I was so tired that I felt like death. I'm not Superman, you know.

The situation is really, really tough. Imagine that you've lived in your house twenty years and then one day somebody tells you to leave. Would you do it? Impossible. Well, I've lived in this house in Beit Jala my whole life, and I'm not giving it up, either.

At the same time, more and more people are saying that if the situation stays like this, maybe they'll emigrate. I'm thinking about this, too. I want a country. I want to know stability and peace. If I get married and have children, I want my kids to have a life. A life without fear. A life that allows you to put your head on the pillow at night and not be afraid that you'll be killed before you wake up. A real life, not like what we're living now. Here we're like birds in a cage.

Yes, if the situation stays like this, maybe I'll leave. I can find work in some other country. Palestinians work wherever they find themselves, in every country in the world. I want to work so I can send money back home to my parents. They raised me and now I want to be able to support them.

The Israelis kill us and steal our land, and at the same time they say that they want peace. How can this be? We're refugees. We're originally from a village near what is now called Beit Shemesh in Israel. UN resolutions have recognized the refugees' right to return to their homes and villages, but none of the agreements between the Israelis and Palestinians confirm this right.

Everyone in the whole world knows what Israel is doing. In America they know what's going on, but they continue to support

Israel regardless. They see all the wrong, and they go on supporting that wrong. Americans should come here and get a better understanding of what we're suffering.

Yeah, maybe I'll finally emigrate to some other country. I don't want to, but are there other options? Any place has to be better than what we're going through now. But then, emigration is no easy thing. In order to get a visa to the United States, for example, you need $150,000 in the bank as collateral. Who has this kind of money?

And even if I leave, I'll never forget my country. This is my country. I have a sense of belonging to it that will never disappear.

Mahmoud, with his son and daughter in Khan Younis

1 2 . MAHMOUD, *owner of a demolished home*

EVERY TIME I VISITED *a new acquaintance in the West Bank or Gaza I was immediately treated to a tour of the family house. No sooner had I walked in the door than my hosts took me to each immaculate room and made sure that I was duly impressed with the polished furniture, ornate pillows, and floors washed down every morning. Even in refugee camps, where a house may have consisted of four cinder-block walls and a leaking asbestos roof, tremendous love and work was devoted to making it as beautiful a home as circumstance allowed. Outside, the gravel streets might be filled with rubbish and the absence of a sewage system might leave wastewater to flow in open channels. Inside, however, a family's home was its pride and sanctuary.*

I was taken through so many tours of family homes that I became an expert on the routine. "How nice! How beautiful!" I said time after time, exclaiming my admiration for trinkets and wedding photographs, fake flowers, and needlepoint pictures of the Jerusalem skyline. I learned to play my role with flying colors, even without thinking.

I was taken aback, however, the first time I visited a family whose house had been demolished. On my visit to a Gaza refugee camp not long after one nighttime raid by Israeli bulldozers, I met a dozen families living in tents near the wreckage of what had once been their homes. To my bewilderment, I found some of them clinging habitually to these customs for the reception of house guests, even though their house was no longer standing.

"Here, let me show you our house," a young girl told me, taking my hand upon my arrival. I followed her as she hopped from one slab of aluminum siding to

another, pointing to various clumps of metal, wood, and plastic chards. "This is our bedroom," she said. "And over there will be the room for my big brother and his fiancée when they get married, and there is the kitchen, and back there is the garden." She spoke in the present tense as if her house were still there, plain to see. I remember looking at the wasteland of debris and managing to mutter what I knew was expected of house guests. "How nice," I whispered, "how beautiful."

House demolitions are nothing new in Israel's policy toward the Palestinians. According to the Israeli Committee Against House Demolitions, Israel has demolished nearly ten thousand Palestinian houses in the Occupied Territories and East Jerusalem since 1967, leaving fifty-thousand men, women, and children homeless. Some 740 homes were demolished during the course of the peace process years, and more than two thousand have been demolished since the start of the second Intifada.

Israel justifies some demolitions as punitive measures against families in which a member is suspected of resistance activity or terrorism. Executed by the army without any requirement of judicial order or verifiable evidence, however, such demolitions amount to extra-legal collective punishment against entire households. Israel rationalizes other demolitions as administrative measures against home owners lacking building permits. Permitless construction by Israeli Jews, on the other hand, is subject to no such repercussions.

What Israeli spokespeople rarely mention is that Palestinian homes targeted for demolition are often located near settlements, bypass roads, or military installations. Demolitions, and the subsequent clearing and confiscation of the property, thus enable expansion of Israeli-held territory in the West Bank and Gaza Strip. House demolitions therefore create "facts on the ground" that redraw the map of Israeli control.

Mahmoud is one of the thousands of Palestinians who have awakened one day to the sound of Israeli bulldozers and the raw awareness that they would never sleep in their houses again. An engineer from the town of Khan Younis in Gaza, Mahmoud received neither warning nor explanation when the army flattened the house that he had built for himself, his new wife, and the family they planned to create together. His land was seized as property of the State of Israel and declared a closed military zone.

I met Mahmoud in the empty apartment that the Palestinian Authority offered him as shelter until he could come up with a better alternative. The apartment complex was filled with other families whose homes had likewise been bulldozed or who had been forced to evacuate their original neighborhoods because bombing had made it too dangerous for them to stay there. The irony was that these apartment buildings had come under shelling from nearby Israeli army outposts. Bullet holes peppered their façades like a bad case of the chicken pox, and children held contests to see who could collect the biggest bullet casings and bomb fragments. Some families, insisting that they were no safer in these emergency shelters than in their original properties, had decided to return home. As one woman told me, "At least there we'll die in our own house."

A swarm of kids playing barefoot outside took me to Mahmoud's apartment when I arrived and asked them the way to the apartment of the engineer. Mahmoud answered the door and invited me to sit on one of the plastic lawn chairs that furnished the stark living room. As his wife made coffee and his toddler crawled in and out of the room on all fours, he sighed and told me his story.

• ◆ •   • ◆ •   • ◆ •

MY NAME IS MAHMOUD and I'm thirty-three years old. My family is originally from Jaffa, but we lost everything in 1948 and came to the Khan Younis refugee camp. My grandfather and father worked hard. They made sure we got an education, and we moved out of the camp to the town of Khan Younis. Now I work in the Gaza airport as an electrical engineer.

During the peace process I worked at the Rafah border crossing as a security representative for the Palestinian National Authority. I had an

Israeli counterpart and we worked together. Things seemed stable, and we felt like there was really going to be a permanent settlement to the conflict. So, three years ago, my brother and two other relatives and I all built new houses here in Khan Younis. My brother is a pediatrician and he had done a special course in Israel in neurology. So he also opened a private clinic in his house for children in the area.

And then the *Intifada* started. Not too far from us, the Israeli army was starting to bulldoze the area beside the main road. They uprooted trees and bulldozed houses so that there was a wide empty space on either side of the street. They bulldozed my relatives' land and destroyed a well.

But there were never any problems in our neighborhood. That is, not until the twenty-first of November. On that day I was just taking an afternoon nap when suddenly I woke up to all of this noise outside. I looked out the window and saw a tank and soldiers surrounding my house. They began to fire gas, but it wasn't regular tear gas. It was a dense gas that blocks your vision. My wife was eight months pregnant at the time, and I was afraid for her and the baby. We managed to escape and made it to the house of some relatives not too far away.

We tried to drive back to our house several times, but each time the army or the settlers would come after us and we'd have to flee again. Finally at ten o'clock that night a bulldozer came. They bulldozed four houses: my house, my brother's house along with his clinic, and the houses of our two other relatives.

It wasn't until later that I found out the story behind the demolitions. Apparently Ehud Barak had visited a settlement in order to reassure the settlers that he was in control of the situation. But on that very day there had been some shooting and a settler was injured at the checkpoint. I guess the Israelis were taking revenge, and they took it out on me.

I had never imagined that they would come for my house. I felt safe and there were never any problems. But on that day the army changed its policy and started to act according to the settlers' wishes. They wanted to scare people, to show another face. And we paid the price.

There was once a great deal of security coordination and cooperation between Palestinians and Israelis. I know; I worked in joint security for five years. I also participated in an American program to bring Jews, Muslims, and Christians together. At that time, everyone had a lot of hope for the future.

I think that the Israeli army wanted to show that it could take care of any problems on the ground on its own, apart from the political arrangements. The military wanted to step in and take charge in a military way. This created a huge gap between us. And now the Israelis say that they want security cooperation again? At this point, any solution is a long way off.

After they bulldozed our house, the Palestinian Authority gave us temporary housing in these apartments. We can stay here until the problem is solved. Sometime after the Israelis demolished my house they also started to bulldoze in the Khan Younis refugee camp. Recently they've also been bulldozing in other places nearby. There is a lot of shelling over there, too. So all of these temporary apartments here have become filled with people who have left different areas and come here because it's safer. But the thing is that we come under shelling here, too. You can see the bullet holes in the buildings. The army just opens fire whenever it wants to.

Anyway, my work at the airport has come to a complete standstill. The airport has been open just once or twice since the *Intifada* started. There are about seven hundred employees at the airport, and we're all out of work. I'll get a new paycheck, but my brother is out of work, and so I give some of my money to him. Or my sister's husband doesn't have work, so I'll give him some, too. Everyone is like this. You try to save some money, but by the tenth of the month, you find that there is nothing left.

The Israelis have closed all the borders: the Rafah border with Egypt, the airport, the civilian crossing to Israel, and the commercial crossing to Israel. There used to be students traveling to study abroad, people traveling to work in other countries. Now people wait at the border for four days in order to pass. People have died while trying to leave for Egypt or trying to return to Gaza. All the people who depend on the airport and the border crossings for a living are out of work. The employees, taxi drivers, people who help with luggage . . . nobody has work anymore. Israel closed the borders as a form of political pressure. It's just another kind of collective punishment against the Palestinian people.

Those of us who haven't lived outside the West Bank or Gaza Strip since 1967 have Israeli-issued identity cards. But Palestinians who went abroad don't have identity cards, and now it is prohibited for them to come back. I have two brothers who are studying abroad, and are forbidden from coming back home. My wife's sisters are also abroad and they can't come here either. The only way you can come is via Israel. Israel decides whether to grant a special visa for a monthlong visit or to deny permission from coming at all. They decide. Families get split up this way.

Imagine that you leave America for a while, but your house is still there. Then someone tells you that it is prohibited for you to return to the United States. They say, "Forget it, you have to stay abroad." You could live abroad for five or ten years, but wouldn't you feel a need to return to your country? A lot of Palestinians get stuck in other countries this way. This, of course, is in addition to those who were made refugees in 1948.

Israel also regulates what goods cross the border. If you can buy something in Israel, you are prohibited from bringing it in from abroad. If you can't buy it in Israel, you can bring it in from abroad, but you still have to get permission from the Israelis. There is just no freedom in anything.

We're living in one huge prison. All of the Gaza Strip and the West Bank have become for the comfort of the settlers. They travel back and forth freely. The settlements that began as one square kilometer have expanded to take up half of Khan Younis. We Palestinians are moving inward under pressure, and the settlements are expanding and expanding. There is no space. Here you find fifty Palestinians living in one house, and Israelis have all the open areas.

And the Israeli settlers don't even live here. The settlements in Gaza aren't homes; they're mostly factories and farms. They call themselves settlers, but the truth is that they're just using the land as a tax-free commercial zone. They don't pay for anything. Water is free for them. They all live inside Israel and just come to Gaza for work. On Friday you can see them all going home for the weekend. You see their cars, two hundred of them going back inside Israel.

So the settlers plant crops and take our water for free. They take our pure water and use it inside Israel. We are left to drink salty water. Everyone in Gaza has yellow teeth and kidney diseases because our water is so filthy. Most of the people leaving at the border crossings and the airport are traveling for medical treatment.

These are problems that we endure every day.

As for the demolitions, the destruction, and the killings . . . that is their way of terrorizing us. We live in fear, but we just have to be patient and endure. There is nothing else we can do. We can't go back to the situation before the start of the *Intifada* unless there is a real solution. But the Israelis aren't giving the Palestinian Authority anything to offer the people.

So we're all under pressure. We're nervous all the time. Many young people who got married before the *Intifada* have since gotten separated or divorced; there is so much stress that problems develop, and they split up. There are no new marriages, either. No one has the money to start a household. And we're all scared for the children. We think, "What will happen if I'm killed and I can no longer provide for them?"

We're not asking for a lot. Originally, all of Palestine belonged to us.

But we have recognized the State of Israel. We don't say that we want all of Palestine. We don't want to take back Haifa and we don't want the Jews to leave. We don't talk about any of that. We only talk about ending the problems that we have to live with every day.

The Palestinians have simple and just demands. We want our land in the West Bank and the Gaza Strip. We want to have control over our border crossings and the airport. We want to share Jerusalem. We want a solution to the refugee problem.

Our solution will come from America more than from Israel. The American people should put pressure on their leadership to be fair. The American government is not worried when Palestinians die, only when Israelis do. Arafat wants a solution. His whole history revolves around searching for a solution. But Israel is always wasting time. Israel wants the Palestinian Authority to be only an administrative apparatus, not a real decision maker. And right-wing Israelis want Gaza and the West Bank. So where am I supposed to go?

That's my story. One day we had a house and a garden and everything was fine. And then suddenly we didn't have a house anymore. We didn't have anything except the clothes on our backs. We had to start over at square one. We had just gotten married so everything was new. I had new furniture, including a television, a refrigerator, a bed and dresser, curtains, everything, everything. I had worked for eight years to get married and buy a house, and it was ruined in a single minute. Everything was destroyed. Now it is prohibited for me to return to the land where my house once stood. The Israelis took control over the entire area. But I want to return. I would like to have my house there. I would like to plant a garden again.

Or maybe I'll change my mind and decide to buy another house. The point is that I should decide. There shouldn't always be someone else forcing me to go here or there. It's an issue of rights. I need to take back my rights. But now there are no rights to take.

PART THREE

Faces of Everyday Resistance

13. Azza, *filmmaker*

14. Saad, *agricultural engineer*

15. Iman, *college student*

16. Sami and Shaaban, *shop owners*

17. Ahmed, *psychologist*

18. Khaled and Marina, *theater directors*

Azza, at a café in Ramallah

13. AZZA, *filmmaker*

"In our country there is room only for the Jews. We shall say to the Arabs: Get out! If they don't agree, if they resist, we shall drive them out by force."
—Professor Ben-Zion Dinur, Israel's first Minister of Education, 1954

"There is no such thing as a Palestinian people. . . . It is not as if we came and threw them out and took their country. They didn't exist."
—Israeli Prime Minister Golda Meir, 1969

IT PERPLEXES ME WHEN *I hear people say that the Palestinians have never recognized the State of Israel. After all, the Palestinian leadership publicly recognized Israel in 1988 when it relinquished its goal of one secular state in all of Palestine and accepted the creation of an independent Palestinian state in the West Bank and Gaza. When the peace process began, the overwhelming majority of ordinary Palestinians likewise accepted Israel as a neighbor with which they would live side by side in equality and freedom. As the negotiations dragged on, opinion polls testified to a steady decline in this faith in coexistence. During the current impasse, violence, closure, and curfew strangulate the spirit of reconciliation more and more with each passing day.*

Palestinians' readiness to accept Israel, therefore, has fluctuated with Israel's demonstrated willingness to accept the Palestinians. Zionism's central myth, "a land without a people for a people without a land," crystalized non-recognition of the Palestinians' roots in the land they called Palestine. After Israel established statehood, many of its leaders continued to make remarks that either denied the existence of a Palestinian people or deemed them to be less than human. Prime

Minister Begin called Palestinians "beasts walking on two legs," and his chief of staff Raphael Eitan pledged that they would be made to "scurry around like drugged cockroaches in a bottle." Just weeks before the start of the second Intifada, Prime Minister Barak likened Palestinians to crocodiles, scoffing that "the more you give them meat, the more they want." Today, classrooms throughout Israel display maps of the Jewish state in which both sides of the Green Line appear as a single entity, absent of acknowledgment that a third of this population is living under military occupation against its will.

The bumpy road to recognition, therefore, is a two-way street. Furthermore, for many Palestinians, real peace requires that Israel recognize not only their right to self-determination, but also the suffering that they have endured. As Vera, a sculptor and art professor, told me:

> *I was very small when I left Jaffa, but I remember the first time I went back with my parents after 1967. They were so emotional, laughing and crying at the same time. I have relatives who always talk about Jaffa. The details of the place are still very vivid in their minds. I have an aunt who talks about Jaffa as if she were still living there now. She will say, "In Jaffa we do this . . ."*
>
> *We've already given so many concessions. How can I forget Jaffa and all of these other places inside the 1948 borders? But if the Israelis would only recognize that they displaced the Palestinians, if they could accept that they committed an historical injustice against the Palestinian people, then I think that I might accept the fact of losing Jaffa.*
>
> *But they haven't done this.*

For Vera, the tragedy and struggle of the Palestinian experience inevitably leaves its mark on her installations and landscapes, whether she is cognizant of it or not. Likewise, for a young filmmaker, Azza, the production of art under Palestinians' current political circumstances is almost inevitably an exercise in bearing witness to injustice, even when it strives only to capture daily life.

I met Azza in one of the trendy cafés where Ramallah intellectuals drink expensive cappuccino and discuss Marx. A confessed workaholic, Azza radiated the style and charisma of an up-and-coming star. I had to hold myself back from asking for her autograph. Yet, the few hours I spent with Azza were memorable for me not only because she was the hippest person I had met in the West Bank. She was also the first person to recognize my last name as being Jewish and tell me so.

In Palestinian society, where faith and culture are intertwined, the topic of religion surfaces regularly. Palestinians often asked about my religion upon meeting me for the first time, and I became expert at changing the subject by replying with a comment on the weather or asking for the way to the rest room.

I did not hide my Jewishness because I believed that Palestinians would be angry or that I would in any way be in danger. Rather, my fear was that people would see me as being first and foremost a Jew, which was not necessarily how I saw myself. This, after all, had happened many times in the United States, and even, if not especially, upon meeting other Jews. In the Palestinian territories as elsewhere, I wanted people to get to know me as an individual, and not as a representative of a certain ethnic or religious group.

In the end, I would come to be ashamed for giving my Palestinian acquaintances so little credit. This was what happened: once when I was living in the West Bank I wrote an article in an American newspaper, which an Italian paper reprinted along with its own identification of me as a Jewish writer. The Italian article was in turn reprinted in one of the Palestinian dailies, which frequently publishes excerpts from the foreign and Israeli press, translated into Arabic.

Thus, after months of hiding the fact that I was Jewish, I was inadvertently "outed" in a forum no less public than the newspaper. When a work colleague in Ramallah showed me the article, I remember feeling an instinctual urge to mumble something about the weather or excuse myself to the rest room. But it was too late. I had been less than honest with all of the people who had welcomed me into their homes and lives, and now the time had come to fess up.

To my surprise, I discovered that none of the Palestinians I knew who read the article cared a wink. In fact, the colleague who showed me the paper told me nonchalantly that everyone in our office had guessed that I was Jewish long ago. They had never mentioned it because they sensed that it was a topic that made me uncomfortable. So much for my clever evasion of the religion question: Palestinians were feigning ignorance for my sake.

It was months before my newspaper exposé, however, that I met Azza and she asked me straight out what it was like to be Jewish in Ramallah. As a filmmaker with a good eye for poignant scenes and telling confessions, she was not about to back away from one of those moments of honest tension in which people reveal themselves. Her words, reassuring yet forthright, reminded me of that most basic principle of recognition: People cannot expect to be recognized by others until they first recognize themselves.

•—•   •—•   •—•

MY NAME IS AZZA. I'm a Palestinian filmmaker. My father is from Haifa and my mom is from Nablus. I was born in Jordan, so I grew up in the Palestinian Diaspora. From Jordan I was raised in Lebanon, where I lived until the Israeli invasion of 1982. Then we went back to Jordan. I came here to Palestine only four years ago following the Oslo agreement, which allowed a very small number of Palestinians living outside to return to Palestine. I was one of the lucky ones.

For Palestinians growing up in the Diaspora, Palestine becomes a mystical place. I think that it is important that all myths are visited; it makes you a healthier person. Remember that it was illegal for us to come here before Oslo, and it is still illegal now. Not even the refugees were allowed to return to their houses. So when I had the opportunity to come back, I thought it was something that I definitely should do.

Growing up I imagined that Palestine was heaven. Here you are secure. It is your land, your place. Now that I'm a proper citizen here I'm no longer nostalgic. It is interesting, because Palestine as a space is not as important to me as it used to be. I'm more interested now in the people and the injustice that they live. Palestine is still occupied, and it hurts to see a nation being humiliated again and again and again.

I lived through the civil war in Lebanon, so I know war that is ugly. There you would see the destruction, but you wouldn't actually see humans doing it to other humans. Here, you see the army and you see the victims. When you cross a checkpoint you see an Israeli soldier lining up the Palestinian workers. It's really painful. You can look at the expressions on the workers' faces and you see that they're broken. They're humiliated. There's something in this that I think is even worse than actual war.

Through my work I see lots of things of this type. I've seen mothers who have just lost their children. I've seen people right after their houses have been demolished. I've seen Palestinian workers in the settlements. Many of these workers used to own that land. When it was taken by settlers, they became laborers. Imagine having to be a hired hand like that on your own land. It's terrible.

I think that if you look at my work you will discover how my relationship with this place has slowly changed.

My latest film is called *News Time* and it takes place now, during the second *Intifada*. It is about me trying to assemble a crew to shoot a film, but I can't because everyone is working on the news. Actually, it's funny because our life in Palestine *is* news. What you see on the news is how we live.

When the current *Intifada* began, I started thinking about why. They say it began because of Al-Aqsa, but in my film this is not the reason. There is an eclipse and I take you back to discover that way before Sharon there was *Al Nakba*, the Catastrophe of 1948. It goes back to

1948 and to the refugees. It is not an issue of living in a refugee camp. It is an issue of being dispossessed. In all of my films there is the theme of dispossession.

So I talk about *Al Nakba*, and then about my own childhood in Lebanon. But then I think that this is too depressing, so I start talking about a love story between my neighbors. But when the Israelis start bombing, my neighbors leave the neighborhood, and I'm stuck with an unfinished film. So then I start filming the boys in the neighborhood. Children have become a main part of this *Intifada* because most of the victims are children. So I follow these four children without any political agenda, just to see their daily lives. I think this summarized the whole situation. You see their confusion and their questions: Why is this happening? What is our role in it? The end of the film is very sad because I lose them to the crowd. This is because the situation is so powerful. We no longer remain a neighborhood. We become part of this "big thing."

I think that what is happening is very damaging for our souls as humans. I always hear people saying, "We're worth nothing." You see that people are killed every day. And this person is you. For example, the kids I was filming. Two boys in their class were killed. So it is not something alien. The violence is not happening in some neighborhood far away. This applies to all of Palestinian society. Different sectors, different people; everyone is being hurt. How can we recover? How can we heal later on?

It is humiliating. You saw the picture of the settlers dragging the body of that man in the street. I think that all Palestinians thought, "This is me. This could be me." Any one of us can be in the wrong place at the wrong time and end up being shot and dragged.

I know that there are people being killed from the Israeli side. But think about the ratio. For example, think about car accidents. Car accidents happen all over the world, but if they happen all the time to the same nation, then there is something going on. You can't even compare the number of Palestinian and Israeli dead.

It is like cattle being slaughtered. It is like your life has no value. Think of how many couples wanted to get married at this time and were unable to. Think about children, like the boys I filmed. This is not part of the film, but I know that they have nightmares. These are children! Where do they get their nightmares from? All of their dreams are about people coming to their homes and shooting them. Another thing I noticed among children that scared me is that they feel that there is no protector. It began with the Mohammed Al-Durrah story, but then it escalated. Mohammed Al-Durrah was with his father, and the father could not protect him. But your father should protect you because he is your father and he is the strongest person on earth! When you talk to children now, you always feel this: we're not protected—what's going to happen to us?

So what you've got here is an insecure nation. I think of our image of ourselves. I'm usually very optimistic, but this is just so damaging. To be honest with you, I believe we're going to win in the end just because we're here and we're staying and they can't get rid of us. No system like that has been able to survive on earth. Even apartheid in South Africa collapsed. So I'm not worried about the political situation as much as I'm worried about the process of healing. How many generations of Palestinians do we need before we can be healthy?

Thinking about Jews and the Holocaust, they should know better. They lived with the horror of the Holocaust, and you can still track it today, this collective memory. To be the subject of violence is not an easy thing. It creates this feeling inside. I'm worried about us.

Regarding the process of recovery, first of all the Israelis owe us an apology. It would mean a lot, because it is an historic acknowledgment of what happened and that it shouldn't have happened. I think that from there we can start thinking of coexisting. Mind you, we already coexist at checkpoints and such. But what I mean is a healthy way of thinking about our relationship and ourselves. But in order for this to happen, somebody needs to say sorry.

I think that the Israelis are very scared of acknowledging what happened in 1948 because they think it challenges their whole existence. But I don't think that reality works that way. In New Zealand they apologized to the Maori, and our situation is similar to theirs, or to that of the Native Americans. We're all indigenous populations.

From there it becomes a different process. We have never been given space. For example, the main theme in Palestinian art is usually Palestine, as if it were illegal to talk about anything else. That is because it is the main issue, the main priority. But human lives should never be unidimensional, so this is very unhealthy. Maybe when this whole issue is settled we can start to be self-reflective and think about our own identities and own culture. We need the space to think of new things.

I'll be honest with you. I really wish that I never had to see this much ugliness. And I'm one of the lucky ones. I'm spoiled. I went to private schools all of my life. I've never had financial problems. But even I have seen a lot of blood and death. I would have liked not to have seen this, and to think that it only happens in faraway places. I would have liked to make films about wild life.

I always laugh because liberal Israelis call me and say, "We're looking for Palestinian films that do not talk about the political situation, you know, films that talk about day-to-day life." I laugh because we don't have anything like that. What are they going on about? We don't have day-to-day life apart from the political situation. I *want* to have day-to-day life.

For example, you should watch Palestinian *Candid Camera*. *Candid Camera* is done all over the world, and they did a Palestinian version on Palestinian TV. They want it to be funny, but it is about Palestinians and Israelis. One of the episodes is about a Palestinian guy who is running from the soldiers and he goes from house to house and says, "Can you hide me?" And this is supposed to be funny! The point is that *Candid Camera* is supposed to be about day-to-day life, and this is day-to-day life for us.

I don't think that Israelis understand what is happening here. We know them better than they know us. We watch their TV and we listen to their music. We are workers, which means that we go into their communities. But they don't come into ours.

I see Israelis in film festivals and some are good friends. But when I meet Israelis for the first time, they insist that I must not really be Palestinian. I think that nothing irritates them more than seeing Palestinians producing culture.

What is nice about a creative profession like filmmaking is that it helps you heal. For example, I was angry about settlements, but then I made a film about settlements and in a way did my part. It's a very personal act. I don't believe that films change the world, but it is my own contribution. Like at the beginning of the *Intifada*, when I thought I was going to have a nervous breakdown. The streets were empty, there were only funerals . . . and then suddenly I started filming, and this helped me. So maybe I'm doing it in order to be able to cope. If I lived somewhere else, maybe I would stop making films, I don't know. But now, it really helps.

Saad, helping farmers prune trees in the Northern West Bank

14. SAAD, *agricultural engineer*

Ah my intractable wound!
My country is not a suitcase
I am not a traveler
I am the lover and the land is the beloved

Mahmoud Darwish, Palestinian national poet

ONE LOOK AT THE *rolling hills of the West Bank, and you understand why both Palestinians and Israelis are attached to this land. It was the view of this landscape that got me out of bed to go jogging each morning when I was living in Birzeit. Trotting on a road paved by the PA with Norwegian donations, I would listen to music on* Voice of Palestine *on my Walkman and look out at the seemingly endless valley of olive trees. It certainly was breathtaking, especially the leg of my jog that was straight uphill.*

Land is the crux of the conflict between Israelis and Palestinians. On the eve of the 1948 War, Palestinians owned about 87 percent of Mandate Palestine, and Jews about 6 percent. A full 78 percent was in Israel's possession when the fighting ended, with the remainder falling under its control in 1967. Even after Israel formally withdrew from the most populated Palestinian areas during the peace process, it continued to confiscate tens of thousands of acres of Palestinian farmland for settlements and settler roads.

Israel has claimed possession of Palestinians' water as well as their land. In 1968, the army declared all West Bank and Gaza Strip water resources to be property of the State of Israel. It set quotas limiting Palestinian use and began pumping water from the territories to Israel. Today, approximately one fourth of the water used by Israelis originates in the West Bank or Gaza Strip.

The upshot of these policies is that nearly every year Palestinians suffer water shortages. In fact, the very summer that the negotiators were at Camp David, faucets throughout the West Bank went dry. My friends in Birzeit talked about frantically filling every vessel in the house each time the water came on for a few hours. During the days of dryness that followed, they got along by creating elaborate systems to distinguish between bottles of fresh water for drinking, less fresh water for dish-washing, even less fresh water for laundry, and the rest for flushing the toilet.

During this and other shortages, Palestinian villages that happened to be on the same water lines as neighboring Israeli settlements were fortunate to find their water flow undisrupted. University students who hailed from these villages would go home for the weekend and return newly showered, the envy of their friends. One student who did not have such a respite explained to me that the water crisis made her feel Israel's power in a way that was disturbingly personal and direct. "It reminds you that they control even whether or not you can wash your own body," she said. "When they want to, they can force you to live like an animal."

Since the start of the second **Intifada**, *Israel's policies toward Palestinian natural resources have gone beyond these long-standing norms of control. After two years of* **Intifada**, *the Palestinian Ministry of Agriculture reported that Israel had destroyed over 100,000 acres of Palestinian agricultural land and uprooted some 700,000 trees. In addition, troops have wrecked Palestinian greenhouses, wells, irrigation networks, and agricultural equipment and buildings. Settlers have attacked Palestinian farmers in their fields, leaving dozens dead and hundreds of others too afraid to face the risk involved in collecting their harvest. Produce has rotted on the trees when Israeli closure prevented farmers from reaching their crop, or rotted at checkpoints when the army blocked shipment within or outside of the Occupied*

Territories. In all, the cost to the Palestinian agricultural sector totals in the hundreds of thousands of dollars.

I will not forget the first time I saw an uprooted olive tree in the aftermath of an Israeli bulldozing. Its spindly roots ripped out of the ground, it reminded me of a helpless giant knocked onto its back. And I will not forget the first time I tried to interview a farmer whose olive trees had been uprooted. He was a white-haired man in traditional dress, a farmer and son of farmers from southern Gaza. He wrung his well-callused hands and told me that the Israeli army had bulldozed his property without warning or explanation. Beyond that, he had nothing to say. After five excruciating minutes of searching for something to ask him, I finally turned off the tape recorder and asked if there was anything I could do. As a matter of fact, he said, there was. He had written an appeal for help, and if I translated it to English, perhaps someone from abroad might come to his aid. To this day I do not know if his letter has reached any eyes but my own:

To whom it may concern,

Upon exhausting all other options and finding all doors closed, I am taking this opportunity to address myself to all those with mercy in their hearts. I am the sole provider for my twelve children. On the night of October 28, 2000, Israeli bulldozers razed my farm. They leveled olive trees, orange groves, and the eleven plastic greenhouses in which I grew tomatoes and green peppers. In addition to completely destroying my land, they demolished my house and all of its belongings.

It had taken over thirty years of toil and sacrifice to build this farm. In less than three hours it was all obliterated.

Today my family and I are living in a tent in a Red Cross camp. With neither work nor shelter, I am powerless. From the Palestinian National Authority I have received no more than a package of flour.

We hope in God Almighty and in those who find it within themselves to extend us a helping hand.

God bless you.

Sincerely,
Amer Jaber Barakat Daheer

Accompanying the letter was an inventory of all that had been lost, including three ceiling fans, a gas stove with five burners, two hundred hens, one motorized sprinkler, and almost three acres of land. Attached were Polaroid snapshots of his children holding the carcasses of some of their rabbits that had been buried alive in the rubble.

Given the enormous economic, environmental, and political gravity of Israel's policies toward Palestinian land and water, I figured that I had better consult an expert in order to make sense of it all. And so I paid a visit to the Palestinian Agricultural Relief Committees (PARC), a nongovernmental organization seeking to promote sustainable rural development in the Occupied Territories.

Founded in 1983 by a group of concerned agronomists volunteering technical advice to poor farmers, PARC has since grown to sponsor an array of projects from reforestation to the building of water cisterns. As three fourths of all Palestinians engaged in agriculture are women, one of PARC's largest undertakings is its Rural Women's Empowerment Project. This venture provides women with vocational training, small-business loans, and assistance in supervising their own savings and credit programs.

Since the outbreak of the Intifada, PARC has had to temper its long-term projects with crisis services designed to meet rural Palestinians' urgent needs. It has carried out emergency construction projects to provide work for the newly unemployed, distributed seeds for home gardens in an effort to help families achieve food security, and helped open hundreds of miles of agricultural roads in order to connect villages cut off by the Israeli closure.

I visited PARC's Ramallah headquarters in order to interview Saad, an agricultural engineer. Searching for his office, I never imagined that during Israel's first reincursion into the West Bank a year later, Israeli troops would storm this very building and station snipers on the roof. Soldiers entered and ransacked PARC's offices, leaving about $60,000 of damage in their wake. Like the half dozen other environmental and human rights organizations whose offices were invaded during the reincursion, PARC gradually repaired its walls and equipment and reopened its doors. Three months later, when troops returned to the streets of Ramallah, the PARC office was invaded yet another time.

All of this was still unthinkable, however, when I met Saad. Raised in a family that tended the land, he was the head of PARC's Plant Division and an impassioned proponent of organic farming. Halfway through our conversation the phone rang and he answered in Russian. "My wife wants me to pick something up on the way home," he said in response to my look of confusion. He added that he gone to college on scholarship in the Soviet Union. He had met his wife, a Bolivian national, in an organic chemistry class, and they had returned to the West Bank together.

A soft-spoken and gentle person, Saad struck me as someone more accustomed to speaking about plants than politics. Nonetheless, as he talked it became clear that, in the Palestinian situation, it is difficult to separate the two.

•◆• •◆• •◆•

MY NAME IS SAAD. For the last ten years I've worked as the head of the Plant Production Division in a nongovernmental organization called the Palestinian Agricultural Relief Committees.

I was seventeen years old when my father taught me how to take a piece of an existing olive tree and use it to plant a new tree. I left to study agricultural engineering abroad when I was nineteen and returned six years later. I remember that when I got back, I didn't leave the house for two full days. On the third day, I left the house and walked four miles to see those trees again. I went on foot because there aren't any roads in the area where I grew up, and my brother came with me. When we finally arrived at the trees I said, "That's enough. I'm happy now. We can turn back now." My brother didn't understand, and I explained that these were the trees that I had planted when I was seventeen. There they were, and I was proud of them.

There is another kind of olive tree that we call a Roman tree because of its old age. My father taught me how to prune them. The first Roman tree I ever pruned was so big that it took me almost half a day. Later, during the harvest, my brother and sister climbed the tree to pick off the olives. But then they started playing around and walking along the branches. A branch broke and I got so angry that I yelled at them to go home. I couldn't stand the idea that a single branch would fall.

This *Intifada* has been as hard on farmers as on everyone else. Almost all the villages were under closure during the olive harvest, and farmers couldn't reach the olive groves or the olive presses. So olive-oil production took a real hit. On top of that, the closure prevented wholesalers from traveling to the villages, so there wasn't even a guaranty that farmers would be able to sell the oil that they produced. In normal times we export a surplus of fifteen thousand tons of olive oil a year. But all of that stopped this year because of the closure.

The same problems go for other crops as well. For example, the roads are closed, so the farmers in Jericho can't transport their produce. All of the vegetables produced in Jericho are just stuck there. The cost of one kilo of tomatoes in Jericho should be about $1, but now there are so many tomatoes there that you can buy fifteen kilos for that price. Meanwhile, in the other cities they don't have enough vegetables. So prices have risen everywhere else in the West Bank.

The closure affects shepherds, too. They can't move their animals from one place to another to graze. And they can't bring fodder from abroad for their livestock.

The closure also affects those of us who work in agricultural associations trying to support farmers. All of our programs have been profoundly affected. We haven't been able to plow the land for our land-renovation project. Our agricultural consultants can't reach farmers in order to provide them with assistance.

For example, we run a program that trains agricultural engineers who have just graduated from college. We've been training a group of thirty-two engineers in Jenin for nine months. The trainers are from Ramallah, Jerusalem, and Bethlehem, and they haven't been able to travel to Jenin. So we've been forced to suspend the program.

The army has also uprooted thousands of trees, bulldozing whole acres to the ground. The uprooting of just one olive tree costs a farmer about $700. When you plant a new tree, it takes five years before it produces anything, and then another five years before it reaches the level of production of a mature tree. So the losses stem not only from the loss of the tree itself, but also from the loss of years of production.

The farmers work all day every day, knowing that the army or the settlers could destroy their crops at any moment. And for us, the trees are more than just trees. Olive trees represent the symbol of our existence, our culture, our identity. All of our folk songs are about olive trees and the olive harvest. For Palestinian farmers, all the important events in life are connected to the olive harvest. A farmer has to wait until the harvest before he can build a house or marry off his son or send his child to study abroad. Now, during the *Intifada*, he must stand there and watch how easily this source of life, the olive tree, gets uprooted and swept away. Can you imagine the suffering of that person? The symbol of his culture and identity—his very presence—is under attack. And there's nothing he can do about it. It's no simple loss.

Every olive tree has a story that connects it to the life of its owner.

Old people are always saying things like, "I was sitting under the olive tree when so-and-so came to us and we ate under the tree." My own father planted a tree for each of my brothers and sisters and me when we were born. He would say to us, "I planted this tree when your mother was pregnant" or "This is the tree where your grandmother and I sat together."

And then the army comes on sweeping campaigns and claims that the olive trees pose a threat to security.

On top of all of this, there are other abuses from the army. In a village in the Jenin region, one farmer came across the Israeli army on his way back from pressing olives. They stopped the car and made him pour out half a ton of oil before he was allowed to go along his way.

But the settlers are the worst. They do whatever they want. They've burned greenhouses, destroyed irrigation networks, and damaged fields. Farmers are afraid for their lives. One fifty-year-old woman was simply gathering figs on her own land when settlers came and killed her. There are cases of farmers and their entire families spending the whole day harvesting the olives. At sunset, just as they are about to head home, the settlers come and kick them out of the fields, ordering them to leave the olives behind.

Israeli settlers have done a lot of damage during this *Intifada*. But "settler" isn't the right word anyway. They don't live on settlements. Those things are colonies. A settlement is when a person goes to live in a place that doesn't belong to anybody else. A colony is built on land that has been taken by force from its original owners.

These colonies have an enormous negative impact on Palestinian farmers and the agricultural sector as a whole. First, the colonies are built on mountaintops, covering up the area where the rain falls and decreasing the amount of water that is available for farmers to use. Second, when Israelis build settlements they don't just confiscate the land where they construct houses and buildings; they also confiscate the surrounding fields. This land is the source of livelihood for Palestinian farmers, and they are being prevented from making full and proper use of it. Third, many colonies cause environmental problems because they're not connected to the sewage system. Their waste just drains down and contaminates the springs and rivers. The dirty water has killed many trees and polluted the water sources on which many Palestinian villages depend. Fourth, there is the issue of the roads that have been paved to connect the settlements. Tens of thousands of hectares have been destroyed for these roads. In order to build a bypass road for twenty-five settlers, Israel destroys thousands of hectares of land that had been the livelihood of farmers and their families. On top of that, when the Israelis want to open a road they cut a mountain in half. This has destroyed the footpaths that farmers use to reach their lands, forcing them to make detours. A trip that used to take minutes may now take hours. Finally, the presence of these colonies is very painful for farmers on a psychological level. Imagine what it is like to have someone come and take your land, and then you have to look at your stolen property every day.

The army and the settlers use any means at their disposal to make our lives difficult, even water. Water is a huge problem here. The average Palestinian consumes less than one fourth of the water consumed by each Israeli settler. Israel confiscates 80 percent of the water that should be for Palestinian use and gives it to the colonies and their residents. In the Israeli media they say that we misuse our water. How can it be that we are using our water poorly when they consume more than four times the amount that we do? Every summer we have water crises. In my village we typically have no water for a month or a month and a half during the summer. None at all. Even the main Palestinian cities will go without water for human consumption. If we just had rights to our own water, none of this would happen.

Meanwhile, the houses in the colonies have watered gardens and swimming pools. They grow water-intensive crops like cotton and use water-intensive technology like hydroponic irrigation. They consume as much water as they like, and we don't even have as much water as we need.

Our population is growing, and we need water to increase the productivity of the land. In the future we won't have enough for either drinking or farming. We're searching for new sources and trying to boost our existing sources, but we're forbidden from using the water that belongs to us. We try to make full use of the natural springs. We try to build greenhouses and pools to collect water in the winter. But all of this is prohibited. They even prohibit us from digging wells to catch the rainfall.

All of this is forbidden because the Israelis say so. They don't need any law to explain why it is prohibited. It just is. There is just one law and that is the law of occupation.

This *Intifada* has had an impact on me personally as well. In 1999, I developed an idea. My plan was to resign from my job at PARC and start my own agricultural project. I thought that I could buy some cows, sheep, rabbits, and chickens and build my own farm. I also know how to keep bees, so I would have beehives as well. I can't do all of this work alone, so my thought was to have two or three workers. They could bring their families and I would bring my family and we could all live together.

This would be enough to survive. It would be a small farm, but a special one. It would be a self-sufficient, organic farm. I visited farms like this in Europe, and I wanted to create something similar in the village where I grew up, near Jenin.

This was my plan for the year 2000. I was ready to take my family, leave life here in the city, and return to nature. Then the *Intifada* started, and everything has had to be delayed. I still hope that I will be able to build this farm someday.

I urge the American people to see the situation from both sides, not only the Israeli side. I don't understand how Americans, who live by the slogan of freedom, can see everything Palestinians do to liberate themselves from occupation as terrorism. We encourage Americans to come here and see what's really going on, to compare our situation to that of the Israelis; to see who is the occupier and who is the occupied, who is suffering and who is engaging in repression. The sum total of all the weapons possessed by Palestinians is less than those in the settlement of Ariel alone. We are a people who want to live like everyone else. We want to build our state. We, too, should be able to raise our flag, just as the Americans do.

Iman, in Hebron

15 . IMAN, *college student*

IT WAS IN HEBRON *that I learned that if you are going to record interviews on a cheap tape recorder, at the very least you have to use good batteries.*

*I interviewed five people in one jam-packed day in Hebron, each one with a
story more remarkable than the last. My first visit was to Najwa, a nurse and
mother of five whose home had repeatedly been hit by shelling. Her son showed
me his collection of bullets that had come through their window, identifying the
caliber of each. Her daughter demonstrated how the whole family piled into the
hallway that had proven to be the only safe place in which to sleep at night.*

*I then met with Shakir, who lived next door to Kiryat Arba, the settlement
that continued to honor the grave of its late resident, Baruch Goldstein. Since
arriving in 1971, the settlers had been relentless in their efforts to intimidate
Shakir's family into abandoning their property. Although one of his children
had suffered a breakdown as a result, he had nowhere else to go.*

*Then I met Hanna, whose house in the Old City was sandwiched between an
Israeli military base and a settlement. Imposition of curfew had forced her to
choose between being trapped at home in her Israeli-controlled neighborhood
or continuing her work as a hairdresser in a beauty parlor located in the part
of the city under Palestinian authority. In order to save her family's only source
of income, she had left home and started sleeping in the beauty parlor. Weeks
had passed without her being able to see her family, under curfew just a few
blocks away.*

*From there I met Hisham, a human-rights activist who attributed his sur-
vival past infancy to serendipity. When the 1967 War began, Hisham's*

family fled to Jordan for fear of a repeat of the expulsions and killings of 1948. Hisham was born there on the last day of fighting. At that time, Israeli troops often shot at Palestinians who snuck back to the West Bank. Yearning to return home, Hisham's family decided to take the risk. They crossed the Jordan River by foot and made it to where clandestine Palestinian taxis waited on the other side. They approached the first car, but the other passengers were afraid that the baby Hisham would cry and attract the soldiers' attention, and thus refused to allow them to ride along. Hisham's family left in another taxi shortly thereafter. A few miles down the road they passed the first car, and saw that everyone inside had been killed. In a twist of fate, Hisham's family made it back to Hebron, where he has lived ever since.

Lastly, I met Taysir. After studying medicine in Europe, he had returned to invest his life savings in the construction of a four-story building in Hebron's Old City. On the first floor he built a fully equipped clinic, and on the other floors he built apartments for his family and those of his brother and sister. When the second Intifada *began the Israeli army seized its roof as a military outpost and observation deck. Such was his reward for having built one of the tallest buildings in the area. His protest letters amounting to naught, Taysir was powerless to stop the soldiers as they established an encampment where his children had once played and three families' worth of laundry had dried in the sun. By the time I visited Taysir, his clinic had long been collecting dust, his stairwell was wrecked, and his yard was filled with the trash that the soldiers tossed from the roof. A prisoner in his own house, he could do no more than beseech the soldiers to stop making noise so that his children could sleep at night.*

I could hardly believe what I saw in Hebron. And when I got back to Birzeit, I could hardly believe what I heard. My five tapes were nothing more than one long stream of static. My batteries had been low the whole day, the tape recorder had not picked up a thing, and I had been too engrossed in people's stories to notice.

"Aren't there machines that can pick up the voices?" I asked every journalist I knew. They all laughed and told me to let it go. Reluctantly, I did so. After all,

if Taysir had lost his house and Shakir his peace of mind, then I could cope with the loss of my recordings.

Still, I wanted an interview with someone who could talk about Hebron, the divided city that some saw as a microcosm of the Israeli-Palestinian conflict at large. Then I thought of Iman.

I had met Iman on a student hiking trip in the Jericho Valley. A native Hebronite and a senior at Birzeit University, she had caught my attention by coming to hike the desert canyon in high-heeled platform boots. She again piqued my curiosity when we broke for lunch later that day. While I had packed a single sandwich for myself, she had lugged along dessert for the whole group. I remember watching as she pulled a ceramic dish, a knife, and napkins out of her backpack, followed by an entire bunt cake wrapped in tin foil. Navigating the rocks in her high-heeled boots, she graciously served us each a piece.

I had thought then that Iman was someone special. Later I was to learn the extent of it. Her father had been in exile or prison for most of her childhood, and her brother was the youngest person killed in the 1994 massacre at the Ibrahimi Mosque. Their family's home had been demolished during the first Intifada on the pretext that it lacked a building permit. Strikingly reflective and resolutely political, Iman was the first person in her family to go to college. She had chosen to major in psychology in the hope of understanding the grief that tormented all of the people she loved.

Iman obligingly agreed to speak with me about Hebron and her life in general. I met her on campus, careful to buy fresh batteries along the way.

·•· ··•· ·•·

MY NAME IS IMAN. I'm twenty-one years old. I'm from Hebron.

The situation in Hebron is really volatile, and we have no protection whatsoever. There are Jewish settlers in the heart of town, which is where you have to go shopping and run errands. We try to avoid getting involved with the settlers, but we always find ourselves in one bad situation after another.

When you're going home at night, you can get beaten by the settlers or by the soldiers themselves. Once we were passing near a park, and they let their dogs out and made them chase us. Another time my mother and I were out walking and a settler lady stopped us. She spit on us and then just walked off. And then there are the settlers' children. They'll follow you on the street and try to provoke you, just because.

We have to take all of this, and we're not supposed to say a thing. If we do they can accuse us of trying to kill them. Or maybe they'll shoot at us from one of the high buildings. So we just have to accept it. We have to swallow what we hear. We have no right to react.

In Hebron, you're not even safe when you go to pray. Not after the massacre in the Ibrahimi Mosque.

That was almost seven years ago, but even now I remember all of the smallest details. It was a day during the month of Ramadan. My father decided that he wanted to take us to pray at the Ibrahimi Mosque. He was working as a laborer inside Israel at the time, and he took a day off from work in order to take my brothers and me to the mosque.

You know what happened after that. My oldest brother and I decided not to go because we weren't feeling well. So my Dad went with my two other brothers. And he came back home with only one of them.

I cannot forget the way that I found out that my brother had been killed. I was fixing up the house when two people came and placed his body in front of us. I had no idea who this person could be. I never imagined that he was my brother. I had just seen my brother leave to go pray moments beforehand. He was only thirteen years old. He was one year younger than I was, and we were practically twins.

I didn't cry. Instead, I was just overcome with dizziness. Then it came time to look at him for the last time and say good-bye. Later I found some of his blood on my hands.

I will never forget these details. I remember the look on my father's face and on my mother's face. I remember where blood stained the ground.

Coping with my brother's death has been very difficult for each of us in the family. My father feels guilty. He feels that it is his fault that my brother died. My mother has become very agitated. She has started to pray and fast more than she did before. Sometimes she blames my Dad for what happened. My older brothers are always fighting with each other.

But it is my younger brother and sister who have suffered the most. My little brother Amin, is now very frightened of the mosque in Hebron. He is even afraid to pray, although he is old enough to start praying. He says that people who pray get killed. My sister Alya, is the same way. She doesn't speak with anyone. And sometimes she gets very upset and anxious.

The situation at home is always tense. Our whole family is on edge, and we don't know how to deal with one another anymore. Our relationships with each other should be warm and positive, but instead there are so many problems separating us. Like yesterday when I spoke with my mother on the phone. She told me that maybe I'll come back home from school and find that the terrible feeling that hangs in our home has finally killed her.

I am agitated, too. But I try to adjust to the situation around me. Now when a settler comes to say something to me on the street, I'm prepared. I know that regardless of what I do I could get killed. I know this for sure. It doesn't matter whether I am being violent with them or not. My brother wasn't using violence. He was only praying when they killed him.

You have to be prepared, and you have to know by heart exactly which area is under Palestinian control and which one is under occupation. It's not easy because there isn't a clear boundary. The dividing line cuts through the city all over the place. In fact, the line runs right through our house. It sounds crazy but it's true. Half of our house is under the control of the Palestinian Authority and the other half is under Israeli control.

I remember the first time I returned to Hebron after they divided it in 1997. I was still not completely familiar with which parts were controlled by the Israelis and which were Palestinian. I was coming home from the university to visit my parents. A settler had just been killed and his wife injured.

I got to Hebron and reached a street near the market. Many people were out, the market was busy, and life seemed normal. That was the Palestinian Authority area. I kept walking in the direction of my house, and suddenly there was nobody on the street anymore. There were a lot of stones on the ground. Can you imagine? Half the street is packed with people and the other half is totally empty.

It had been a long time since I'd been able to come back home to Hebron, so the situation was new to me. I was really confused. As I approached the next street I asked someone, "Is it OK for me to cross?" He told me it was no problem. So I kept going.

I crossed, and it turned out that I was approaching the Israeli-controlled section of town. The Israelis were restricting the area, of course, and they had a big iron door at the entrance of the street. Israeli soldiers were stationed there, and one of them yelled at me, "Where are you going?" I told him that I was going to my parents' house. He asked me what my family name was, and I told him. He said "OK, that is correct. Your family lives here." And he gave me permission to go through. So they know about all the Palestinian families and where each one lives.

When I was about halfway home some settlers spotted me. Some of their kids started calling to each other, saying "An Arab! An Arab!" I heard this and knew it meant, "Look, there's an Arab. Come and hit her." They started throwing things at me and then came running toward me. I didn't know what to do. I thought it was over for me. Fortunately, the soldiers kept them away and told me to run.

So I hurried back to the Palestinian area. Meanwhile the commanding officer at the gate had changed. The new officer saw me and asked what I was doing. I told him that I had just entered the area, but he didn't believe me. He told me that he knew that I was really coming from the Palestinian section and trying to enter the Israeli section. My house was back in the direction where the settler kids had started chasing me. I had to return there in order to get home. But the soldiers refused to allow me to go back.

I kept going around and around in circles. I did everything I could to get out of there, but I just didn't know how. I didn't know where the Palestinian area ended and the Israeli area began. I was so tired because I was lugging my bag with everything that I had brought from school. The settlers kept yelling at me the whole time, and I didn't know anyone in that neighborhood who could help me.

In the end, I spent about an hour and fifteen minutes going from one soldier to another. Finally, one of the soldiers told me, "I'll give you five minutes and then I don't want to see you here again . . . or else!" When I told the soldier that I didn't know where I was going, he told me that I was lying and made me stand against a wall.

I started to cry because I was so tired. The soldier started mocking me. He pushed me and asked me what my name was and where I was from. I was just so exhausted that I told him that I didn't know. Then a Palestinian woman appeared. She was coming from the hospital and had permission to pass through to the Israeli-controlled section. The soldier told her to take me with her, and I went.

What I'm saying is that I don't believe all Jews are bad. Look at the differences in their behavior. One of the soldiers wanted to hit me. Another one, who was stationed near the mosque, tried to calm me down. He even gave me tissues to wipe my tears.

You know, in the past I wouldn't have minded if Jews lived here with us in peace. After all, Jews lived in Mecca with the prophet Mohammed. But now they are coming here to throw us out. This is especially the case with the Orthodox groups that feel that Palestinians have no right to this land at all.

They have come and planted a fight here and we have come to hate them. I feel like I'm being besieged from all sides. In Hebron, settlers walk around carrying very sophisticated weapons. At the same time, if the Israelis find a Palestinian carrying a weapon, they put him in prison immediately.

There have to be some equal rules here. In some areas the Israelis don't even allow us to build. At the mosque they make you go through a full inspection before they let you go in and pray. It's so humiliating. Imagine. I wash and get ready to pray, and then a soldier comes and does a body search on me.

I really hope that one day I can live without this torture. I just don't want to have to deal with the Israelis anymore. After all the killing that has taken place, it is going to be impossible for us to live side by side with them. Still, my ultimate goal is peace. I want this very much. I try to be optimistic and believe that Abu Ammar will negotiate with the Israelis and everything will turn out OK.[1]

My family suffered tremendously during the first *Intifada,* too. My father used to work in Jordan. He was a member of *Fatah* and trained with *Tanzim*. When he came back to Palestine the Israelis said that *Tanzim* had confessed to crimes against Israel. So they arrested him and

1 Abu Ammar is the commonly used nickname for Yasser Arafat.

put him in prison for two years. This left my oldest brother to become responsible for the family. But then he was also imprisoned several times. Once they put him in jail for six months because they said that he had thrown a stone. He was released, but later he was put in jail again for another three months.

My brother was tortured a lot in prison. Now he is terribly thin and weak, and his face is always very pale. In prison the soldiers used to hit Palestinians in the knees with their guns, or would just stand on their kneecaps. My brother's knees continue to hurt him a lot, even today. The soldiers would also stand on his stomach, or put out cigarettes in the palms of his hands, or force him to stay standing up for several days in a row. This is why his health is so bad today.

My father went through the same thing when he was in prison. Now he can't work anymore. His stomach is always hurting him because of the food that he had to eat while he was in prison. His back and legs ache because of the ways he was tortured.

I imagine that no one who enters Israeli prison comes out with a sound body.

Today my brother has a hard time dealing with people. He got married but he couldn't get along with his wife. After just six months they got divorced. He has become an extremely anxious, nervous person. He gets upset at even the tiniest word.

My father is similar. There has been a wall between him and the rest of us since he was released from prison. There is so much distance separating us from him. Sometimes it doesn't feel like he's really our father.

There are so many difficulties in our lives. Sometimes you feel like you want to run away from reality. We just keep holding on until we reach the point where we can't endure it any longer.

And we've all suffered during this *Intifada*, too. As a people, we are both dead and alive at the same time. Even children feel it. They're always sad. They watch other kids on TV throwing stones and they say that they want to go throw stones, too. They don't realize what the consequences could be.

TV is filled with news about funerals and bombings, so I don't watch it anymore. I don't even listen to the radio because they just play nationalistic songs and news about those who've been killed. I've started listening to Israeli stations instead, because they don't broadcast bad news.

I tell myself that I can't surrender. I have to cope with the situation and give my support to those who have lost loved ones and homes.

But I also have to live. It's hard. For example, one day a student brought a cake to the university to celebrate his birthday. Those days the news was filled with stories about all the Palestinians who were being killed. The other students couldn't believe that he wanted to celebrate at a time like that. We were all talking about it, but then one of the professors told us to stop. He said that this person was committed to carrying on with life, and we should respect that.

Sometimes I feel that it is selfish to be a student when so many people are suffering. At the same time, I need to graduate so I can be of service to my people. I want to go on to graduate school, but I'm not sure if that will be possible, given my family's economic situation. I have to work to help them.

And I also feel that there is a cause that is more important: Palestine. We can't just rely on Abu Ammar to do everything for us. Each one of us has his own duty. We must look beyond our own personal problems. We have to stand together and do something to get our freedom. It is when we act as one that we can make a difference.

Shaaban, in the tourist sector of the Old City in Jerusalem

16. SAMI AND SHAABAN, *shop owners*

WHEN I MOVED TO *Gaza City in June 2001 I looked at several apartments before splurging for one a few blocks from the Mediterranean coast. My excitement about my first taste of beachfront property ended in the wee hours of the morning, however, when I was rattled awake by the sound of construction on the roof. After days of the same, I confessed to the clerk at the corner shop that had I known about the construction, I would have chosen another apartment. He laughed and explained that had I chosen another apartment, there never would have been any construction. My landlord had begun building a new top story years ago, but had stopped due to lack of funds. The very day I appeared with a month's rent, he resumed.*

This, it seemed to me, represented something of the stalled Palestinian economy at large. Throughout the West Bank and Gaza Strip I met men and women with big ideas and an eagerness to create. The problem was that opportunities for industrious people to pursue their ambitions—like an American tenant in Gaza—were the exception to the rule.

According to Harvard University political economist Sara Roy, Israeli policies in the Palestinian territories have been designed to promote not development, but "de-development."[1] From the early years of the occupation, Israel regulated trade to secure a captive Palestinian market for Israeli goods while blocking the entry into Israel of Palestinian products that could compete with Israeli ones. Although

1 Sara Roy, *The Gaza Strip: The Political Economy of De-Development* (Institute for Palestine Studies, 1995)

legally responsible for the well being of the population under its administration, the occupation government neither made meaningful investment in Palestinian infrastructure nor permitted such investment from outside sources.

It was widely believed that the peace process would bring economic improvement. As Roy explains, the opposite occurred:

> *Arguably, at no time since the beginning of Israeli occupation in 1967 had the Palestinian economy been as weak and its people as vulnerable as during the seven Oslo years. . . . During the Oslo period, the economic fundamentals of occupation remained unchanged. Israel retained full control over the Palestinian economy by virtue of its control of key factors of production—land, water, labor, and capital—and of external (and in the West Bank, internal) borders. Furthermore, Israel continued, almost wholly unchallenged, to engage in practices that further dispossessed Palestinians of their lands, their homes, and their livelihoods.[2]*

Compounding these long-standing elements of de-development, the Oslo years also saw the introduction of a new shackle on Palestinians' economic possibilities: an unprecedented stranglehold on freedom of movement. Before the peace process, people and goods traveled within and between the Occupied Territories with relative ease. Six months before the signing of the Declaration of Principles, however, Israel implemented "general closure," a system of checkpoints and prolonged searches at border crossings. Israel could stiffen this policy at will, declaring "internal closure," which further restricted movement within the West Bank, or "total closure," which completely prohibited Palestinians from leaving the towns in which they lived. A decade after the imposition of general closure, it had yet to be lifted once.

---

2 Sara Roy, "Palestinian Society and Economy: The Continued Denial of Possibility," *Journal of Palestine Studies*, Vol. 30, No. 4 (Summer 2001).

Largely due to closure, real GNP in the Occupied Territories declined by 20 percent from late 1992 to late 1997, with per capita GNP dropping nearly 40 percent. When Israel eased the closure in 1998 and 1999, GNP began to grow immediately. Nonetheless, the recovery fell far short as compensation for the harm that closure had already inflicted upon the Palestinian economy. Closure obstructed Palestinian exports and the import of both consumer goods and materials needed for construction and manufacturing. It also stifled trade between the West Bank and Gaza Strip, cutting both areas off from Jerusalem. Before the imposition of closure in 1993, half of the goods produced in Gaza were marketed in the West Bank. By 1995, the number had dropped to 8 percent. Where closure did not block movement altogether it distorted outlay such that 35 percent of production costs were spent on transport, three times more than any regional world average. In addition to its impediment on trade, closure severely limited the number of Palestinian laborers allowed inside Israel. This signified a nosedive in the income upon which hundreds of thousands of Palestinian families had come to depend, especially in poverty-stricken Gaza.

In spite of its advances in the building of public infrastructure, the Palestinian Authority aggravated many of the economic weaknesses that it inherited. According to Roy, the PA's heavy-handed control of the market stifled the growth of the private sector and its failure to institute rule of law scared away investors. Its distribution of opportunities on the basis of personal connections and political loyalty gave rise to a new class of elites who, in alliance with Israeli security officials and contractors, created their own monopolies in key sectors. As the poor got poorer, the rich built large villas and opened foreign bank accounts. With the advent of the peace process, patronage politics and corruption became the norm in the Palestinian territories as throughout the developing world.

The result of these multiple economic distortions was that Palestinian living standards were higher on the eve of the Oslo process than on the eve of its collapse. At present, the Palestinian economy is at an all-time low that worsens by the day. When the Intifada began, about 20 percent of Palestinians were under the poverty line of $2 a day. By the time that it ended its second year, the number had risen to 75 percent. During the same period, unemployment tripled *to over half the workforce, with losses of $3 million daily. In addition to income losses are the losses stemming from the destruction of homes, land, and both public and private property. Israel's damage of Palestinian infrastructure totaled $350 million from the eruption of hostilities until the reinvasion of the West Bank in March 2002. During that reincursion, Israel demolished another $361 million's worth of property in a single month.*

Despite the enormity of this destruction, the main source of economic crisis in the Palestinian territories remains their slow and steady strangulation by closure. As the Director of the World Bank in the West Bank and Gaza put it:

> *If the closures are lifted, the Palestinian economy will recover. If closures persist or intensify, the economy will eventually unravel. Public services will break down. Unemployment and poverty rates will continue to climb. Helplessness, deprivation and hatred will increase, and this unique chance for reconciliation will pass.* [3]

That the Palestinian economy continues to operate at all seems a function of individuals' creativity in developing nonviolent ways of defying the blockage of freedom of movement. I heard stories about villagers trudging clandestine paths through the hills of the West Bank in order to reach the city, and about truck drivers bribing Israeli soldiers in order to get shipments of strawberries out of Gaza. I met a manager at a granite company that, in a desperate attempt to transport its materials to harbor, used its own cranes to remove unguarded Israeli road barricades in the middle of the night. It would replace the concrete barriers upon clearing the path for its trucks such that the shift of soldiers arriving the next morning would never know what had happened.

3 The World Bank, "Fifteen Months—Intifada, Closures and Palestinian Economic Crisis" (the Assessment), available online:http://lnweb18.worldbank.org/mna/mena.nsf/61abe956d3c23df38525680b00775b5e/81299af1b1220c528525680e0071d721?OpenDocument

This capacity to adapt aside, evidence of economic suffering remains everywhere you look in the Palestinian territories. In Gaza, one sees refugees lining up for United Nations rations of flour and rice, their main source of nutrition. In the West Bank, one sees boys selling anything from coffee to clothing to the people walking through checkpoints—perhaps acting as the only wage earners in their families. And, in the tourist sector of the old city of Jerusalem, one sees hardly anything at all.

The near evaporation of tourism since the outbreak of hostilities has been devastating for Palestinians and Israelis alike. In the hope of gaining some insight into how merchants were coping with the economic ramifications, I visited the empty souvenir shops of the Arab quarter. I entered one large shop and found an abundance of leather briefcases, hand-painted ceramics, and trinkets designed for visitors of every religion, but not a customer in sight. When I asked Sami, the tall, thin shop-owner, if I could ask him a few questions, he obliged. Before long we were joined by Shaaban, the owner of a shop farther down the winding cobblestone road. Sami and Shaaban willingly put aside their newspapers in order to talk to me, both mumbling something about this being the most business they had seen all day.

•✦•   •✦•   •✦•

Sami

My name is Sami. I'm a merchant and shop owner. I've lived in this country nearly all my life. I've been living in Jerusalem and the West Bank since the occupation began.

For those of us in business, the most difficult and draining thing about the *Intifada* is its economic aspect. Those of us in the tourist sector have suffered a lot, even before the *Intifada* began. The Israeli tour guides don't let customers come to the Arab parts of the city. They take them to Ben Yehuda Street or to Bethlehem, where they get a 30-percent commission to take tourists to just a few select shops. That way nobody else gets any business. When the *Intifada* began, most of the merchants had to leave their businesses and go work as waiters in Israeli restaurants or garbage collectors or something. The businessman is no longer a businessman. He gets no respect.

The first *Intifada* ruined us merchants. It left us broke. When my grandfather owned this shop we had ten employees. Today I've had to hire some guy who doesn't even know how to put three words together to greet people.

Then the first *Intifada* ended and they started what they called the "peace talks." There were some positive results. What we had saved in the seventies we invested in the eighties, and hoped everything would work out. But then in 1995 and 1996 the bus bombings started and tourism in the area was destroyed again.

We kept on moving toward destruction, and that's what led to this current *Intifada*. What we have now is complete destruction. There's not a single store here that has any business. I had to divide my shop in two so I could rent out half of it. But now I can't even rent it. In the end there's only one option in this part of the Old City: either we close our shops altogether and go home, or we just keep on like this, silent and doing nothing.

Unfortunately, nobody is listening to us. There is just no income. If someone sells $10's worth of merchandise in one day, he is like Superman. That's a really good day.

We're asking for just one thing: for the Israelis to exempt us from paying property taxes. We don't want anything more. We don't want to be millionaires. We just want to stay here in this country and live with dignity.

The situation is a total disaster. Psychologically, people are destroyed. The average merchant sits all day thinking about how he can bring a little money home to support his children. How can I pay the shop's expenses? I told the accountant, I'm not ready. I have no income whatsoever. Zero. How can I pay income taxes to Israel on top of everything else? I'm practically suffocating. I can't pay, not this year. I owe 60,000 shekels. That's $15,000 dollars. Where am I going to get the money? And my situation is better than that of a lot of other people.

During Ramadan, Orient House gave each merchant 1,000 shekels in assistance.[4] The merchants went and took the money, but I don't want any handouts. As long as I'm able, I have to work. I'm not asking for the impossible. All I ask is for a simple lifting of the property tax and the repressive conditions that are imposed on us. Those who have money should still pay. But those who are struggling to make a living in the destroyed tourism sector should be exempted.

I've been working here in the tourist sector for twenty-three years, and I can tell you that the situation has never been as bad as it is right now. My five brothers used to work here with me, but when the Intifada began I told them, "Forget it, there's no use." Everyone left tourism and went to seek a living in his own way. Now I'm alone. I never used to just sit here and read Maariv. Now I just sit and waste my time. Every so often I look at the clock.

You can see that all the shop owners just play backgammon all the time. I told them that we should hold an international backgammon competition because we could win big. You'll see that everyone acts happy when someone wins. They all clap because they're boiling inside and they need something to take their minds off the trouble.

I live in Kufr Aqab, where a lot of clashes take place. There's an Israeli military camp there and there are always the frightening sounds of shelling. They bombed the whole area about two weeks ago.

I have five children, and every day when I go home, all I can think about is the shop. When I go to the shop, all I can think about is the kids. Maybe they'll come back from school alive, maybe they won't. What might happen to them? In our apartment we can hear the sounds

---

4 Orient House is the office of the PLO's representative in East Jerusalem.

of stones being thrown. I don't know . . . maybe my son is involved. I listen to the news. This happened in an area that is near my house, or that happened in an area close to my kids' school. I worry about this kind of thing day and night.

The first thing that I did when the *Intifada* started was tell my kids to turn off the TV. I wanted to make sure that they didn't see the news because the scenes are really horrific. During the first few days my youngest daughter, who is five years old, told me, "Daddy, I saw someone on TV, and his hand was blown off." How will this affect her when she grows up? She is really scared. Whenever there is a noise or shooting by the house, my daughter gets scared. I have to tell her, "Sweetie, don't go out to play in the parking lot or the park." What if something happens to her while she is outside?

My daughter knows that I have to cross a checkpoint to get home. She asks me, "Daddy, the soldiers didn't see you, did they?" She's so afraid. All of this has a big effect on kids' psyches.

As a resident of Jerusalem, I can tell you that Jerusalem is totally closed off. Ramallah, Hebron, Bethlehem, they're all blocked off. I can't go and check up on my daughters who are married in other cities, or on my other relatives, even though it is a religious requirement to visit relatives on the holiday. Twice a year one must go to his family and tell them, "May you be well for the coming year." But this year I just could not go and face the danger. This year is the first time that I didn't go and visit my family. What I'm going through here is enough. My psyche can't take any more than this. We've all become ill in this country. We need six hundred psychiatrists to cure everyone. We're addicted to the news, and soon we'll all be on Prozac. If anyone said to you, "I am not sick about all this," he's crazy.

All I can say is, "Please God, bring some good."

We only want one thing: for the world to support peace for the Palestinian people. We are disciples of peace, not warmongers. War brings only blood and ruin. We just want what's in our right. If the world understands this, maybe peace can be achieved through dialogue. We want to live in our land in peace. I want my son to come and go in peace. I want my wife to come and go in peace. I don't want to have to give my son a cell phone so I can call him every minute and ask, "Son, where are you?" I want to be able to sleep and know that my son is safe in the next room. That's all I want. God willing, some good will come.

• ◆ •   • ◆ •   • ◆ •

SHAABAN

MY NAME IS SHAABAN, and I fear no one but God.

My friend here is talking about peace, but I want to add one thing. Does the other side really want peace? Because we are not going to give up our rights. Israel was established on the basis of U.N. resolutions. The same resolutions have not been applied to us, because we're weak. When something happens to the Israelis, when someone is hurt or killed, for example, the whole world is enraged. Meanwhile, we die by the hundreds and no one does a thing, as if they don't even know about it.

They talk about human rights. I spent a lot of time in prisons in Israel and let me tell you, when they interrogate us there is no such thing as human rights. So when someone gets out of jail he is filled with rage at the whole world. At the same time they tell him, "Let's start a new chapter in life."

In jail we used to go on hunger strikes for days on end, consuming nothing but water. One time we were on a hunger strike for twenty-one days. They force-fed us milk and eggs through a tube. The conditions in prison were terrible. The common criminal faces a better situation than those who are in jail on political charges. And if there hadn't been an exchange of prisoners we would probably still be in jail today.

Then the Palestinian Authority came. In the beginning the people said, "The nightmare of occupation is gone, and now there is someone here to protect us and make our lives better." But the opposite happened. There's a lot of corruption, but how many people have been put on trial for this? Not one.

A few years ago I was in Bethlehem and someone came up to me and said that four men were going to be executed for collaborating with Israel. I said, "I'm against these conspirators, but why are they going after these little fish and not the big ones?" He responded, "Because Oslo has prevented us from doing anything to the real conspirators."

On TV the other day they had a Saudi who donated $1 million to the families of those who've been killed or injured. He called Faisal Husseini on the phone, and Husseini said, "Only two-hundred thousand dollars has been distributed." The Saudi said, "Where's the rest?" Husseini told him, "In addition to the charities, we have to distribute money to Palestinian Authority agencies." The Saudi said: "I don't care about the PA. I donated it for the people."

This is an example of corruption. It was exposed on TV, but what has been done about it? Nothing. Everyone heard about what happened, so now potential donors won't give assistance. Other organizations are insisting on donating their money directly to the people rather than going through the PA, because there's no longer any trust.

Still, even those in the PA know that there are certain things they cannot surrender. A newspaper reporter came to my shop and did an interview with me when they were negotiating at Camp David. They asked me what I thought would happen if it failed, and I predicted that there would be a reaction.

In this current *Intifada*, all of the families here are suffering. I'm suffering, too. I have a shop, and thank God there are still some customers who come and spend 100 or 200 shekels. Other shops might make only about 50 shekels every three or four days. It is especially hard here in Jerusalem because we have the huge burden of a lot of expenses. We have to pay the property tax and other taxes to Israel. In the West Bank they don't have such taxes. But here if the property tax isn't paid for two months, they'll take you to court. Then you have to pay the amount due as well as the lawyers and all of the other court expenses.

I don't let my kids watch TV either. But if they don't see it in my house, they'll see it at someone else's house. So even if "peace" happens, this new generation is not going to go along with it. If they sign a document but the situation does not improve, in another twenty years this generation is going to burn all the peace treaties. Then we'll end up going through the same thing all over again.

We have to make clear the people's point of view: public opinion, not the official opinion. The official is sitting in his office. He doesn't know what's really happening. I'm one of the people and I'm talking to you in full honesty. I tell you that we hope for peace and we want to feel safe.

But no one feels safe. When we leave the house, we're afraid that we'll never come back. If you do make it back to the house safely, you feel as if you've been born anew.

Ahmed, on the beach in Gaza City

17. AHMED, *psychologist*

WHAT MAKES A SUICIDE *bomber tick? In the wake of September 11, many experts have turned to the Palestinian case for clues about the terrorist psyche. Ignoring context, the media has produced a flood of newspaper articles and television specials delving "Inside the Mind of a Suicide Bomber." The result has been the emergence of a litany of theories.*

• *An October 2000 edition of the* New York Times Magazine, *its cover bearing a daunting photograph of a Palestinian protestor, argued that religious fanaticism was the chief culprit. After visiting the Gaza Strip, the correspondent spoke with Israeli experts who maintained that the promises of paradise "are taken literally, not metaphorically, by those who surrender their lives to jihad. Miss that point and you miss the overarching fact that it really is a holy war . . . a clash of cultures that cannot be resolved by a negotiated agreement."*
• *Writing in the British daily* The Guardian, *an Oxford University professor blamed sexual frustration. "Testosterone-sodden young men too unattractive to get a woman in this world might be desperate enough to go for 72 private virgins in the next," he argued. A Purdue University professor agreed, writing in a separate article that "the young Palestinian male who seeks the 'martyrdom' of a 'suicide bomber' is presently at a loss for any alternative validation of his maleness."*
• *The journal of brain science,* Cerebrum, *contested that the problem*

was biological. As a neurobiologist explained in one of six essays on terrorism and the human brain, "chronically elevated levels of cortisol and disruptions in serotonin function" can lead antisocial persons to "cold, premeditated violence." A second essay by a medical doctor added that fundamentalism stunts cognitive growth, "freezing the emerging critical powers of the frontal cortex."

I cannot claim to explain suicide bombings, but somehow I find that these ways of turning the phenomenon into a question of psychology say as much about "us" as about "them." Neurobiologists blame neurotransmitters, non-Muslims target Islam, and a large audience of Westerners is luridly fascinated by those virgins in paradise. It seems as if we are making sense of Palestinian suicide bombings by putting them in our own terms, all the while ignoring the terms that dictate real life for Palestinians.

The psychological dimension of the current violence in the Palestinian territories is central, but in ways quite distinct from mainstream "terrorology." Upon touring Israel and the Occupied Territories as a member of a three-person United Nations commission of inquiry, Princeton University professor Richard Falk argued that Israel was waging no less than a "psychological warfare" against the Palestinians. Many Israeli policies, he explained, appeared to be calculated and designed to cause emotional pain.[1]

Falk supported his claim with a host of specific examples. First, settlement expansion strikes Palestinians psychologically as well as materially because it "casts doubt as to whether Israel ever intends to withdraw from the Occupied Territories." Second, the assassination of Palestinian political activists causes widespread anxiety as far as it is "designed to make Palestinians feel that no matter who they are or what they do, Israel has the capacity to kill them at its discretion." Third,

---

1 Richard Falk, "The Need to Protect Palestinians from Israel's Psychological Warfare" Palestine Center Information Brief No. 77 (24 May 2001). Available online at: www.palestinecenter.org

the bulldozing of Palestinians' homes—carried out without warning in the middle of night—is so "notable in its cruelty" that it seems to be a deliberate effort to traumatize. On home demolitions, Falk observed that "there appears to be no genuine security justification. And even if there were, Israel could proceed in a far less inhumane manner."

These and other policies, Falk argued, showed that Israel's objectives aimed at Palestinians' psyches in a manner that went well beyond self-defense:

> The circumstances of the Palestinians are worse than my moral imagination is capable of depicting . . . Israel's larger design includes a desire to break the will of Palestinians to resist and to fasten a permanent structure of dominance onto the territories. The Israeli public, with some notable exceptions, lacks any real understanding of the Palestinians' daily suffering.

One facet of the psychological warfare that Falk did not mention is the emotional fallout of Israel's dispatching of tanks, helicopter gunships, warplanes, and missiles to Palestinian towns and refugee camps. In addition to killing or injuring hundreds of innocents, the spectacle of this combat arsenal has systematically terrified the entire population. My foreign friends who spent time in the Occupied Territories found that their contact with these weapons of war left them shell-shocked long after they returned home. Moving from the West Bank to Boston, Gretchen would jump at the roar of the "T" because it reminded her of F-16s. Once settled again in France, Laetitia confessed that she panicked one morning when she heard the sound of tanks outside. When she saw that they were just garbage trucks, she did not know whether to laugh or cry.

It is children, however, who have been most devastated by the psychological impact of the violence. UNICEF's investigations led it to report that "all Palestinian children in the West Bank and Gaza are exposed in some form to increased psychological stress." The most common manifestations of trauma were nightmares, bed-wetting, insomnia, and irregular sleeping patterns. A close second was fear:

> . . . fear of darkness, fear of sleeping alone, leaving the house, strangers, loud noises and sudden movements. Children find it difficult to concentrate. Some are more anxious and irritable. Children are experiencing psychosomatic symptoms, such as headaches, stomach cramps and skin problems. And others are withdrawing from friends and family, rebelling or becoming aggressive themselves.[2]

One of the Palestinian organizations working to help children and adults cope with these and other aspects of trauma is the Gaza Community Mental Health Program, a nonprofit organization specializing in counseling, rehabilitation, training, and research.

I visited the Gaza Community Mental Health Program headquarters, located on an unpaved road, a five-minute walk from Arafat's Gaza City residence. Ahmed, its executive director, was in the midst of last-minute preparations for an important meeting, but insisted that he had time to chat with me. He gave me his full and calming attention, unperturbed by the assistants who periodically knocked on the door to get his approval of one memo or another. Ahmed was a therapist by training, indeed.

Many months after I met Ahmed I would see the Gaza Community Mental Health Program again in a most unlikely place; CBS's 60 Minutes. The organization's founder Dr. Eyad El-Sarraj had been called in as an expert for a story entitled "The Mind of a Suicide Bomber." Asked about psychological abnormalities among suicide bombers, he replied that there tended to be none. Had he been asked about social abnormalities in the environments from which suicide bombers emerge, however, he might have had the chance to respond, as he did in one of his articles that never made it into the American press:

---

2 UNICEF press release, Geneva, 15 November 2001; see http://www.unicef.org/newsline/01pr87.htm.

It is a well-documented observation that throughout the vicious cycles of violence, suicide bombing is a phenomenon that is inversely related to the degree of hope. Whenever there is hope, death and dying travel away.[3]

In other words, we will never understand suicide bombers as long as we concentrate on looking inside their minds and ignore the world in which they live.

·•· ·•· ·•·

MY NAME IS AHMED. I am a clinical psychologist and executive director of the Gaza Community Mental Health Program. The founder of the organization used to work in a psychiatric unit run by the Israeli Civil Administration that ran the occupation in Gaza. The Israelis were not concerned with mental-health services, and he was fired due to his ongoing criticism of their policies.

Our organization was established about two years after the start of the first *Intifada*. At that time it was very difficult to find a single Palestinian who had not experienced multiple traumas. People were traumatized from tear gas, broken bones, home demolitions, shootings, detentions, the loss of family members, curfews, etc. During the first *Intifada*, the Israelis used to impose long curfews on Gaza. For example, during the Gulf War, the Israelis imposed a twenty-four-hour-a-day curfew for a period of forty-five days. They only allowed people to go out of their houses for two hours once every two or three days in order to do their food shopping. These and other kinds of traumatic events have left a big impact on the psychological character of Palestinians. Adults and children, men and women, everybody has been traumatized.

3 Dr. Eyad El-Sarraj, "Why We Have Become Suicide Bombers: Understanding Palestinian Terror." Available online at: www.mediareviewnet.com

Palestinian women have experienced a double suffering. Some women have been beaten and tortured inside Israeli prisons. Hundreds of thousands have lost their husbands when they were killed, detained, or deported. Our traditional ways have not prepared Palestinian women for the responsibility of being the sole head of household in a husband's absence. Our organization's Women's Empowerment Program offers support, counseling, and training for women facing the challenge of raising children in addition to working and guaranteeing the future of their families.

We can't talk about the current *Intifada* in isolation from the larger context. The story, in my opinion, started after the signing of the Oslo agreement, which raised a lot of expectations among Palestinians. We all expected that the problems would end, that refugees would return to their homeland, that there would be no more wars or conflicts. But the Oslo agreement just added to the overwhelming problems from which the people were already suffering. Our economic status was much better before the Oslo agreement than it is today. There used to be more than 150,000 Palestinians who worked in Israel. Now nobody is going to work there. In addition, Palestinians haven't been able to export their products because of the closure. And on top of that, Israelis kept expanding settlements, occupying more land, making the Palestinians travel on back roads, etc., etc.

The people have reacted to this.

The clashes have resulted in a tremendous number of killings and injuries. And we know from our experiences with victims of the first *Intifada* that many psychological disorders might develop as a consequence of all that is happening now. Some children are developing Attention Deficit Disorder and hyperactivity. Others are suffering from more serious conditions. Two weeks ago we received a twelve-year-old who had been shot. He is from my village and lives very close to an Israeli settlement. Every day he must pass by the settlement on his way to and from school. One day he was passing by with a group of other children, and Israeli settlers shot at all of them. Sixteen children were injured in that incident. We know that the settlers used silencers on their guns because the children told our professionals that none of them heard any shooting. They just suddenly found themselves on the ground in a pool of blood.

That is why children have become afraid to go outside. They are undergoing a sort of social phobia. They're not safe at home, they're not safe at school, they're not safe on the streets, and so on. This has created a crisis for children.

Of course, there are other psychological disorders. We have also worked with people who have post-traumatic stress disorder, depression, and anxiety attacks.

I work in Gaza City, but I live on a farm in a small village called Deir al-Balah, in the middle of the Gaza Strip. There is a settlement just one kilometer from my house. There the Israeli settlers and soldiers have this daily routine. After seven or eight in the evening, they start shooting and bombing houses. In addition, they have bulldozed thirteen houses in my village. The soldiers come without any previous warning and demolish the house, right in front of the people's eyes. Some farms have been completely destroyed by the Israelis. Some families have now started to leave their homes because they cannot stand living in such a situation any longer.

One night my kids were watching TV and they heard the news that Israeli helicopters were bombing Gaza City. Then my oldest daughter said, "Maybe in a few minutes they'll come bomb Deir al-Balah." She started to cry, and then all of my other children got anxious, too. They said, "What can we do? Where should we go?" I told them that we couldn't go anywhere, but I thought that we would be safe here. After a few minutes a helicopter came and started bombing very close to our house. My children started crying and shouting. So I started something like a debriefing session with my kids, my wife, and my mother, who also lives with us.

The Israelis keep saying that this is for their security. But you can see how well these settlements are protected. Palestinians don't have the weapons to hurt the settlements or the settlers living there.

I think that what the Israelis are doing now in places like Deir al-Balah is a planned process to force the Palestinian citizens to emigrate. They shoot at civilians' homes and destroy farms because they want us to leave and abandon our land.

I have friends in my village who come to me almost every single night asking for help. Sometimes you feel powerless as a professional. You feel that you cannot help people. There is one man who lives just a hundred meters from the settlement. The Israelis occupied his home. They just came and made a military outpost on the roof of his house. His family can't leave or do anything without informing the Israeli soldiers. His five-year-old child can't sleep at night because he hears the soldiers shooting from the roof. This man is trying to provide some peace for his child so he can sleep. That's all he's asking for.

Of course there are others who've lost their homes completely. I know another man who worked in Saudi Arabia for twenty years. He came back here after the Oslo agreement and spent all of his savings to build a house. And then the Israelis destroyed it, just like that. I expected this man to develop some sort of psychological disorder. He just couldn't believe what happened. He kept going back to visit the place where his house had been. He keeps talking about the rooms, the furniture, how expensive everything was. He keeps talking about his home, as if he is in denial that it has been destroyed.

Another one of my neighbors is now under treatment in the hospital because he had a heart attack after they destroyed his farm. He had inherited that farm from his father and his father had inherited it from his grandfather. So the farm carried a very long history. And now it's gone.

All of these people feel that they have been uprooted from their lands. And after a farm has been destroyed, the owner doesn't have the right to go back and cultivate it again. The army confiscates the land. So it's all lost.

My brother-in-law's land was occupied and his farm was destroyed. They expanded the nearby settlement and his land simply became part of it. Just ten days ago, other settlers near Deir al-Balah destroyed thousands of *dunums* of very productive and fertile farmland. My farm is very close to there, so I am expecting that one night I'll go to sleep and wake up in the morning and find that my farm is no longer there. And there will be nothing that I can do about it.

How? Why? These are questions to ask the Israelis. They just come with their bulldozers and destroy things in a matter of seconds. That's it. You can't prevent them from doing it. If you try, they'll beat you. There is no logic. You can't find any explanation for it; just like there is no explanation for the shooting of those children on their way home from school.

It is a matter of power and aggression. The Israelis know that many Gazans rely on their farms, and that is why they are destroying farms. They want people to emigrate. They want them to leave Gaza.

This is easy to understand in our long history with Israelis. They forced the majority of Palestinians to leave their homeland, and now they are not allowing them to come back, in violation of the United Nations resolutions on Palestinians' right to return. People who have experienced this uprooting still have the keys to their homes. They still have the documentation that shows that they own land in Palestine. Some of these older people ask their children to take them back to their original villages, just to pass by, just to see.

I studied with Israelis in Tel Aviv University for three years, and I believe that the threat that they feel is not from the outside. They have to investigate their feeling of lack of security inside themselves rather than projecting it on others. Then they can stop always seeing others as planning to destroy them and kill them, which is the whole justification for their actions now. We have discussed this issue with our Israeli friends who are mental-health professionals.

Ask the Israelis, "What if you banished the Palestinians? Then would you feel safe and secure?" Then they might say that the Iraqis are threatening their security, or the Iranians, or who-knows-who-else. It is as if they need an enemy in order to keep a kind of psychological balance. And they must kill, as if by killing children they prove that they are still the stronger ones. They say that they are protecting their security. But how can a child with a stone threaten a soldier with an M-16?

You know, I think that peace would be the most dangerous thing for the Israeli community. Peace means that the outside enemy is no longer there. If they didn't have an external enemy, then they would probably have to look for another enemy among themselves. This was the psychological process behind the killing of Rabin. Rabin was serious about making peace with Arabs and Palestinians, and that is why an Israeli killed him.

Israeli soldiers have to ask themselves: Why are we killing Palestinian children? Now they justify this by saying that Palestinian mothers hate their children and send them to clashes with the Israelis to get rid of them. But this is just a way for them to avoid asking themselves why they are behaving like killers. What do they want to achieve? What is the message that they want to convey? These are questions that must be answered if Israelis are serious about wanting to make peace.

I was invited by Israelis to attend a conference on conflict resolution in 1994. I delivered a paper entitled "A State of Mind and a Change of Peace." In it I talked about how Palestinians and Israelis perceived each other and how this would affect the peace process. And I talked about the idea of hate. Afterward one old Jewish lady came up to talk to me. She still had the number on her arm from the Nazis. She told me, "We don't hate you. You have black hair and black eyes like us. Those who we hate have blond hair and blue eyes."

Israeli soldiers must ask themselves, "Are we getting revenge? Revenge against whom?" You know, in the Knesset they discussed forcing Palestinian laborers to wear some sort of sign so they would be recognizable as Palestinians. That was what the Nazis did during the Second World War. So, you see—it is an unconscious psychological process.

I don't think that any sort of peace accords will solve the conflict between Palestinians and Israelis until Israelis recognize the rights of Palestinians. Without that, it is an ongoing conflict that might last for generations into the future.

I hope that some Americans will come here and investigate, and see what is happening with their own eyes. I hope that they will listen to what we have to say.

Khaled and Marina, in Khaled's house in Beit Jala

18. KHALED AND MARINA,

theater directors

FOR YEARS, THE WESTERN media has reported that the Palestinian media incite children to violence, Palestinian textbooks indoctrinate children in anti-Semitism, and Palestinian parents encourage children to become martyrs. Given these stories, a visitor to the West Bank or Gaza must expect to find children to be veritable fireballs of rage. Watching them stream out of school in their matching uniforms, backpacks and pigtails flying as they race to the corner stores for 25 cent candy bars, one must wonder how such well-trained instruments of hate can look so much like children anywhere.

Yet these are not like children anywhere. For all the stories about how Palestinian children are socialized to be agents of violence, relatively little has been written about these manifold ways in which they are targets of violence. During the first three months of the Intifada, more than a third of Palestinians killed by Israeli soldiers or settlers were children. As the organization Defense for Children International (DCI) expressed it, the killing of a proportionately equivalent number of school-age children in the United States would amount to the equivalent of two Columbine High School massacres occurring every day for three months.[1]

Palestinian children's exposure to violence has only intensified over time. As the current Intifada approached the end of its second year, over three hundred

---

1 Defense for Children International/Palestine Section, *A Generation Denied: Israeli Violations of Palestinian Children's Rights* 2000, p.62; Available online at: www.dci-pal.org/english/publications/viol00/violpg.html

children had been killed. Of these, a third were under the age of twelve. Half were killed by live ammunition and another third by missiles, shelling, or machine-gun fire. Nearly 90 percent were killed in situations unrelated to the occurrence of any armed confrontation. At least another seven thousand children have been injured, over two thousand of them on their way to or from school. An estimated five hundred had been disabled for life.

Apart from the deaths and injuries, no Palestinian child has been unaffected by the hostilities' disruption of the educational process. After two years of Intifada, the Palestinian Ministry of Education reported that over one thousand school days had been lost due to closure and siege. In addition, some eight hundred fifty schools had been temporarily shut down, 185 schools had been hit with Israeli shells or bullets, and 23 had been used as Israeli army barracks or detention centers.

In other words, Israel's policy of bombings, shootings, and closure affect children no less than they do adults. As one mother in Gaza told me, Palestinian children do not need textbooks to teach them to resent Israel. Their own lives give them virtually no opportunity to feel otherwise.

When I arrived in the West Bank, I found Palestinian parents at their wits' end trying to help kids cope with the traumatic effects of violence. Dozens of local organizations had mobilized to assist them. In Ramallah, I spoke with social workers at the Treatment and Rehabilitation Center for Victims of Torture, which was sponsoring group-therapy sessions in area schools as well as support groups for families of martyrs. In Gaza, I visited a YWCA camp that tried to take kids' minds off the bombing through sports, drawing, and a much-anticipated trip to the beach. And in Beit Jala, I met with the directors of the Inad Theater, dedicated to empowering children through drama, dance, and song.

The word "inad," meaning stubbornness, is meant to capture a distinctive trait of children growing up under occupation. Yet it also expresses the spirit of the theater itself. Founded in 1987, the Inad troupe persevered through the difficult years of the first Intifada before it was at last able to establish a permanent theater. During the second Intifada, the theater was hit by repeated shellings, as had dozens of other buildings in Beit Jala. Nevertheless, the Inad troupe remained inad.

I came to the theater early one morning before it had opened for the day. When I sat on the stoop and prepared to wait, a man on the street called to me that I should go visit Khaled, one of Inad's founders and lead actors. I declined shyly, but he insisted on driving me to Khaled's house himself.

A few moments later I was knocking on Khaled's door. His expectant wife answered. She was still in her pajamas and Khaled was in the shower, but of course I should come in, come in. When Khaled emerged he graciously let me ask him questions as he sipped his morning coffee. He spoke with the patience and perfect enunciation of a professional performer accustomed to communicating tough issues to children. Later, when I translated the tape recording of the interview, I would be grateful for this style.

By the time Khaled had guided me through all of the playbills and newspaper clippings of his scrapbook, it was time for the theater to open. We drove to Inad, where we found his colleague Marina already at work. A woman with a small frame and boundless spunk, she eagerly told me more about the theater, its work with children, and the bombing of Beit Jala.

Khaled and Marina's passion for drama was inspiring, as was their belief that it could provide children with some comfort, hope, and techniques for facing violence without turning to violence themselves. Yet they both insisted that there was a limit to what such social and cultural activities could achieve. In the end, they told me, only a political solution that guaranteed Palestinians' rights would bring the security and justice necessary for Palestinian children to flourish and make peace with their neighbors. Until then, all of the summer camps, art lessons, and good intentions of civil society could do little more than stem the damage that was being wrought, day after day after day.

• ◆ •   • ◆ •   • ◆ •

KHALED, *actor and director*

MY NAME IS KHALED. I was born in Jerusalem in 1971. I finished high school in Bethlehem and then went to Chile to study theater. A lot of my friends also left to live in different countries and decided not to return to Palestine. But there was something inside me that made me come back home. In all of Palestine there are no more than thirty professional actors. So here I can make a difference. My country needs me.

I started working in the Al-Kasaba Theater in Jerusalem and Ramallah. Then a small group of friends and I founded the Inad Theater here in Beit Jala. We worked together day and night for years. In the beginning we spent from our own pockets in order to cover expenses. We did rehearsals in our own homes and used our own things as costumes and props. We struggled until we got to this point, where we have our own studio and are able to dedicate ourselves to theater fulltime. Building a theater wasn't easy. It was the result of over ten years of work.

So then one night, on the twenty-first of October, when they bombed the theater . . . when they bombed the theater it was very, very sad.

I also teach drama to kids and work in television and radio. I do a radio program for children in which we use songs and word games to talk about children's rights, society, and the environment. The show also has a hotline for kids to call in and talk about their problems. We talk about how we can work together and support one another. Before the show started in 1993, there was no such program for children in Palestine. We started out small, but worked until we were able to reach children throughout the Palestinian territories.

Now during the *Intifada* the big problem for children is fear. Children are scared to go home. They want to move, to look for another home in which they can feel safe. There are also problems of bed-wetting, anger, anxiety, violent behavior, and deteriorating performance in school. Children want to understand why this is happening, how it is happening, and for how long it will continue. They want to know how to cope with the situation and how to protect themselves. They call in and ask questions like: What should we do when there is a lot of shooting going on?

On the show we'll also talk about checkpoints. I have a big problem with checkpoints. The Israeli occupation imposes checkpoints on us to stop the course of our lives. And the checkpoints are not just on the roads between cities. They also put checkpoints inside our minds and our hearts. For example, when Israel decides to close a school, this is a checkpoint. Or when it says that you can't build here, this is another checkpoint. Or, when there is a public oven, and you make bread but aren't allowed to get to the oven to bake it—this is also a checkpoint. Our lives are filled with checkpoints at every turn.

I try to use laughter to help people deal with checkpoints. I use stand-up comedy to tell everyone, "You have a problem. And your problem is like my problem. But what are we going to do about it? Are we going to throw our hands up in the air? Or are we going to laugh about it?" If we laugh maybe we can lighten our burdens, brush them aside, and keep moving forward.

That is why I do stand-up comedy about checkpoints, soldiers, the closure, and the situation in general. But I don't speak just about the Israelis. I also speak about us. I say that we need to open our eyes. We can't look at the situation from a narrow point of view. We have to takes risks and take advantage of opportunities to have new experiences and learn. We have to open our hearts. We have to forgive, if there ever comes the opportunity to forgive.

And I try to say that we can't always remain in the past. We have to look to the future.

The Inad Theater in Beit Jala works with children of all ages. You can see that all of our plays deal with the situation that we are living. Here in Palestine there is an element of struggle in our daily lives, and there is something beautiful in this. It makes you feel that you really exist, that you are really here.

In addition to performances at the theater, we also go to schools to teach drama. Inad Theater tries to get to children wherever they are. We try to reach them in the remote areas, where they aren't able to make it to the theater or can't afford to buy a ticket. What we do is get in a van and go from Beit Jala to Hebron, the refugee camps, the villages, etc. We stop in the main square, perform for a half hour, and head on our way again. We do this every year. Theater is not only when the audience comes to us, but also when we go out to the audience.

As an actor, my first major production was *Romeo and Juliet*. It was a joint production between the Palestinian Al-Kasaba Theater and a theater in Israel. I don't think that I am ready now to make another coproduction of this sort. At that time, back in 1994, it was possible. Everyone was talking about peace, and I also believed that real peace was possible. We in theater thought that we had an important role to play. If genuine peace is going to be a reality, culture can be more important than all of the meetings between political leaders.

And we believed that the other side also respected peace and respected how we think. We respected them. We made a big effort and worked together with them. And they also worked with us. And we all agreed that theater should reflect reality. What happens onstage has to be in sync with what is happening on the streets.

It was a very big and expensive production. But we agree that it is not right to continue with the production right now. Romeo and Juliet love each other. Romeo is Palestinian and Juliet is Israeli. But if they see each other on the streets today they are not going to love each other. I don't want actors to be liars. As an actor, I cannot lie.

Doing *Romeo and Juliet* was a nice experience. I have many close friends from the production, people who I like very much. For example, there is one Israeli actress with whom I became very close. When Israel bombs us, she calls me to see if I'm OK. And when there are problems in Tel Aviv, I also call her and other friends to say that I hope that they are alright. There are good people on both sides, just like there are bad people on both sides. The important thing is that we learn how to respect one another.

In the future, if there is real peace, it might be possible to do such a production again. Here there is one land, and two people living on it. In order for there to be peace, we don't have to love one another, but at least we have to respect one another. This means that they have to accept me as their equal. They can't look down at me like something inferior to them. I have to have my freedom. I have to feel that I have my land and my country. I have to be able to stand up and be strong, and not feel like I have to bow my head before them.

Peace in not just words on paper. If we cannot see those words actually applied to our lives, it's not peace. For example, if I teach in a school in Jerusalem and I can't get there, this is not peace. If my theater is in Jerusalem, and I can't get there, this is not peace. My radio program is in Ramallah, and for three months now I have not been able to get there to do the show. Children are waiting to hear my voice, and I'm waiting to hear their voices and learn about their news.

I don't think that Palestinians' hearts are filled with hate. Their hearts are filled with sadness and anger. We just want our rights. Give us just one chance to experience living with our basic rights. Humans don't live on bread and water, alone. We want our identity and dignity. And Israelis are not the only ones worried about their security. We want our security, too. We want to be safe from them.

We have children who come to the Inad Theater to do ballet. This is the first time in the history of Beit Jala and Bethlehem that we have ballet. People here don't know what ballet is. Palestinians have *debka*, a traditional folk dance. We don't have ballet. But people see ballet on

TV and they see that it is something beautiful. So we brought in a ballet instructor, and people loved it. This is culture. It's learning about other people and other ways of life.

So one day the children were at the theater practicing, and then Boom! Boom! Boom! They started bombing outside. All of the girls got scared. Two of my coworkers were at the theater at the time, and they took the girls to take cover in the kitchen during the shelling.

Another time they started bombing when we were in the middle of a drama class. So you see that Israel is not only bombing buildings and the outside of things. They are destroying our insides, too. They are destroying how we work and the strategies we use to go about our lives. Now children are scared to come to the theater. We have to think of alternative ways to encourage them to come again.

Our children here in Palestine are not like children elsewhere in the world. It can be difficult to deal with them sometimes because they grow up so quickly. They grow up, but inside they remain children. They're not used to people playing with them. Maybe the child's father has to go to work in Israel. He wakes up at 5:00 A.M. to get to the military checkpoint. He comes home exhausted, and then there is no time to play with his child. On top of that, there is no money because of the economic situation. So the mother and father are dispirited. They're so worried about how to feed their children that they don't have time to think about how they're going to talk with their children.

For example, this Christmas I took my ten-year-old cousin to a toy store and asked her what she wanted. She told me that she was big now and had no need for toys. But if you looked in her eyes, you could see that she loved every single thing in the shop. She is a child and would love to have a Barbie or this toy or that. But she knows that her father and mother are both out of work. So she says that she is big now and doesn't need to play anymore.

Children are people, too. They have feelings and politics has a big impact on their lives. Put yourself in the shoes of that child. He is sleeping in his room. Someone comes in the middle of the night and destroys his room and makes him leave his house. The next day when that child goes to school, he's not going to be happy. When he sees a soldier, he's not going to go and give him a flower. He's going to express his anger with a stone. Let him go ahead and do it. The stone is just symbolic. No one is going to bring down the State of Israel with a stone. But somehow, Israel is still frightened.

I tell children to carry a stone in one hand and a pen in the other. I say, "Today you are small and you carry a stone, but tomorrow you'll be big, and you'll carry responsibility for the nation."

In spite of all of this, we teach our children to say no to violence. We teach them to study and learn and talk to others—even to talk with the other side. And we try to encourage children to be positive. There is a song we always sing to the children that goes, "Come, my friends, let us build a small house in our country. Tomorrow we will grow up, my friends, and the whole world—even the little house— will grow along with us." That is the right path—come and let's build and create.

"This is the way. I tell the children, if they tear up a tree, then we have to plant ten new trees in its place."

•◆•   •◆•   •◆•

MARINA, *director and manager*
MY NAME IS MARINA and I'm from Beit Jala. My great-grandparents had a house in Jerusalem, and they became refugees because it was taken. The house is still there and when we go to Jerusalem we see it. I studied at Bethlehem University for my first degree in English and

then I got scholarships to get two master's degrees in Britain. I live here in Beit Jala with my parents.

I'm executive director of the Inad Theater. For the past four months we haven't been able to work at the theater because it was hit several times by Israeli bombs and missiles. The theater is located opposite the Gilo settlement. Any time they shell Beit Jala the theater gets hit. We've collected loads of bullets and shrapnel that have come through the walls and windows. All of our electrical equipment was ruined one day when a bomb hit the electrical generator in the neighborhood. Our water tank was badly hit and we didn't have water for a month and a half. We had to get water from the neighbors and carry it in buckets.

This is basically a residential area of families. Many people have left their houses because they're very scared for the lives of their children. Whoever has been able to move to the house of a relative where it is safer has done so. But some people have had to stay in their houses because they don't have any other place to go.

When they first started bombing we were not sure whether or not to continue to perform. Then we got a phone call from the principal of a school. He said that the children were in a state of shock and that we needed to come and do something. He wasn't sure what the result would be, but he wanted us to come and try.

We went and performed, and the children responded really well. We included a workshop to let them talk about what they were going through. Talking helped the children discover that everyone else was scared, too. It wasn't a cure, because what we're talking about here is trauma. But at least the children could see that they were not alone. And we tell them that we're scared, too. Our theater was bombed, and now we have to rebuild it.

Once we were going to perform in a village near Hebron. It took three hours to get to the Halhoul Junction, which should usually take only half an hour. When we got to the junction there was an Israeli military jeep. We were waiting to ask permission to cross when suddenly one of the soldiers comes out of the jeep and points a gun at our car and started shooting. We all got down on the floor of the car. I don't know how the driver turned the car around, but he did and we got away.

The children in Hebron, meanwhile, had been waiting for hours to see us. We finally had to call them and say that we just couldn't make it.

Since then we've decided that we can no longer go to perform in Hebron. It's too dangerous because soldiers and settlers attack people on the roads. When the situation calms down we'll go to Hebron again, and to the refugee camps because they are neglected. It is amazing when we go to the camps and some fifteen hundred children come to see a performance. They all come out because they've never seen anything like theater before.

It's amazing to see how children are coping with things. They know all the different types of bullets. They'll tell you that this is a 500 and this is an 800. You can see children carry toy guns because they think that this will help them defend themselves. There is one little boy who had a missile crash inside his room. He asked his parents to buy him a toy tank so he could use it to protect his family.

Another boy went to school once wearing five T-shirts, one on top of the other. When his teacher asked him why, he said, "This way, if I'm hit by a bullet it won't hit my body." There is another boy who came to dinner once carrying his mother's dress. He told his mother that they were shooting boys, but not girls, so maybe dressing like a girl could save him. But the thing is, girls have been shot, too.

I don't think this generation is going to forget what has happened very easily. I don't know if they'll ever be able to have personal contacts with Israelis. I can't even imagine going to West Jerusalem to go shopping like we used to. I am scared just to be around Israelis.

Every time Beit Jala was bombed I would immediately sit at the computer and write about what I thought or felt or what was happening with my family. One night I really panicked because I didn't think we were going to make it through alive. So I got on the Internet and sent an e-mail to my friends that said, "I don't know if I'm going to see you again or not. Beit Jala is being bombed. Our theater has been hit, and that's it."

That was the first time I wrote. But then I decided that I should write more people and tell them what's happening here. Gradually I developed a list of about fifteen hundred people. And every time Beit Jala was bombed I would describe what it was like.

Writing the e-mails has been emotionally draining. And sometimes the electricity would get cut off or there would be no connection or something would happen to someone in my family. So I would have to write at three or four in the morning, or the next day. Still, I felt a responsibility to write. If I stopped, people might think that everything here is OK. Some people have written to me and said that the newspapers say that the violence has calmed. I have to write them and say, "Not at all! We're still getting bombed! People are still getting killed."

An American journalist once asked me to ask Palestinian mothers why they send their children to confrontation sites. I was so furious. First, I think it's racist to even suggest that Palestinian mothers would do this. Second, there is no mother in the whole world who would tell her child to go to his own death. Third, children in the Palestinian community feel that they are part of the struggle. They feel that they have to do something. They know that by throwing stones they're not achieving much. But they think that this is the only way that they can participate.

The Ministry of Education has tried to make the school day longer in order to keep children at school. They've also tried to prohibit children from leaving school unless a parent comes to pick them up. And many organizations have tried to create programs to keep children away from the clash points.

Anyway, there are so many cases of children who were killed when they were nowhere near confrontation sites. They've gotten shot when they were going to school or were sitting on their mothers' laps in a taxi.

Palestinian mothers would give their lives for their children. Some mothers say that the only way to stop children from going out to throw stones is to lock them inside. But children will find ways to escape. They have many excuses and ways of leaving the house when they want to.

The violence still hasn't stopped. But we hope that this year will be better than last year. This morning I saw that the people who live next door to the theater were beginning to rebuild their home. Maybe this means that they have hope.

POSTSCRIPT

IT IS A FEW DAYS before the first of the year 2003, and my plane touches down in Tel Aviv. I am nervous. Israeli security does not seem to like people poking around the Occupied Territories and reporting on what they see there. I have heard many stories about foreigners coming to Israel and the West Bank and Gaza Strip on peace and solidarity trips, only to be stopped at the airport and sent back home. I am worried that the same will happen to me. My grandmother, whose patience for my visits to dangerous places has run dry, hopes that this will be the case. But I am prepared for obstacles. This semester I have started studying Hebrew, and in class we memorize the lyrics to a new Israeli song each week. If the airport security guards deny me entry, I will charm them with my rendition of *Yelda Hachi Yafa b'Gan* ("The Most Beautiful Girl in the Kindergarten"). They will see that I am no threat to the State of Israel, and let me through.

My worry is for naught.

Within minutes I am out of the airport and in a taxi headed to East Jerusalem, and, from there, to the West Bank. Laying to rest my first fear, that I will not make it to the Palestinian Territories, I steel myself for my second fear: that I *will* make it to the Palestinian Territories and have to come face-to-face with how terribly the situation has deteriorated since I was there last.

The two years that have passed since I recorded the occupied voices in this volume have been marked by milestones of seemingly ever-escalating death and destruction: recurrent Palestinian suicide bombings inside Israel and unremitting shootings of Palestinians in the Occupied Territories; Israeli assassinations of Palestinian activists and Palestinian attacks on settlements and army outposts; Israelis and Palestinians' common plunge into lives governed by worse and worse economic desperation and greater and greater fear.

Against this backdrop, the unprecedented events of the spring of 2002 stand out as a turning point in the course of the violence. On March 27, a Palestinian blew himself up in a hotel in the Israeli resort of Netanya, killing twenty-eight people gathered for a Passover Seder. It was the eighth suicide bombing in a month that had seen over one hundred Israelis killed. At dawn two days later, hundreds of Israeli tanks and armored personnel carriers reoccupied the streets of Ramallah and bombarded Yasser Arafat's compound. In the days that followed, Israeli tanks and troops battled Palestinian fighters and reoccupied seven other West Bank cities, imposing curfew on approximately one million civilians.

Over three hundred Palestinians were killed from the start of the invasion until the end of May, at least fifty of them children. Almost thirty Israeli soldiers lost their lives, as well. Some six hundred Palestinians were injured, over nine thousand arrested en masse, and hundreds of millions of dollars' worth of public and private property destroyed. Officially, the Israeli army's aim was to strike terrorist infrastructure. In practice, it also struck the infrastructure of civic, cultural, and political life in the Palestinian territories at large. Noting the army's particular assault on governmental and nongovernmental institutions, Israeli journalist Amira Hass argued that a more accurate name for "Operation Defensive Shield" was "Operation Destroy the Data":

It's a scene that is repeating itself in hundreds of Palestinian offices taken

over by IDF troops for a few hours or days in the West Bank: smashed,
burned and broken computer terminals heaped in piles and thrown into
yards; server cabling cut, hard disks missing, disks and diskettes scattered
and broken, printers and scanners broken or missing, laptops gone, tele-
phone exchanges that disappeared or were vandalized, and paper files
burned, torn, scattered, or defaced—if not taken. And it's all in rooms
full of smashed furniture, torn curtains, broken windows, smashed-in
doors, walls full of holes, filthy floors and soiled bathrooms . . .

The scenes of systematic destruction show how the IDF translated into
the field the instructions inherent in the political echelon's policies:
Israel must destroy Palestinian civil institutions, sabotaging for years to
come the Palestinian goal for independence, sending all of Palestinian
society backward. . . . That way, the Israeli public can continue to be
deceived into believing that terror is a genetic problem and not a socio-
logical and political mutation, horrific as it may be, derived from the
horrors of the occupation. [1]

While Israeli troops were reoccupying the West Bank, I was in Massachusetts struggling to pass my statistics class. As had been my experience in Cairo during the beginning months of the *Intifada*, I found that
the news from the Occupied Territories made it a bit difficult to concentrate. Each day I received e-mails describing horrors ranging from
the stench of cadavers to the fear of families cowering in the dark and
surrounded by the sounds of war. I read articles about people who died
in their homes when ambulances were prevented from getting them to
hospital, and the loved ones who stayed by their side. I watched TV
footage of old women crying over their demolished homes, imploring
someone, anyone, to come to their aid. I saw photographs of cities I
had once known to be full of life and possibility, and I could hardly recognize their ravaged streets. I listened to the White House call upon

1 *Haaretz*, 24 April 2002.

Israel to stop its incursions and withdraw to recognizable borders, and then waited as Israel continued to use American-made weapons against Palestinian civilians.

Although the Israeli army formally withdrew from the last of the West Bank cities forty-five days after reinvading, it returned to many of them shortly thereafter. Israel now enters Palestinian towns and refugee camps at will, rendering the Oslo distinction between Areas A, B, and C all but meaningless. It is not strange for tanks to drive around Palestinian neighborhoods at night, and house demolitions occur so regularly that they hardly make headlines anymore. It is rare for a day to pass without at least one Palestinian being killed by an Israeli soldier.

In the background of this military activity looms Israel's building of an eight-meter-high "security wall" and its appropriation of sur-rounding Palestinian land as closed military zones. The wall is being built not along Israel's 1967 borders but inside Palestinian territory. Palestinian analysts forecast that approximately 10 percent of the West Bank will be annexed in order to complete the wall, leaving hundreds of thousands of Palestinians either hemmed in or stuck on the Israeli side of the divide. In the northern West Bank construction is currently under way.

"*Intifada*" no longer seems an apt idiom for this latest phase of the Israeli-Palestinian conflict. The first *Intifada* witnessed concerted civil disobedience as diverse sectors of society participated in popular com-mittees, strikes, and boycotts. The current conflict, in contrast, has come to resemble a semiwar in which competing Palestinian military groups sponsor armed attacks or suicide bombings against Israelis, and the Israeli army employs an arsenal of military and nonmilitary weapons against activists in these groups, the Palestinian Authority, and the Palestinian population at large.

In the first year of the second *Intifada*, some Palestinians called for the need to "bring the masses back to the battlefield and directly confront the structures of occupation . . . through massive, nonviolent resistance."[2] Over time, however, popular participation has contracted to the point that most ordinary people can focus on little more than keeping themselves and their loved ones alive. For most Palestinians, their role in the *Intifada* consists less of "directly confronting the structures of occupation" than of enduring suffering and pledging their commitment to continue doing so until national independence is achieved. Palestinians, no less than Israelis, refuse to submit to force.

Such is the nature of the stalemate that I find when I return to the Palestinian Territories, now in the third year of what began as the Al-Aqsa *Intifada*. I have returned to the West Bank and Gaza Strip with the goal of revisiting the men, women, and children whom I interviewed two years ago. Laura has come from London in order to join me and take photographs. For some of our interviewees I have a phone number or an e-mail address, for others just a name or a vague recollection of the location of their home or office. Given the family-based nature of Palestinian society, where everyone seems to know everyone, word travels fast, and people go out of their way to help guests, I am not worried that I will be able to track them down.

My first visit is an easy one. I meet the doctor Mohammed precisely where I met him two years ago, at Ramallah Hospital. He welcomes me warmly, apologizing periodically to take calls regarding a patient who cannot get from his village to the hospital in the city. Mohammed can empathize with this dilemma. He explains to me that he also lives in a village and must cross multiple checkpoints on foot in order to get to work. In total, he walks about four miles each day.

2 Ghassan Andoni, "A Comparative Study of Intifada 1987 and Intifada 2000" in Roane Carey, ed., *The New Intifada: Resisting Israel's Apartheid* (London and New York: Verso Books, 2001), p. 218.

I find Mohammed as I saw him last, busy juggling dozens of patients and manifold administrative duties. Yet something in the hospital itself seems to have changed. During the spring 2002 reincursions no sooner had tanks reinvaded Ramallah than they encircled the hospital, cutting off its water and electricity supplies on the charge that gunmen were hiding inside. At one point, some thirty Israeli troops stormed the halls of the hospital itself. They checked the ID cards of those present, broke down the doors of locked offices, contaminated a sterilized room, and arrested one visitor.

The Israeli army reentered Ramallah under a hail of missiles, tank fire, and live ammunition, and many Palestinians throughout the city were killed or injured as a result. It was not long after troops reoccupied, therefore, that the hospital morgue was overflowing. Although bodies continued to accumulate as one day and then another passed, the curfew made it impossible to transport them to the cemetery for burial. It was not until the fourth day of the reincursion that curfew was at last lifted for two hours. As Ramallah residents rushed to buy food, water, and supplies, hospital officials had just enough time to bury the twenty-five cadavers in a mass grave in the hospital parking lot.

Mohammed had seen many horrors during his long career as a surgeon, from broken bones during the first *Intifada* to bodies torn apart by explosive bullets during the second. The mass entombment of cadavers in a parking lot, however, was something he had never imagined possible:

> When in history has a hospital had to bury bodies in a lot? Even in times of war, people have always been allowed to bring their dead to church or mosque cemeteries. Anywhere else in the world this would be something utterly inconceivable. But it happened here in Ramallah. And more than that, it also happened in Nablus and Jenin.

Mohammed lived at the hospital for the first month of the reincursion. If the sheer amount of patients to care for had not been enough to prevent him from going home, the curfew and closure would have been. While he was sleeping at Ramallah Hospital, Suzanne and her twin, Jehan, were on the other side of town, spending terrified nights in the safest place in their apartment: the kitchen floor. I meet both sisters at a new Ramallah restaurant called Sangrias. Checkers, the hamburger joint where I interviewed Suzanne the first time, had closed after the shopping center in which it was housed was destroyed by Israeli shelling.

Suzanne and Jehan come to the restaurant directly from their respective offices, each with the poise and drive of Manhattan career women. I remember how Jehan once told me that, since they were young, the two sisters have been keenly aware of the lack of opportunities for work and study that Palestinians face. They realized that if they were to succeed they would have to work twice as hard as everyone else, and that is precisely what they had aspired to do. I motion the two of them to my table and am struck by their maturity and style. As we exchange kisses, I push my backpack under the table so they will not see that, two years since they saw me last, I still have not learned to carry a purse.

Suzanne has a number of new stories to tell from her work as a reporter. Once when she was reporting from the checkpoint her cameraman was shot. He went down before her eyes and she dragged him to an ambulance herself. On another occasion Suzanne herself took a rubber bullet, although in a less typical way. Lethal at a close range but harmless beyond a certain distance, the rubber bullet came right toward her, lost momentum, and then gently fell into her wide-necked summer blouse.

After months of coolly reporting from checkpoints, funerals, and hospitals, however, Suzanne found that the accumulated violence was becoming too much for her. A small quiver in her hands when she gripped the microphone worsened until it became obvious on the screen. When the editor at the station told Suzanne that she had to bring her nerves under control, she opted to take a leave of absence. She returned and began a new job reporting for an Arab satellite channel. A few months later, she decided that she needed a more extensive break from journalism, and accepted a new position in the public relations department of a Palestinian marketing firm.

It is not her career as much as the reoccupation, however, that dominates Suzanne's reflections as she speaks to me about her experiences during the past two years. When tanks returned to Ramallah, Palestinians from different political factions came out with guns to fight them off. Suzanne and Jehan's block happened to become one theater for some of these battles between gun and tank, and from their window they saw a number of armed Palestinians shot and killed. Their building was hit so badly by tank fire that all of the other residents fled, leaving the two of them alone to listen to the shells being discharged and then count the seconds that passed for them to hit their target. When tank shells hit their own apartment, Suzanne found herself thinking of something that she had heard months earlier when reporting from the field:

> *Once I interviewed a little boy whose home was hit by shelling. When I asked him what it was like, he told me that it made him feel like he wanted to hug his house. I remember thinking that this was a strange thing to say. But when our house was hit, I understood.*
>
> *Your home is supposed to be a secure place. But when the bullets can hit you wherever you are, you feel like there is no difference between sleeping in your bed and sleeping in the street.*
>
> *We've lost any feeling of security. Something inside has changed, and things will never be like they were before.*

Without telephone, water, or electricity, Suzanne and Jehan invented a homespun way of recharging their cell phones with loose batteries. Although their parents in Jenin called frequently, they worried about conserving power and would hang up immediately upon reassuring them that they were still alive. Besides, Jehan had to keep the phone open for the calls she received day and night in her capacity as a staff member at a local association supporting prisoners' rights. It was her job to check on inquiries from the panicked friends and families of men who were being rounded up and trucked away to detention centers by Israeli troops. Jehan investigated repeated calls about one missing person only to discover that he had not been arrested but killed. "His friend kept calling," Jehan recalled. "But I couldn't bring myself to tell him the truth."

After the fighting had subsided and the Palestinian Authority repaired the damage to their apartment, the sisters settled into a period of tortured waiting under curfew. Days went by without the twins even talking to each other. Unbearable for Suzanne was the cutting of the water supply, which made it impossible to bathe for days on end. "They make you feel so filthy that you begin to loathe your own body," she said. "I looked at my face in the mirror and I could hardly recognize myself." For Jehan, the worst part of being trapped in the house was the feeling of lost potential:

The waiting kills you. You are trapped at home, waiting and waiting and you don't even know what for. Waiting for curfew to be lifted? Waiting to be killed? You miss everything that you can no longer have, like going outside and seeing people.

And when you finally go outside you see that everything is different. There are soldiers everywhere and so much has been smashed. There used to be a tree where you passed by every day and now it has been crushed by a tank. You feel like the city is no longer your city. You feel a stranger to it.

There were times when I thought, Why does all this have to happen when I am young and filled with life? You feel that the situation is crushing you, squeezing your insides. Your ambition kills you. It is like your whole life is on hold. It is like your life is a film, and someone has pressed pause.

While Jehan's life was a film being paused, Azza's life, her films, was being rummaged through. Soldiers stormed her house on two separate occasions that spring, the second time leaving a havoc of strewn papers and photographs and walking off with a CD player and some jewelry. Her car, as well as that of her American housemate, were run over by tanks and squashed flat. Both cars were later displayed in a multimedia installation designed by Vera, the artist who had once spoken to me about her parents' longing for their native Jaffa. She had lined up a dozen crushed cars in a Ramallah soccer field and inside each played a tape of the music that she imagined the driver would have enjoyed.

Azza was out of the country at the time that her house was searched and her car transformed into a steel pancake. When I met her two years earlier, she was putting the finishing touches on *News Time*, her movie about the starting months of the second *Intifada*. She went on to exhibit the film in fifty countries, winning several awards and eventually selling its rights to the BBC. While the film's success opened many doors for her to work abroad, her reasons for taking a break from the West Bank were as much personal as professional:

When I left in February, I just couldn't deal with it anymore. I was nervous and crying all the time. It was the first time in my life that I simply could not cope. After a while I felt better and came back, but I don't know if I can handle it on the long term. There used to be a small community of filmmakers here, but at this point I'm the only one left.

On the other hand, I have attachments here, and I feel a sense of responsibility. To be honest, I'm not finding it easy to abandon this place.

Azza's new film, *Three Centimeters Less*, explores these conflicted feelings. It centers on the lives of a number of Palestinians of her generation who resented the sacrifices that their parents made for the national struggle, only to find themselves coming of age and doing the same.

Looking to the future, Azza confesses that she no longer sees a solution. She attributes the success of her film *News Time* to the natural innocence of its real-life protagonists, four boys in her neighborhood. "I see these boys now and that innocence is gone, totally gone," she says. Azza feels violence developing even within herself, which frightens her. "All of us, without exception, are angry," she says. "There is a degree of anger here now that you cannot even fathom." The anger, she explains, is a reaction to Israeli conduct aimed at degrading Palestinians:

This is not just occupation anymore. It has gone beyond that. Now it is about humiliation.

I don't think that Israelis see us as human beings. I can see no other explanation for their behavior. If they saw us as humans, they would not be able to do what they do. I think they want to tame us. They want to destroy our political structures so that they negotiate with us when we having nothing left.

My own walks around Ramallah and other Palestinian cities confirm Azza's assessment. Public infrastructure that was built over the course of seven years of peace negotiations was destroyed in a matter of weeks. In Hebron, I see schools wrecked and roads gutted by tank tracks. In Jenin, lampposts on every corner have been hit by tanks and twisted into some perverse modern art exhibit. In Ramallah, Arafat's compound—the complex of governmental offices that had once been the center of the Israeli Civil Administration—looks like the site of something worse than an earthquake.

Nowhere has Israel's strike at Palestinian state-building been more total than in the sphere of security and law enforcement. When I ask a friend why there is not a Palestinian policeman to be found on the streets, she remarks that they, like the young guys who had taken up guns against Israelis, were all dead, in Israeli prisons, or in hiding to save their lives. In every West Bank city with the exception of Jericho, PA prisons and detention centers have been completely or partially destroyed by Israeli bombardment. The PA released detainees in anticipation of the siege; to continue to hold them in buildings targeted for missile attack would have amounted to a mass execution. In contrast to the common accusation that the PA released terrorists, however, the acting Palestinian ombudsman notes that four hundred of the seven hundred detainees freed in anticipation of Israeli attacks were being held for collaborating with Israel. The majority of the others were charged with criminal offenses.

In the long term, this halt and reversal of Palestinian public development promises to be disastrous for Palestinians and Israelis alike. In the short term, however, Palestinians' daily distresses seem less focused on the political realm than on the economic. During my month in the West Bank and Gaza Strip, there is no comment I hear more than the frank observation, "There is no work." From what I can tell, ordinary Palestinians are not thinking about how to use violence to bring Israel to its knees. Far from it, they are absorbed in a battle to feed their families from one day to the next.

I go to the Old City in Jerusalem in the hope of discussing the economic situation with Sami and Shaaban, the two merchants who were already grappling with a commercial crisis when I met them two years prior. I find Shaaban in his shop. He has managed to keep afloat by running an informal money-changing service from his store in addition to selling souvenirs. His hair is grayer than when I met him the first time, but he is no less energetic and candid in his criticism of the Palestinian leadership, Israeli policies, and the political situation in general.

When I get to Sami's store, however, I find its metal door locked and dusty. The owner of the shop next door directs me to Sami's nephew, who gives me the details. After months in the red, Sami finally decided to close his store, even though he must continue to pay thousands of dollars in property taxes to Israel's Jerusalem Municipality each year. Selling the shop is not an option, as current market conditions would force him to relinquish it at a fraction of its worth. Besides, the store had belonged to Sami's father and is meant to belong to his children. "The family has invested so much in the shop," Sami's nephew explains. "We just have to hold on to it and hope for better times." If tourism to the Holy Land was on its deathbed in the early months of the *Intifada*, he tells me, the events of September 11 sealed its coffin. The common wisdom is that even were Palestinians and Israelis to go back to negotiations tomorrow, it would take another five years for tourism to return to prior levels.

The week that I come looking for him Sami happens to be in Jordan, where he is currently making ends meet by trading everyday goods between Jordan, East Jerusalem, and Israel. Like many in the tourist business, he abandoned his area of expertise in order to try his luck with commerce for the domestic market. Sami's nephew himself has done likewise. After eight years of working in both the souvenir trade and in Jerusalem hotels, he opened a women's clothing store in the East Jerusalem shopping district. That store, however, is faring little better. The market is flooded, he sighs, and consumers cannot afford to buy anything but the necessities.

In Batir, the village outside Bethlehem, Sultan has also shifted gears in order to rescue his ceramic souvenir factory from bankruptcy. As gifts with Christian or Jewish motifs are no longer selling for lack of foreign visitors, he has refocused production on Islamic items to market within the Palestinian territories and elsewhere in the Arab world.

Sultan's wife, Narimen, has started working with him in the factory, although she tells me that she still hopes to find a job in the city that will give her an independent livelihood. When the *Intifada* began the souvenir shop where she once worked in Bethlehem closed and never reopened. She has not seen her former work colleagues since.

Although Sultan and Narimen's business has picked up a bit, the stiffening of the Israeli closure presents them with ongoing obstacles. The only way for Sultan to ship his wares from Batir is to drive them to the checkpoint, get out of the car, and carry them across the roadblock, one heavy and fragile box at a time. He must repeat the same routine at every other checkpoint until he reaches his final destination. When the city of Bethlehem is under curfew, as it has been on and off for months, getting out of the village is simply impossible.

Closure and back roads have become a daily fact of life for Sultan and Narimen's friend Jamila, as well. After her job at a temporary crisis intervention project at a Bethlehem refugee camp ended, she was hired for a second temporary crisis intervention project, and subsequently a third. All of the jobs, which focused on helping kids with trauma, were financed by grants channeled from foreign governments or foundations to Palestinian non-governmental organizations. Many Palestinians, who have cynically referred to NGOs as "stores" since they began cropping up en masse with the peace process, snicker that the international community uses such donations to create the impression that they are doing something while they avoid taking the political steps necessary to produce real change. Their charity amounts to a form of sugar coating on the occupation and a cover for the world's acquiescence to Israeli dictates.

Jamila's job is located about fifteen miles away at a refugee camp near Hebron. Due to the army's closure of the direct road, the only way for her to get to work is via several hours on the infamous "Valley of Hell" back road. I traveled this mountain path coming southward from Ramallah when I visited Jamila for the first time two years ago.

This time I complete the saga by coming northward from Hebron. Whereas settlers jet smoothly between Hebron and Bethlehem in twenty minutes, the journey takes me about four hours, two shared taxis, and one maddening walk over the mounds of dirt that the Israeli army has heaped for no apparent purpose. Bumping along the narrow path that serves as a makeshift two-lane highway, I grip anything I can to keep from sliding from one side of the minivan to another. No barrier separates us from the steep drop to the valley below. The woman in the seat in front of me holds a plastic bag open for her four small children, each of them on the verge of nausea and one of them crossing the line. Months later, when friends in the United States ask me if I ever feared for my life in the West Bank, I would say no—but then recall this trip as the one exception.

Although Jamila spends hours on this torturous path nearly every day, she somehow still finds time for an endless stream of life projects. She continues to do everything from helping her three boys with their schoolwork to baking bread in their wood-burning oven. In addition, she has become a founding member of the village's new women's center, a collective that combines day care for children with an initiative to help local women market their handicrafts.

The women's center strikes me as just one manifestation of what seems to be a quasi-feminist revolution bubbling in this small village near Bethlehem. Like communities throughout the West Bank and Gaza, menfolk who once supported their families by working as laborers inside Israel are now entering their third year of unemployment. Women, who often have more luck in finding or keeping their jobs as teachers, social workers, and functionaries, have therefore become the sole breadwinners in many families.

The reversal of traditional gender roles appears to be fanning the flames of social relations that have already been strained by two years of violence and uncertainty. In Batir, many wives are fed up with husbands who neither bring home an income nor compensate by doing more to help with the children or household chores. Their husbands, meanwhile, seem to be struggling with an unchosen idleness that undercuts their sense of self-respect.

Jamila's family has found some respite from this conflict in her husband's undertaking of a major refurbishment of their house, a project that serves both as an investment in the worth of the property and as an outlet for the carpentry skills he had used as a construction worker in Israel. Their home is over one hundred years old, and he is working to restore the traditional Arab architectural style. The result is beautiful, but as Jamila's employment is funded by a temporary grant, the family does not know for how much longer they will have extra funds for house repairs.

What the unemployed and Palestinians at large are feeling, Ahmed tells me, is a sense of powerlessness to provide for and protect their families. I meet Ahmed back at the Gaza Community Mental Health Program, where he has resigned his position as executive director in order to return to more hands-on therapy work. He continues to confront in his own life many of the fears and frustrations he sees among his patients. He spends sleepless nights listening to shooting from the settlement located near his home in Deir Al-Balah, and he copes with closure and checkpoints as have all Gazans. Upon returning from an international conference, he once spent two days and two nights sitting on the Egyptian side of the border before Israeli security allowed him to cross back to the Gaza Strip.

Ahmed explains to me that one of the most grave losses of the past two years of violence has been ordinary Palestinians' sense of security. Related to the feeling of vulnerability is the growing sense of hopelessness. Echoing an explanation I hear many times over from Palestinians of all walks of life, Ahmed tells me that it is this desperation that drives Palestinians to become suicide bombers:

So many people are willing to blow themselves up because their current lives have no meaning. They can't even satisfy their basic needs. So they try to cross through this miserable life to get to a better one. If they defeat the enemy, they win. If they die, they win, as well. They have no control over this life, so they concentrate on the control they have over the next one.

While some people have come to believe that this life is no longer worth living, others show an amazing will to absorb adversity and survive. As illustration, Ahmed tells me about the army's blockade of the road connecting his village to Gaza City:

The Israelis piled up two mountains of sand on the road. Cars could not cross, but people could go by on foot. The army could have stopped people from going altogether, but it didn't. Its aim was simply to make things more difficult for people.

At first people were very angry. But after a few days they adjusted and dealt with the mountains as if they were just another part of ordinary life. People would talk and students would tell jokes as they climbed across. Other people started selling things there, and it became a regular free market zone.

I myself witness similar scenes of Palestinians' adaptation to checkpoints throughout the Palestinian Territories. On the path to Hebron, I meet boys who try to make a bit of money by carrying people or their belongings in wheelbarrows across the dirt roadblocks. At the southern entrance to Nablus, I come upon a group of female university students denied permission to cross the checkpoint in order to make it to campus. They decide to wait until the military commander changes his mind and, six hours later, he does so. On the other side of Nablus, I see an ill person forced to ride a donkey for several miles on his return from the hospital. As the army has closed the road that leads directly northward, travelers have devised a new route that circumvents the roadblock. They now take a taxi to the foot of a certain hill and walk about an hour on a dirt path through the mountains to a clearing where other taxis wait to take them to their next destination. Entrepreneurial men spend the day charging people $1 to take them the length of the path on donkey back. I opt to walk when I travel this route, and halfway along I am astonished to find a handful of Israeli soldiers in the middle of a field. They order Palestinians to wait as they inspect their ID cards, and occasionally send people back in the direction from which they are coming. One asks for my passport and, seeing that I am an American, cheerfully tells me that he went to high school in Ohio.

As the closure becomes more and more severe, however, Palestinians find fewer opportunities to adjust and keep going. When I arrived in January 2001, I found the checkpoints separating Jerusalem from the West Bank to consist of a few jeeps and half a dozen soldiers inspecting vehicles and stopping pedestrians at whim. When I return two years later, I am surprised to find foreboding concrete shelters, Palestinians waiting in a single-file line, and soldiers scrutinizing the ID cards of each and every would-be passer-by. Only foreigners and holders of Jerusalem IDs are allowed in and out; residents of the Occupied Territories are generally prohibited from leaving. In my conversations with Palestinians, I find them to be very pessimistic about where this increasing institutionalization of the closure is headed. Several people with whom I speak predict that the day is not far when Israel will implement a full replica of the South African Bantustan model, in which each Palestinian will register as a resident of a given town and will only be allowed to exit that town with prior written permission from a military authority.

For now, however, Palestinians cope, help one another, and carry on.

With time, people even adapt to the sounds and jolts of Israel's use of heavy weaponry and the possibility of being killed. Iman jokes with me that she is so accustomed to shelling that when a stretch of time passes without some, she feels like something is missing.

I meet Iman in Hebron. She has graduated from Birzeit University with a B.A. in psychology and moved back to her hometown. For the past year she has been working as a psychological counselor offering emotional support for Palestinian Red Crescent ambulance drivers. The position was created after a foreign researcher visited Hebron and concluded that emergency crews are experiencing severe distress due to both the horrors they witness and the real dangers they face in their contact with the army.

Thus, while Hebron has come to depend on the fearlessness of its rescue workers, they in turn have come to depend on Iman as the person to whom they can admit to being afraid. Iman tells me that she often arrives at her office in the morning and finds one of the guys waiting for her, needing to talk or even to cry. She has become a key part of the medical-relief team. When curfew prohibits Hebronites from leaving their houses, her colleagues make sure that she gets to work by driving her to and from her office in one on their fleet of ambulances.

Iman's daily work, therefore, deals with the trauma of violence. Her daily life, however, reveals what some observers call its "banalization." She tells me that the first time her neighborhood came under shelling she was shocked and terrified. As nighttime bombardment became routine, however, she learned to roll out of bed instinctively, drop to her knees, and crawl to the safer side of the house, all without being more than half awake.

Iman also tells me dispassionately about how Hebronites deal with the curfew intermittently imposed on the city. During curfew, anyone who dares to go outside or look out the window can be shot.

Nonetheless, people risk it when there are compelling reasons to do so. In the Israeli-controlled Old City, neighbors share food when no soldiers are looking by passing them along from roof to roof or from balcony to balcony. Elsewhere in Hebron, people venture out of their houses stealthily when the tank turns the corner and the coast seems clear. Iman says that people often seize such opportunities to run to grocery stores that keep their doors open a crack in a veiled signal that they are open for business. Sometimes when the soldiers catch these stores defying curfew, they throw a tear-gas canister inside and lock the door from the outside.

In general, Iman explains, Hebronites have learned unspoken rules that guide their sense of how and when they can attempt to disobey the Israeli army's orders. "Approximately once a month the army kills someone who breaks curfew," she says about the most fundamental of these rules. "For the first few weeks after that, people know that it is relatively less dangerous to go out. But once the month has passed, you have to be careful again because the time is approaching for them to issue a 'new warning.'"

Not too far from where Iman now lives at her parents' house, Sana' and Sami have also come to deal with shelling and curfew as fixtures of daily life no less invariable than homework and household chores. Sana' is now in her final year of secondary school, preparing for the major certification exam that largely determines university admissions for young Palestinians. When she finished middle school and started at her new high school, it was located in the section of Hebron under Palestinian control. In recent months, however, Israel has unilaterally extended the boundaries of its sovereignty in the city. Sana's school happened to fall within the Palestinian territory that was annexed, and as a result the soldiers tend to declare it closed more often than they used to.

Sana' has plenty of new encounters with the army to recount. Like most kids her age, the bulk of her reflections center on school life:

Once the soldiers threw a sound grenade outside. My teacher told us "Don't worry, it's just firecrackers." As if we couldn't look out the window and see what was going on!

Another time they started shooting in the street. The girls weren't too afraid, but then all of a sudden we noticed that our teacher disappeared. Then we saw that she was hiding under the table.

And then there was the time when I was on my way to school when they declared curfew. I had gone a little ways when I ran into some soldiers on the street. There were six of them, and they closed in on me from all directions. I looked around. The road to school was blocked by soldiers. The road back home was blocked by soldiers. What was I supposed to do? Finally, they said that they would follow me back home. So I went back home, with six soldiers walking behind me, each one with a gun.

Sana' giggles when she recalls this story, but her older sister is stone-faced as she listens in. It is another case of soldiers using Palestinians as human shields, she explains to me. The soldiers were on patrol and made Sana' go before them and lead the way. That way, if anyone threw stones at them, they would hit her first.

Sana's brother Sami is now in the ninth grade. His mother tells me that he not only earns top grades, but also holds down an after-school job sewing the flat mattresses that serve as couches and beds in many Palestinian homes. He spends a lot of his free time tending the garden, especially when curfew is imposed and school is canceled.

Sami, his mother adds, has grown up a lot in the past years. His older brother is now attending law school in Morocco and, in his absence, Sami has decided to assume the man's role in the family. His mother warns me that he speaks with a maturity that belies his age, and when he comes home after finishing his workday, I see what she means. Sami answers my questions about work and school concisely and is no less pointed in his assessment of the political situation:

Everything is a mess—economically, culturally, and socially. Peace with Israel isn't in our hands, it's in the hands of the Israeli leaders. In the future, things will either stay like they are now, or get worse. We're expecting Sharon to commit massacres here when America goes to war in Iraq. What does America want with Iraq, anyway? Everyone knows that Bush just wants control of the oil. But our own president is a traitor, too. When we die, he doesn't say a thing. But when there's a suicide bombing, he goes on and on apologizing and condemning it. If that isn't a traitor for you, what is?

Middle schoolers are not the only ones I find in the West Bank and Gaza to be critical of the Palestinian leadership. In fact, hardly a day passes without my hearing expressions of exasperation, ranging from "Arafat and Sharon are the same thing" to "the Palestinian Authority no longer exists." In Jenin, people tell me that when Arafat announced his intention to visit after the invasion, locals were furious. "How dare he come to the city of resistance," they said, "when he himself only caves to Israel's demands?" A stage erected in anticipation of Arafat's public address was burned to the ground in protest, and rumors circulated that he would be shot if he dared to set foot in the refugee camp. In the end, Arafat made the long trip to Jenin but hardly stepped out of the car before turning around and heading back to Ramallah.

I visit Mohammed, and find him to have harsh words for the Palestinian leadership as well. Mohammed's injury healed and he had made it out of the Ramallah hotel where he had been recuperating and back to his home in Jerusalem, where he resumed his work in carpentry. A few months after recovering from that injury, however, he was shot and injured yet again. After another stint in the hospital he assumed a leadership position in the Injured Persons' Committee, which seeks to offer support to and information about Palestinians injured by soldiers and settlers. Although the committee is officially sponsored by the

Palestinian Authority, Mohammed explains that most in its ranks, including himself, identify with opposition parties:

> I like the people who came back with the Palestinian Authority as people. They are Palestinians and have a right to return to their home-land. But as an Authority, it is little more than a mafia. As officials, each one of them specializes in a different kind of theft. This one spe-cializes in stealing cars, that one specializes in stealing contracts. Where is the nation?
>
> We Palestinians have a problem, and that is that we like to blame Israel for everything that's wrong on our side. OK, Israel is an occupying power and I have a right to resist it. But not with suicide bombings or Kalashnikovs—with politics, words, writing, demonstrations. Just as I want to live, so does an Israeli citizen have the right to live. Just as I don't want my son to die, I don't want his son to die.

I find Saber to be even more severe in his censure of the Palestinian leadership and the shape of the *Intifada* in general. When I first met him, he had come to Birzeit University as a visiting professor for the fall 2000 semester. Due to closure and the repeated delays that accompanied the start of the *Intifada*, that semester did not end until March 2001. After grading the last of his final exams, Saber headed back to Texas.

Saber returned to the West Bank about a year later to lead an informal fact-finding group of students and community members from San Antonio. They visited Gaza, met with Jewish groups in West Jerusalem, and toured the Jenin refugee camp in the immediate aftermath of the Israeli invasion. He tells me that he has since found it impossible to relieve his memory of what he heard and saw in Jenin, in particular the sight of children's clothing under the rubble. As some houses had been bulldozed on top of the heads of their residents, he finds that he still wonders about those children and if they were among those who were killed. Saber tells me that the other Americans who participated on the trip are likewise yet to recover from what they encountered in the West Bank and Gaza. To this day, some of them cannot talk about it without crying.

Saber has continued to be active in raising awareness about the Palestinian cause in addition to his work as a professor and editor of a mathematics journal. He confesses that if there is one topic that shakes his professional demeanor and makes his blood boil, however, it is the Palestinian Authority:

> The PA is the worst thing that has ever happened to the Palestinian cause. Even my mother understands this, and she is illiterate. We have an expression in Arabic that she always quotes: "You fast and you fast, and then you break the fast on onions." That's our situation. We've suffered for over fifty years, only to get this destructive, anti-democratic government. It's like our dreams have been shattered. Not only are they corrupt, but they are trying to corrupt the population, as well.
>
> When this Intifada began, we thought it would be like the first Intifada, but better because we would build on the lessons we'd learned. In the beginning, kids would go to the checkpoint and throw stones. But then the PA changed the entire scenario by militarizing things. Hamas was becoming more popular, so the PA started to mimic them in order to stay in power.
>
> Palestinians think that they can ignore the PA and achieve something in spite of them. But with bad leadership, you just can't win.

Despite overriding frustration with the PA, Palestinians insist that it is for them, not Israel or the United States, to choose their leaders. They also clarify that it is not the PA that started the *Intifada,* as both its spark and its staying power stem from the general population's sense that it is the only way to end the Israeli occupation once and for all. Moreover, some Palestinians with whom I speak give PA ministries credit for their work trying to rebuild what Israel has destroyed.

The Moslets, for example, are in their home again thanks to repairs carried out by the PA. I return to Beit Jala, where Manoa brings me up to date. When I visited the family the first time, the top floor of their house had been bombed and they had moved their life activities to the bottom floor. When the bottom floor was also bombed shortly thereafter, the PA evacuated the Moslets to a hotel, where they lived for several months with other families in similar situations. As weeks passed and their original neighborhood remained unsafe, they were moved to a small apartment on the other side of the hill. The PA offered them rent for two months, after which time making the payment became a monthly struggle. At last the shelling calmed a bit, the PA repaired the two floors of the Moslets' house, and they returned home about a year and a half after they had left.

Manoa takes me on a tour of the house, which looks as good as new. Her children have grown so much that they also seem as good as new. Ahmed is nearly a foot taller, and I hardly recognize him when he comes into the room in a baseball cap and baggy jeans. Amal has gotten married, and her father drives me to pay her a visit in the new apartment she shares with her husband across town.

The Moslets' good news, however, cannot completely mask the ongoing difficulties of their lives in Beit Jala. The army continues to fire upon the village periodically, tanks often rumble through town in the middle of the night, and the imposition of curfew confines the family indoors from time to time. Manoa's middle son Mohammed, was shot in the heel as he was standing outside a local grocery store. Their neighbor, a mother of two, was inside the store and was shot in the neck and killed.

Neither have the family's economic troubles lessened since I met them for the first time two years earlier. Manoa's eldest son Ibrahim, is on edge after two and a half years without work. "I wake up, walk around the village, and then come home at night, and sleep," he tells me. "Every day it is the same thing. Nothing changes here." There are no jobs to speak of in Beit Jala, and his mother refuses to allow him to try his luck getting into Israel for fear that he will get shot or arrested when crossing the checkpoints. Ibrahim tells me that he and a buddy of his have spoken with a Greek priest in the area about getting visas to work in Greece, and they plan to submit their applications to the consulate that very week. He had tried for a visa to work in Belgium a few months back, but his application had been denied.

Given the hardships that surround them, the Moslets seem to be holding themselves together by deriving all the solace they can from their family and home life. I see intimations of something similar when I return to the house of the martyr Mohammed Nabil Hamad Daoud. Not long after I met Mohammed's mother Muna two years ago, her husband opened an Internet café a few blocks from their house. For the Daoud family, the café was not only an economic venture, but also an effort to offer a safe after-school activity to boys in the neighborhood— a positive alternative to going to the checkpoint and risking their lives by throwing stones. Moreover, the Internet café has enabled the Daouds to continue to have contact with Mohammed's friends and to watch them grow up.

I visit the Daouds at their home in Al-Bireh, where they treat me to a lavish lunch filled with laughter and warmth. Soha tells me about her job at the Palestinian cell-phone provider, her continued study of finance at a local university, and, most important, her recent engagement to be married. She is so elated that she literally glows. At one point, she asks me how to say "I love you" in as many languages as possible.

The Daouds' home is no more than a five-minute walk from Arafat's compound, and the blasts that turned the complex into a wasteland no doubt shook them for nights on end. Nevertheless, I find the family to be in such good spirits in anticipation of Soha's wedding that I lose my nerve to ask them about how they have coped with the siege. Neither can I bear to ask them about Mohammed. It is enough for me to notice that photographs of Mohammed hang in nearly every room in their home. In addition, a memorial some eight feet tall has been erected outside the corner store farther up their street. It consists of a long pole strung with plastic flowers and topped with three large posters of Mohammed. Each faces a different direction so that anyone coming and going meets his gaze.

As the lunch plates clear and tea is served, Soha brings me the pictures from her engagement party, and conversation turns to her preparations to move to her fiancée's village after the wedding. I catch Muna's eye. I feel that I must ask her about her son the martyr in order to come full circle, but I cannot bring myself to do so. When I finally bid their family farewell several hours later, it is with the awareness that there is no such thing as a full circle. There is simply life, and the will to be free.

In Gaza, I find that marriage serves as a similar testimony to the continuance of life for people who feel that death can come at any moment. I make it to Rafah, where the Israeli soldiers along the Egyptian frontier open fire day and night at nothing in particular. There are no Palestinian gunmen to speak of, but shots ring out from the Israeli military installations on the border relentlessly. I go to buy oranges on Rafah's main street and practically drop to my knees when I hear the crack of bullets. The soldiers are a few miles away, but the sound is so terrifyingly shrill that I feel it echo in my chest. The people around me, however, do not seem to flinch. In Rafah, gunfire has become the background music for Palestinians' day-to-day lives.

And against this background, people continue to get married and have children, two rare but time-tested slivers of happiness. In a refugee camp not far from the border I meet Issam and discover that he, too, has recently tied the knot. He and his new wife are living in a single room in his parents' house in the camp where he was raised. Given the scarcity of funds and the reigning sense that it is wrong to rejoice when society at large is suffering, the two married without any sort of celebration.

Issam, like the majority of men in Gaza, is unemployed. The temporary job he held at an UNRWA school when I met him ended long ago, and he has not been able to find any other formal work since. He has also been forced to sell the car that he had used as an informal shuttle service and had served as his main source of income. The increase in the price of gasoline, combined with soldiers' intensified shooting at Palestinian cars on the roads, convinced him that the car was no longer a good investment.

Since then Issam has pursued other entrepreneurial projects and watched each fall before it got off the ground. He and his best friend tried to start a business offering services and materials to university students, but could not find a sufficient market. When I meet him he is testing out a new venture. His wife has long kept a few birds as pets, and Issam has begun to breed them in the hope of selling them to others. Two cages of chirping birds share their single-room apartment, but Issam does not seem to mind. "They are beautiful," he says in the soft voice that captured my affection the first time we met.

I have coffee with Issam and his new wife and am heartened to find them laughing and gently teasing each other. When I ask about the source of his good cheer, however, he tells me not to be fooled by appearances:

> As long as I am alive, I will try to laugh and make it bearable. But you cannot call our lives here truly living. Sure, maybe we're able to eat and sleep, but isn't there more to life than this? Here there is no work, no opportunity, nothing we can make of ourselves.

After I was injured, I was unconscious for days. I was near death then,
so I don't fear death now. The dead do not feel anything. It is only the
living who suffer. That is why it is better to be dead.

I don't think that people who go and blow themselves up inside Israel
are going to bring a solution to our situation. But here you can get
killed at anytime.

Israelis live and work. They go out and travel wherever they want.
They don't pay any consequences for what they are doing to us. That is
why someone here, who has suffered all his life, will go and blow himself
up. Then they might suffer one percent of what they have made us suffer.

There may have been a time when such words were shocking. In my
travels throughout the West Bank and Gaza Strip, however, I hear them
echoed so often that I come to understand them as the norm. Time and
time again, Palestinians tell me they feel suspended between life and
death. Empathy with the kind of desperation that pushes people to violence cuts across all ages, genders, and class backgrounds. It seems that
nearly everyone, at one point or another, has felt that they too could be
pushed to violence. As one young professional in the West Bank told
me, "at this point the Israelis have left us with only one choice: life
without dignity or dignity without life."

Not far from Issam, on the Egyptian border, Israel is constructing a
steel wall six and a half yards high, reinforced by concrete, and
entrenched many feet below the ground. The Israeli army has
destroyed over 350 Palestinian homes and damaged some 500 others
in the building of this wall and the clearing of the surrounding "buffer
zone." Twelve more homes are bulldozed the day that I arrive, and
when I visit the wreckage I see a repeat of the scene that I encountered
the last time I was in Rafah: a doorway and stairwell still intact among
a wilderness of shards; an old woman trying to pull a blanket from
under a collapsed wall; dozens of children, now homeless, looking on.

A man standing on the pile of concrete that was once his kitchen says that he would offer me a cup of tea if he could. He was a child when his family fled their home in the Negev in 1948, and now he has been made a refugee a second time. "Ask your president where I am supposed to go now," he tells me.

I tell him that I will ask my president, but first I ask Mahmoud, who has now seen two years pass since his home was similarly demolished. Mahmoud has resumed work in the Gaza International Airport, although the airport is not functioning in any real sense, his job consists mostly of shuffling papers. After bulldozing his house in Khan Younis, the army used the land to expand a settler bypass road. The area remains a closed military zone, and Palestinians are strictly prohibited from coming near it. When I ask Mahmoud about the distance between his current residence and his former property, his answer surprises me. "What lies between me and my house," he sighs, "is a solution to the Palestine question."

Meanwhile, life lingers on in the apartment complex to which the PA relocated Mahmoud's family after his house was demolished. Mahmoud has a new baby son, and his daughter, who was still crawling when I visited the first time, is now a precocious three-year-old scuttling around the room on a tricycle. Knowing that his former property has been lost for good, Mahmoud's major worries these days revolve around meeting twin challenges: the financial challenge of providing for his family and those of his relatives who are out of work, and the security challenge of protecting his children from the gun- and tank-fire that frequently hails upon his neighborhood.

The latter has proven especially difficult. Mahmoud recounts how he and his daughter were coming home one day when Israeli helicopters began to shell the area. As they pulled into the parking lot, they watched two neighbors get hit and drop to the ground. One was killed and the other injured. Knowing the difficulty of ambulance access, Mahmoud carried the bodies to his car and drove them to the hospital himself.

"Dina saw everything, understood, and started sobbing," he says as his daughter climbs onto his lap. "Now, whenever she hears an airplane she remembers that incident." Shelling of their neighborhood continues constantly, and other neighbors have been injured or killed as well. Both of his children panic at the sound of the bullets, and Mahmoud shows me how he rubs his son's wrists in a traditional approach to calming nerves and how he holds his hands over his daughter's ears to deafen the blasts. His daughter is often agitated, he says. She cannot bear being stuck inside the apartment all the time, but there is nowhere else to go. Outside, it is simply not safe.

Khaled's daughter, a few months younger than Mahmoud's, is experiencing similar distress. When I met Khaled the first time at his home in Beit Jala, his wife was pregnant with their first child. When I arrive the second time, his daughter, Daniella, answers the door and his newborn Joseph, is asleep in his crib. The house is filled with Christmas decorations and children's toys. Daniella even has one of those inflatable castles that children bounce on that I always dreamed of having when I was a kid.

Despite the family's clear efforts to create a safe and loving space for their children, a heaviness hangs in the air. "Many people think that it is wrong to celebrate the holidays at a time like this," Khaled tells me. "My wife and I gave it a lot of thought, and we decided that we would go ahead and get a tree and make the traditional Christmas cookies. We don't want to let them take everything from us. We want to try to continue on with our lives."

Khaled talks to me about curfew and the repeated shelling of Beit Jala. He was on tour with his Inad Theater company in Egypt when Israeli troops reoccupied Beit Jala the first time. From the TV in his hotel room he saw tanks fire upon what he recognized to be his own home. His house was badly damaged, but his wife, daughter, mother, father, grandmother, and siblings survived by gathering in the basement storage closet. His wife sang to his daughter in an attempt to block out the sound of the explosions as they waited out the attack.

Khaled tells me that he has tried to avoid speaking with his daughter about the occupation and the army, because he wants to protect her from such things. Even at age two she hears and sees what happens around her, however, and has questions. "My surroundings are stronger than I am," he says, "and so I have had to start explaining things to her." Nevertheless, Khaled insists that he is incapable of teaching hate:

> To teach hate is something inconceivable to me. I would not even know how to do it. I lack the tools to do it. I could not imagine telling my daughter a bedtime story, and saying, "When you grown up, you are going to kill Jews. When you grow up, you are going to throw Israelis into the sea." No human being who wants peace and dignity could teach this to his children.
>
> I want Palestinian children to be safe and to have hope. And I want the same thing for Israeli children and for all children in the world.

Although the closure forced Khaled to cancel his Ramallah-based children's radio show long ago, he has continued to bring drama to children at the schools that he is able to reach. He recalls a visit he made to one classroom in which he instructed children to clap their hands overhead in song. When one child named Nicholas waved his hand from side to side, Khaled thought that he had misunderstood the directions. Then he learned that Nicholas had lost an arm when he was struck by a tank shell in the garden of his home. Khaled notes that academically and socially, Palestinian children seem to be going backward. "You look in their eyes and can see that they are searching for what has been lost," Khaled tells me. When I asked what was lost, he responds simply, "Life."

Khaled continues to believe in the role of theater even, if not especially, during such difficult times:

> It does not surprise me that people can't bear to talk about the news
> anymore. We have reached the point where killing and destruction have
> become daily life. Now when something happens, people don't even talk
> about it. That is why this is the moment for theater. Theater goes beyond
> Yasser Arafat and Ariel Sharon. It is a way of recording history from our
> point of view . . . from the point of view of real people living their lives.

Khaled's work, as a form of both artistic expression and resistance,
offers some source of hope. But these days it is a struggle to believe in
the future. "What we want is to be treated as equals," he says. "My
grandfather, my father, me, and now my son all living under occupation. I don't understand how they think that we can continue under
occupation like this forever." When I ask him what he thinks occupation means, he falls silent for a long time. As I begin to fidget in my
chair, I notice that he has started to cry. When Khaled speaks at last it
is with a tremble in his voice. "Occupation," he says slowly, "is when
you want to celebrate Christmas and you cannot."

From Khaled's house I walk to the Inad Theater to speak with his
colleague Marina. On the way, I come upon a procession headed
solemnly to the Catholic church. It is the funeral of Farah Al-Araj, the
former mayor of Beit Jala and Honorary Consul of Honduras. I pay my
respects and continue on to Inad, where I find the troupe distraught
with worry. For months the theater has been planning a trip to France
to perform a play in which actors improvise their own experiences
under shelling and curfew. All the plans are set when a double suicide
bombing occurs in Tel Aviv and the Israeli government announces that
Palestinians under the age of thirty-five will no longer be allowed to
leave the country. While the four female members of the cast receive

special permission to fly from Tel Aviv, two male members are instructed that they simply must go to the Jordanian border and hope that the soldiers decide to let them out of the West Bank. One of Inad's lead actors is told that security reasons forbid him from leaving the country under any circumstances. This actor is Khaled.

At the theater, the cast scrambles to restage the play without Khaled. It is the day before the men plan to try their luck at the border crossing. Marina, as theater manager, is on the phone with the French embassy and anyone else who might be able to help. When I get her attention for a moment, I ask her if she plans to write about these difficulties in the mass e-mails she sends to people abroad about the situation in the West Bank. She tells me that she no longer writes those e-mails. She stopped after the invasion of the Jenin refugee camp and the United Nations' decision to cancel its investigation of what happened there. "I have given up hope," she says. "There are good people throughout the world who are our friends. But those in power don't care about what happens to us."

Marina looks at me with dark circles under her eyes and continues. "Sometimes I feel that it is useless even to speak about what is happening. Sometimes . . ." And then the phone rings, and she excuses herself to take another call.

I hear Marina's words echoed throughout the West Bank and Gaza Strip. Looking back, I have the sense that the *Intifada* began for many Palestinians as an expression of their will to live with dignity. After seven years of negotiations that guised settlement expansion and rendered Palestinians less free to move around than ever before, they were standing up. They were saying that they could not be fooled into waiting for a viable and independent state forever. They had a right to control their land and their lives no less than other nations do. Given the peace process's failure to deliver, they would seize that right themselves.

Two years later, I find that the sense of possibility with which the

Intifada began has all but eclipsed. The occupation must and will end, Palestinians are now saying, but perhaps not in this generation. "Maybe it is our fate to suffer," I hear from one taxi driver. "All we can do is trust in God." A hopelessness that I have never seen before has come to cover the Palestinian territories mercilessly. Only a just compromise can provide an enduring end to the Israeli-Palestinian conflict, but these days there is no justice to be found.

I meet Samia in the library at the Rawdat Al-Zuhur school in East Jerusalem and ask her opinion. She agrees that the loss of optimism is among the most tragic casualties of the violence:

The situation had affected everyone, educated and uneducated, rich and poor. What is scary is that the people are now beginning to lose hope. You can feel it in the air.

We must keep struggling because justice is on our side. It is like the parable in Luke about the widow who brings her case before a very difficult and stern judge. He throws her out of the court but she keeps coming back and coming back. Finally he says, "This is a persistent woman and I must recognize her rights or she will keep bothering me."

This is what we have to do. We have to be persistent, because we have a just cause. And eventually I hope that the world will be bothered.

Samia's family, meanwhile, is dealing with stern judges of their own. For years, her son-in-law, an American citizen registered as a resident of the West Bank, lived in Jerusalem with his wife and children, all of whom hold Jerusalem ID cards. With the tightening of the closure, however, he has become confined to the West Bank and prohibited from entering Jerusalem. The family's three attempts to appeal to the Israeli courts for family reunification rights have been denied, the last of which ended when the judge cited a secret file whose contents could not be revealed for security reasons.

For Samia, this solidification of borders and separation of peoples represents a turn farther away from what she has long held as her ideal of a free and open country for all people:

> *Anyone with any common sense dreams of a single, unified secular state for everybody: Jews, Muslims, and Christians. It is Israel that insists upon having a Jewish state. So we said OK, if you want a Jewish state, then, for the sake of peace, we'll have a Palestinian state.*
>
> *If there were a properly signed agreement with set borders, of course Palestinians would be committed to it. We have said this repeatedly. If they don't believe us, there is no way we can prove it to them. Let us try, and if we do anything to violate it, then they can put sanctions on us. But why do they have to assume that this will fail before ever giving it a chance to succeed?*

In the absence of an overarching resolution to the Israeli-Palestinian conflict, some Palestinians are concentrating on the smaller steps that can be taken to advance the national cause. I find Saad acting in this spirit in his continued work to safeguard Palestinian land and support those who tend it. After eleven years as an agricultural engineer for the Palestinian Agricultural Relief Committees, he has taken a new job overseeing environmental education at a Ramallah school. In this position, as well as in his continued work training agriculturalists, he advocates organic farming as a strategy for protecting the soil, reducing diseases, and eliminating dependency on chemicals imported from Israel. He also talks to the community about home gardening in order to promote Palestinian self-sufficiency and end reliance on international food relief. Saad insists that alternatives exist to the purchase of the Israeli-made products that continue to line shelves in most Palestinian supermarkets. For example, his own family joined with fourteen other families in Ramallah in developing a cooperative arrangement with a Palestinian farmer. They pay in advance and he supplies them with organic produce to meet all their needs.

Saad tells me that Palestinians can create new ways of challenging the occupation by altering their relationship to the land and their own consumer habits. The first change, however, must occur in the mentality of the public:

Now we have two frameworks for action: the use of force and negotiations. Neither one has worked, so we need a completely new way of thinking.

Do you know how Mahatma Gandhi started his revolution? He announced that he wanted to kick the occupiers out of India. Once a British journalist asked him how he planned on leading his revolution. Gandhi told him, "Come with me to the sea."

They went to the sea and Gandhi took a piece of cloth and laid it on the sand. Then he took a can, scooped up water, and poured it onto his cloth. The journalist asked him what he was doing, and Gandhi responded, "This is my revolution. Wait a few hours."

A few hours later they came back. The water had evaporated and left salt. Gandhi said, "My revolution will begin from this salt." Within weeks, thousands of Indians came to the sea and collected salt in this way. And then, they did not have to buy salt from the British anymore.

After a while, it was not just salt; it was everything. Eventually, the British decided that it was useless to stay in India, and they left.

The same can happen here.

Given the difficulty of identifying any light at the end of the tunnel, I find Saad's conviction to be no less than inspiring. When I ask him about other developments since I met him two years prior, he blushes and says that the most important change in his own life is that he has started practicing a new sport. When I ask which one, he blushes again and says,

"Yoga." I wonder to myself if it would be possible to nominate Saad as a candidate for president. I make a note to ask my no-nonsense Birzeit University political science professor, who has recently been appointed General Secretary of the new Palestinian Election Commission.

With my visit to Saad, my month in the Palestinian Territories draws to a close. I am packing my bags when a long letter arrives via e-mail from Osama, now in Europe. After being turned away at the Israeli-Jordanian border crossing three times, he finally made it out of the West Bank last year in order to move with his wife to her native France. There she has started a new job, and Osama has been tending to the house while he slowly learns French. In spite of his university degree, fluent English, and eight years of professional experience, his lack of French has made it difficult to find his place in French society, and countless job applications have amounted to naught. The experience of being a foreigner, he writes, is filled with both beauty and pain:

> In Europe, for the first time I enjoy the freedom of movement. I walk, bike, drive, and travel wherever I want without fear for roadblocks. I explore the mountains, the sea, and the forest. I have even learned to ski. There are so many things to discover, things that are completely normal for my Western friends, but extraordinary for me as a Palestinian.
>
> For me, real happiness continues to lie in the hope of seeing my country free, open to all, and with no more pain and bloodshed. By leaving, I got a chance to open my eyes to new people and issues. But I have not been able to shed the heavy load of occupation. Here I must constantly prove my innocence, and this brings new worries.
>
> I know that sooner or later my wife and I will go back to Palestine. We miss the land and its tradition of hospitality and simplicity. We miss the feeling of integrity. If I am to be a free man one day, my life's energy must be dedicated to helping build my homeland.
>
> I had wished to be a simple citizen of the world. But I cannot help

but think of the sorrow of my people. I know that my country needs me now more than ever.

And so the day of my departure arrives, I head back to the Tel Aviv airport, and before long I touch base in a United States preparing for war in the Middle East. Like Osama, part of me remains in Palestine. Like Osama, I know that I will not be completely free from the heavy load of occupation until it has at last freed itself.

The semester begins, my Hebrew class resumes, and we sing our new Israeli song for the week. We go around the circle and talk about our winter vacations and my professor tells us about the month she has just spent in Israel visiting her children and new grandchild. A Sabra, she confesses that she has never seen her country so sad. Restaurants are empty and anyone going to the mall must pass through multiple security checks. Government-issued pamphlets instruct citizens how to prepare for potential Iraqi missile attacks, laying out everything from how to seal a bunker to how many bottles of water each person should keep in reserve. My professor tells us that, in the end, most Israelis feel that a war in Iraq will serve their national interests. But for now, people are simply focusing on getting their new gas masks.

Ariel Sharon wins another landslide victory, and is elected to a second term as Prime Minister of Israel. I try to stay in touch with the Palestinians I have met in the West Bank and Gaza Strip. There is curfew again in Bethlehem, and an ambulance has come under fire in Hebron. Israeli bulldozers raze another refugee neighborhood in Gaza, destroying the two wells that supply half of Rafah's drinking water. An ambush attempted by two Palestinian gunmen against an outpost of Israeli soldiers results in the deaths of the former. A would-be suicide bomber is caught trying to cross a checkpoint near Nablus. Palestinian families have not been issued gas masks, although any Iraqi strike against Israel would put them in danger, too. Like Israelis, they brace themselves for a future that is dominated by unknowns. They expect the worst.

Another week passes and the new song in my Hebrew class is "Yoshav al Ha-Gadayr," or "Sitting on the Fence." "In Israel, it is impossible to sit on the fence," my professor tells us. "There is always war, always terror, and you need to take a stand." She lets the tape roll, and I cannot help but think that she might be right for Israelis as individuals, but not for the political system as a whole. The occupation has become an untenable purgatory that no one seems to think can last, yet no one has the courage to end. Israel is sitting on a fence with one foot on each side of the Green Line, and that fence is caving under the weight of its contradictions.

I listen to the song and think about the Israeli voices that lie behind the policies that have shaped the lives of the Palestinians whose voices I have recorded. Who are Israelis? For over thirty years, they have refused either to give Palestinians rights within their state or to grant them a state of their own. They boast a vivacious democracy yet deny freedom to 3.5 million people forced to live under their rule. They pledge their allegiance to a Jewish state in which at least one in every five citizens is not Jewish. They maintain one of the strongest militaries in the world, yet fear for their very existence as a nation. They embody the Zionist dream to replace diaspora weakness with a fighting and pioneering spirit, yet cannot extricate their national policy-making from the collective memory of the Holocaust. They have accepted the principle of land for peace, yet remain unable to let the land go. They wait for a partner on the other side while sanctioning a siege that renders it unthinkable that one will come forward. They decry Palestinians for raising their children to hate at the same time that they make the lives of these children insufferable.

Perhaps I will do a book of interviews with Israelis some day, I say to myself. Perhaps I will call it *Occupied Voices*.

The song ends with a line about someone who reads the newspaper and hears the news on time, but wraps himself in a smokescreen. I do not know for how much longer Israel will act on the belief that denying an entire people self-determination will make it secure. I do not know for how much longer the United States will underwrite this strategy and the international community will watch in silent complicity. History shows that no amount of force—neither the pounding force of the weapons of war nor the strangling force of blockaded horizons—can suppress a people convinced of the justice of their cause. Palestinians of all walks of life say this, loud and clear. Each Palestinian man, woman, and child says it in his or her own voice, and together they say it in the voice of a people.

A fence constructed in the no-man's land between genuine peace and total war cannot protect a nation, no less two nations. The time has come to listen to voices that express the humanity in the other we fear, and to choose a new course.